¡VIVA!
LIBRO 1

Teacher Guide

ALWAYS LEARNING · PEARSON

Published by Pearson Education Limited, Edinburgh Gate, Harlow, Essex, CM20 2JE.

www.pearsonschoolsandfecolleges.co.uk

Edited by Polita Caaveiro
Cover design by Miriam Sturdee
Cover photo © Miguel Domínguez Muñoz

Text © Pearson Education Limited 2013

First published 2013
18
10 9 8 7

British Library Cataloguing in Publication Data
A catalogue record for this book is available from the British Library

ISBN 978 1 447 96030 0

Copyright notice
All rights reserved. No part of this publication may be reproduced in any form or by any means (including photocopying or storing it in any medium by electronic means and whether or not transiently or incidentally to some other use of this publication) without the written permission of the copyright owner, except in accordance with the provisions of the Copyright, Designs and Patents Act 1988 or under the terms of a licence issued by the Copyright Licensing Agency, Saffron House, 6–10 Kirby Street, London EC1N 8TS (www.cla.co.uk). Applications for the copyright owner's written permission should be addressed to the publisher.

This product is accompanied by downloadable editable Word files. Pearson Education Limited is not responsible for the quality, accuracy or fitness for purpose of the materials contained in the Word files once edited. To revert to the original Word files, redownload them from the given URL.

Printed in the UK by Henry Ling Limited, at the Dorset Press, Dorchester, Dorset DT1 1HD

Acknowledgements
Every effort has been made to contact copyright holders of material reproduced in this book. Any omissions will be rectified in subsequent printings if notice is given to the publishers.

Contents

Introduction 4

Module 1 **Mi vida** 15
Module 2 **Mi tiempo libre** 49
Module 3 **Mi insti** 87
Module 4 **Mi familia y mis amigos** 120
Module 5 **Mi ciudad** 153

Introduction

Course description

¡Viva! is a differentiated 11–14 Spanish course in three stages – ¡Viva! 1 for Year 7, ¡Viva! 2 for Year 8 and ¡Viva! 3 for Year 9. In Year 7 pupils can be assessed at National Curriculum Levels 1 to 5.

¡Viva! 1 and ¡Viva! 2 are suitable for use on their own as a two-year Key Stage 3 course.

The course has been written to reflect the world pupils live in, using contexts familiar to them in their everyday lives and teaching them the vocabulary that they need to communicate with young Spanish people of their own age on topics that interest and stimulate them. They are introduced to young Spanish people and given insight into the everyday life and culture of Spain and other Spanish-speaking countries, encouraging intercultural understanding.

At the same time, ¡Viva! ensures that pupils are taught the language learning skills and strategies that they need to become independent language learners. The elements of the 2014 Programme of Study for Key Stage 3 Modern Languages (grammar and vocabulary, and linguistic competence) are fully integrated into the course. In addition, pupils have the chance to experience cross-curricular studies and are given regular opportunities to develop and practise the personal, learning and thinking skills required to operate as independent enquirers, creative thinkers, reflective learners, team workers, self-managers and effective participators.

¡Viva! ActiveTeach (see details on pp. 5-6) provides easy-to-use and exciting technology designed to add dynamism and fun to whole-class teaching. For individual pupil use, ¡Viva! ActiveLearn (see details on pp. 6-7) provides a wealth of exciting differentiated material for pupils to access individually via computers or mobile devices, in class or for homework.

Differentiation

¡Viva! 1 and 2 provide one book each for the whole ability range. Pupil requirements are catered for in the following ways:

- There are differentiated activities at a range of NC Levels in listening, speaking, reading and writing throughout the Pupil Book.
- Ideas are given in the Teacher's Guide for reinforcing and extending the Pupil Book activities.
- *Skills* spreads towards the end of every module contain in-depth work and some higher level activities which give pupils the opportunity to work on language learning skills at a deeper level and pull their learning together, producing longer pieces of speaking and writing.
- The *Te toca a ti* section at the back of the Pupil Book provides extra reading and writing activities at reinforcement and extension levels.
- The workbooks are differentiated at two levels: reinforcement (*Cuaderno de ejercicios A*) and extension (*Cuaderno de ejercicios B*).

¡Viva! 3 is differentiated by means of parallel books:

¡Viva! 3 Rojo	NC Levels 4–7
¡Viva! 3 Verde	NC Levels 1–5

¡Viva! 1

Pupil Book

- One book for the whole ability range in Year 7
- Full coverage of the 2014 Programmes of Study for Key Stage 3 MFL
- Assessment right from the start at National Curriculum Level 4
- Exciting video introducing pupils to the lives of young people in Spain
- Fully integrated grammar explanations and practice ensuring logical and rigorous progression
- In-depth work on listening, speaking, reading and writing skills to promote greater levels of achievement and linguistic competences
- Integrated cross-curricular work linking to topics covered
- Fully integrated opportunities for PLTS

The Pupil Book consists of six core modules which are subdivided as follows:

- A fun, double-page opener quiz to whet pupils' appetites for a new topic and make them aware of things that they may already know about it.
- Four double-page core units (five in Module 1) – these contain the core material that must be taught to ensure that all the key language and grammar is covered in Year 7.
- Two double-page skills units (one in Module 1), which allow pupils to work on one receptive skill and one productive skill in greater depth.
- *Resumen* – this is a checklist of 'I can' statements, allowing pupils to check their progress as part of Assessment for Learning.
- *Prepárate* – optional revision activities that can be used as a 'mock' test preceding the end of module *Prueba* in the Assessment Pack.

© Pearson Education Ltd 2013. Copying permitted for purchasing institution only. This material is not copyright free.

- *¡Viva! Gramática* – two pages where the key grammar points introduced in the module are explained fully and accompanied by practice activities.
- *Palabras* – two pages of word lists for vocabulary learning and revision, with an *Estrategia* tip box to help pupils acquire the skills they need to learn vocabulary more effectively.
- *Zona Proyecto* – one or two optional units in which no new grammar is introduced, but which extend the module topic into an exciting cultural and practical context which allows for cross curricular and project work.

At the back of the Pupil Book there are three further sections:

- *Te toca a ti* – self-access differentiated reading and writing activities. *Te toca a ti A* contains reinforcement activities for lower-ability pupils, and *Te toca a ti B* contains extension activities for higher-ability pupils. These are ideal for use as homework.
- Verb tables – two pages showing the present tense conjugation of regular -ar, -er and -ir verbs, stem-changing verbs, and the four most common irregular verbs: *tener, ser, ir* and *hacer*, as well as the near future tense.
- *Minidiccionario* – a comprehensive Spanish-English glossary, organised alphabetically and containing all the vocabulary encountered in *¡Viva! 1*. There is also a list of the Spanish rubrics used in the Pupil Book.

Teacher's Guide

The Teacher's Guide contains all the support required to help you use *¡Viva! 1* effectively in the classroom:

- Clear and concise teaching notes, including lesson starters, plenaries and PLTS references for every unit
- Full cross-referencing to the 2014 National Curriculum Programmes of Study
- Overview grids for each module highlighting grammar content and skills coverage
- Answers to all the activities
- The complete audioscript for all the listening activities in the *¡Viva! 1* Pupil Book
- Guidance on using the course with the full ability range

With the Teacher's Guide there is an accompanying customisable Scheme of Work offering complete help with planning, and showing how the course covers the National Curriculum Programme of Study.

The Teacher's Guide and Scheme of Work are available in the following ways:

- As a printed, spiral-bound book (Scheme of Work supplied as downloadable word files with instructions on how to access them inside the front cover).
- Alternatively both the complete Teacher's Guide content and Scheme of Work can be purchased and accessed as Word files online (via the ActiveTeach Library). From there they can be downloaded and printed off as necessary.

Audio

The audio files for the course contain all the recorded material for the listening activities in the Pupil Book. These audio files are also contained on *ActiveTeach* so only teachers who do not purchase *ActiveTeach* will need to buy the audio files. The different types of activities can be used for presentation of new language, comprehension and pronunciation practice. The material includes dialogues, interviews and songs recorded by native speakers.

After purchasing the audio files for *¡Viva!*, you can access and download them online from the ActiveTeach Library. From there they can be saved onto your computer or network for future use.

This audio material is also contained on *ActiveTeach*. Therefore, if you buy *ActiveTeach*, you can play all the listening activities from there without further purchase of the audio files.

Please note: the audio files and ActiveTeach do not contain the listening material for the end-of-module tests and end-of-year test. This material can be found in the Assessment Pack (see right).

Workbooks

There are two parallel workbooks to accompany Studio 1: one for reinforcement (*Cuaderno de ejercicios A*) and one for extension (*Cuaderno de ejercicios B*). There is one page of activities for each double-page unit in the Pupil Book. The workbooks fulfil a number of functions:

- They provide self-access reading and writing activities designed to offer the pupils enjoyable ways of consolidating and practising the language they have learned in each unit.
- They give extra practice in grammar, as well as reading and writing skills, with integrated activities throughout the workbooks.
- Revision pages at the end of each module (*Prepárate*) help pupils revise what they have learned during the module.

- Module word lists (*Palabras*) with English translations are invaluable for language learning homework.
- The *Progreso* pages at the end of each module allow pupils to record their National Curriculum level for each skill and set themselves improvement targets for the next module.
- NC level descriptors in pupil-friendly language at the back of the workbooks allow pupils to see what they must do to progress through the NC levels in all four Attainment Targets.

The Workbooks are available as print books sold in packs of 8 or can be downloaded as PDFs from the ActiveTeach library.

Assessment Pack

The Assessment Pack contains all the assessment material required to assess pupils in Year 7 in all four skills, as well as self-assessment sheets.

- End-of-module tests in all four skills – listening, speaking, reading and writing
- End-of-year test in all four skills
- Covers National Curriculum Levels 1 to 5
- Optional Extra Level 5 test
- Target setting sheets

The audio material supports the listening tests. The assessment pages and the audio can be downloaded after purchase from the ActiveTeach Library. There you will find Word files and PDF versions of the test sheets, alongside the audio files for the listening tests.

ActiveTeach

ActiveTeach is a powerful and motivating resource combining the 'book on screen' and a wealth of supporting materials – providing you with the perfect tool for whole-class teaching.

- Use the on-screen Pupil Book with all the listening activities included.
- Zoom in on areas of text and activities to facilitate whole-class teaching.
- Build your own lessons and add in your own resources to help personalise learning.
- Use fun and motivating electronic flashcards to teach new vocabulary.
- Consolidate language using the whole-class interactive games.
- Use the video clips to introduce your pupils to the lives of young Spanish people.
- Teach and revise grammar using PowerPoint® presentations, followed by interactive grammar activities on key grammar points.
- Download and print off a variety of extra worksheets for starters, plenaries, consolidation of grammar, thinking skills, language-learning skills, extended reading comprehensions, self assessment and vocab lists. These are ideal for follow-up work, cover lessons and homework.
- You can also download and print off worksheets with a current topical and cultural focus. These are updated half-termly, and, once up online, will remain there to be accessed or downloaded at any time.

The wide variety of worksheets in *Active Teach* (mentioned above) can be used to consolidate and extend pupils' learning as follows:

Module 1

Grammar: Personality adjectives

Thinking skills: Number crunching!

Grammar: What a lot of animals!

Extension: All about me!

Module 2

Grammar: Find the endings

Extension: All muddled up!

Learning skills: Recognising cognates

Module 3

Extension: I think the opposite!

Grammar: Adapting a verb pattern

Learning skills: High-frequency words

Module 4

Extension: What a picture!

Thinking skills: Where do they live?

Grammar: To be or not to be?

Module 5

Thinking skills: Marta's day in the city

Grammar: Stem-changing verbs

Extension: A holiday in Chile

These worksheets can be found in the page resources section of the relevant page or by searching by keyword or resource type in the ActiveTeach search.

ActiveLearn

ActiveLearn is a motivating new digital resource for individual pupil use in school or at home. It is accessed online and follows the same topics as the Pupil Book. The *ActiveCourse* part of the product comprises sequences of exercises that will help pupils to work on their language skills, in particular listening, reading, grammar and vocab.

Activities in the *ActiveLearn ActiveCourse* are structured in the following way:

© Pearson Education Ltd 2013. Copying permitted for purchasing institution only. This material is not copyright free.

- Interactive listening skills activities at two levels (lower A and higher B) matched to each core teaching unit (Units 1-4 of each module, or 1-5 of Module 1).
- Interactive reading skills activities at two levels (lower and higher) matched to each core teaching unit (Units 1-4 of each module, or 1-5 of Module 1).
- Interactive grammar activities, one per core unit, covering key grammar points.
- Key vocabulary from each core unit, drilled and tested through a unique system of activities.

Pupils' performance in the activities is tracked and recorded, making it easy for themselves and teachers to review their progress throughout the year.

In addition, through *ActiveLearn*, it is possible to purchase a digital version of their Pupil Book (the *ActiveBook,* accessed online) which includes all the audio files for the listening activities in the Pupil Book.

Group speaking activities

The group talk icon indicates group speaking activities involving more than 2 students with approximately equal levels of participation. Many of them incorporate the Group Talk ethos (developed at Wildern School in Southampton), encouraging students to sustain conversation through opinion, conjecture and debate using phrases such as *¡Ni hablar!* and *¿Estás loco/loca?*

Grammar coverage

Grammar is fully integrated into the teaching sequence in *¡Viva!* to ensure that pupils have the opportunity to learn thoroughly the underlying structures of the Spanish language. All units have a grammar objective so that pupils can see clearly which grammar structures they are learning. The key grammar points are presented in the *¡Viva! Gramática* boxes on the Pupil Book pages and fuller explanations and practice are provided in the *¡Viva! Gramática* pages at the end of each module. In addition, there are grammar PowerPoint® presentations in *ActiveTeach* for presenting new grammar concepts to classes, followed by interactive practice activities that can be used with whole classes or for individual practice. Worksheets focusing on the key grammar topics taught in *¡Viva! 1* are also provided in *ActiveTeach* and can be printed off for individual pupil use.

Grammar points explained and practised in *¡Viva! 1*:

- article 'the' (*el, la, los, las*)
- article 'a' (*un, una*)
- adjectival endings: *-o(s) -a(s), -e(s),* consonant(*+es*)
- position of adjectives
- present tense of *ser, tener, hacer, estar, ir*
- stem changing verbs: *jugar, querer*
- present tense of *-ar, -ir* and *-er* verbs
- negative: *no*
- *me gusta* + infinitive
- *me gusta(n)* + noun
- possessive adjectives: *mi(s), tu(s), su(s)*
- 'a', 'some', 'many': *un(a), unas/unos, muchas/muchos*
- *ir + a +* infinitive (near future tense)

Coverage of the National Curriculum Programme of Study in *¡Viva! 1*

In *¡Viva! 1* the 2014 National Curriculum Programme of Study is covered comprehensively. The Programme of Study is as follows

1 Grammar and vocabulary

Pupils should be taught to:

- identify and use tenses or other structures which convey the present, past, and future as appropriate to the language being studied
- use and manipulate a variety of key grammatical structures and patterns, including voices and moods, as appropriate
- develop and use a wide-ranging and deepening vocabulary that goes beyond their immediate needs and interests, allowing them to give and justify opinions and take part in discussion about wider issues
- use accurate grammar, spelling and punctuation.

2 Linguistic competence

Pupils should be taught to:

- listen to a variety of forms of spoken language to obtain information and respond appropriately
- transcribe words and short sentences that they hear with increasing accuracy
- initiate and develop conversations, coping with unfamiliar language and unexpected responses, making use of important social conventions such as formal modes of address
- express and develop ideas clearly and with increasing accuracy, both orally and in writing
- speak coherently and confidently, with increasingly accurate pronunciation and intonation
- read and show comprehension of original and adapted materials from a range of different sources, understanding the purpose, important ideas and details, and provide an accurate English translation of short, suitable material

- read literary texts in the language, such as stories, songs, poems and letters, to stimulate ideas, develop creative expression and expand understanding of the language and culture
- write prose using an increasingly wide range of grammar and vocabulary, write creatively to express their own ideas and opinions, and translate short written text accurately into the foreign language.

Activities throughout ¡Viva! are specifically designed to give pupils opportunities to cover the Programme of Study. As the Programme of Study is intended to represent learning through Years 7, 8 and 9, not all aspects of it are covered in Book 1. However ¡Viva! 1 and 2 cover the Programme of Study in full. After Book 2, Pupils could either move on to GSCE if time is short, or continue with ¡Viva! 3 (which also covers the Programme of Study) in Year 9.

The table below outlines the points from the Programme of Study in short form, and shows examples of where they are covered in ¡Viva! 1 and 2. The content of the course is also matched to the Programme of Study unit by unit throughout this Teacher's Guide.

1 Grammar and vocabulary (GV)	
GV1 Tenses	M2U2, M3U4, M5U4
GV2 Grammatical structures	M1U3, M3U3, M4U2, M5U2
GV3 Developing vocabulary	M2U5, M4U1, M4U5
Opinions and discussions	M2U1, M2U4, M3ZP, M4ZP
GV4 Accuracy	M3U2, M3U6, M5U6
2 Linguistic competence (LC)	
LC1 Listening and responding	M2U4, M3U5, M5U5
LC2 Transcription	M1U4, M2U2(Starter), M4U2(Starter), M5U1(Starter)
LC3 Conversation	M1ZP, M2U6, M5U3
Conversation (dealing with the unexpected)	M1U2, M1ZP M3ZP
Conversation (using modes of address)	¡Viva! 2

LC4 Expressing ideas (speaking)	M2ZP1, M3ZP, M4U6
Expressing ideas (writing)	M1U6, M3U6, M5U6
LC5 Speaking coherently and confidently	M2U6, M4U4, M4U6, M5U2
Accurate pronunciation and intonation	M1U1, M2U6, M4U6
LC6 Reading comprehension	M2U5, M4U3, M4U5, M5ZP1
Translation into English	M1U2, M2U2, M4Gram, M5Gram
LC7 Literary texts	M1U4, M5ZP1
LC8 Writing creatively	M1U6, M3U3, M4U3, M5U6
Translation into Spanish	M2Gram, M3Gram, M5Gram

National Curriculum Levels in ¡Viva!

The 2014 National Curriculum no longer includes Level Descriptors for Levels 1-8 and exceptional performance. In order to ensure sound progression, as well as to aiding progress tracking and reporting, ¡Viva! keeps the levels in place, using the level descriptors as they were in the previous curriculum. In the course they feature in the following ways:

- All activities in the course are levelled (in the Teacher's Guide) from Levels 1-7.
- End-of-module Assessments for ¡Viva! have been written using the National Curriculum Levels to indicate the level of challenge.
- Workbooks contain self-assessment and target setting pages based around the old National Curriculum Levels.

As the new National Programmes of Study become established in schools from 2014, their use in ¡Viva!, as well as the use of the older NC Level descriptors, will be reviewed to make sure that the course provides the most valid and up-to-date account of how achievement is measured and progress is tracked.

© Pearson Education Ltd 2013. Copying permitted for purchasing institution only. This material is not copyright free.

Coverage of Personal Learning and Thinking Skills in ¡Viva! 1

Activities supporting PLTS development are included throughout the course. One PLTS is identified in each unit, with Modules 1–5 all featuring the full range of PLTS. Each PLTS is given in the table below, with a selection of examples and details of how they meet the curriculum requirements.

Personal Learning and Thinking Skills	
I Independent enquirers	Pupil Book activities throughout the course (e.g. M1 *Zona Proyecto*, M5 *Zona Proyecto 1*)
C Creative thinkers	Regular activities developing skills strategies (how to improve listening/speaking, etc.) (e.g. M2 U5, M4 U6); Starters requiring pupils to apply logic and make connections (e.g. M3 U5 Starter 2); regular activities encouraging pupils to identify patterns and work out rules (e.g. M4 U1 ex. 4); activities requiring creative production of language (e.g. M3 U6 ex 7)
R Reflective learners	Ongoing opportunities to assess work and identify areas for improvement (e.g. M3 U6), including all *Resumen* pages and Plenaries (e.g. M3 U6 Plenary)
T Team workers	Regular pairwork activities (e.g. M2 U2 ex 6, M5 U3 ex 2), group talk opportunities (e.g. M3 *Zona Proyecto*) including many Starters; regular peer assessment (e.g. M3 U6 ex 8, M5 U6 ex 8)
S Self-managers	Ongoing advice on managing learning (e.g. M5 U6), including strategies to improve learning (e.g. M4 U6 exs 7 and 8)
E Effective participators	Opportunities throughout the course for pupils to contribute (e.g. M2 U4 ex 8), including presentations (e.g. M4 U6 ex 8) and all Plenaries (e.g. M4 U3 Plenary)

Pupils may find the following short forms useful as a reference in class:

I am a/an...		Today I...
Independent enquirer	I	worked on my own to find out something new
Creative thinker	C	used what I know to work out or create something new
Reflective learner	R	thought about what I've learned and how I can improve
Team worker	T	worked well with other people
Self-manager	S	took responsibility for improving my learning
Effective participator	E	took part in the lesson in a positive way

Coverage of the Foundation Certificate of Secondary Education in Spanish (Revised Specification) in ¡Viva! 1

¡Viva! can be used to teach the Key Stage 3 FCSE qualification from AQA. The following table shows where each of the FCSE units and sub-topics for the Revised Specification (2014) can be taught using ¡Viva! 1. Many of the FCSE units and sub-topics that do not appear in ¡Viva! 1 are covered in ¡Viva! 2 or ¡Viva! 3 Rojo/Verde.

Unit 1 – Relationships, family and friends

Sub-topics	Where in ¡Viva! 1
Reading and listening	
Family and step family	Module 1 Unit 3, Module 4 Unit 1
Personal details about family	Module 1 Unit 2, Module 1 Unit 3, Module 1 Unit 4, Module 4 Unit 1, Module 4 Unit 2, Module 4 Unit 3
Mini biography of family (Set A only)	
Rank in family (Set B only)	
Personal details about friends (Set B only)	Module 1 Unit 2, Module 4 Unit 2
Girlfriend, boyfriend	
Relationships and reasons for good and bad relations within family and friends	
Issues (Set B only)	
Taking sides in an argument (Set B only)	
Pets	Module 1 Unit 5
Clothes (Set A only)	
Family celebrations	Module 1 Unit 4
Prepositions	
Numbers	Module 1 Unit 3, Module 1 Unit 4, Module 4 Unit 1
Speaking and writing	
Personal information	Module 1 Unit 2, Module 4 Unit 2, Module 4 Unit 3
Family/friends	Module 1 Unit 3, Module 4 Unit 1, Module 4 Unit 3
Meeting up with friends/activities	
Descriptions	Module 1 Unit 2, Module 4 Unit 2, Module 4 Unit 3
Hobbies/free-time activities	Module 2 Unit 1, Module 2 Unit 2

Unit 2 – Education and future plans

Sub-topics	Where in ¡Viva! 1
Reading and listening	
Education	
School – teachers	Module 3 Unit 2
problems	
transport	
timetable	Module 3 Unit 1
uniform	
facilities	Module 3 Unit 3, Module 3 Zona Proyecto
type of school (Set A only)	
location (Set A only)	
subjects	Module 3 Unit 1, Module 3 Unit 2
rules (Set A only)	
school clubs (Set A only)	
sport	
progress report (Set A only)	
items in school bag (Set B only)	
Future plans	
Plans for after school	
Plans for jobs and careers	
Plans for future study	
Advantages and disadvantages of jobs	
Advantages and disadvantages of staying on at school (Set B only)	
Time	Module 5 Unit 2
Prepositions of place	
Alphabet (Set A only)	Module 1 Unit 4
Numbers (Set A only)	Module 1 Unit 3, Module 1 Unit 4, Module 4 Unit 1
Sequence (Set B only)	Module 3 Unit 4

© Pearson Education Ltd 2013. Copying permitted for purchasing institution only. This material is not copyright free.

Speaking and writing	
Physical description of school	Module 3 Unit 3
School activities	
Opinions	
Uniform	
Future plans	

Unit 3 – Holidays and travel

Sub-topics	Where in ¡Viva! 1
Reading and listening	
Holidays	
Types of holiday	
Camping (Set A only)	
Activities (Set A only)	
Travel	
Accommodation	
Weather on holiday	
Problems on holiday (Set B only)	
Holiday experiences (Set B only)	
Speaking and writing	
Destination	
Travel	
Accommodation	
Activities	

Unit 4 – Leisure

Sub-topics	Where in ¡Viva! 1
Reading and listening	
Hobbies	Module 2 Unit 1, Module 2 Unit 2, Module 2 Unit 4
Free time/hobbies	Module 2 Unit 1, Module 2 Unit 2, Module 2 Unit 4
Television	
Films (Set A only)	
Cinema (Set B only)	
Music	
Gardening (Set A only)	

Going out (Set A only)	Module 5 Unit 2, Module 5 Unit 4
Theatre visit (Set A only)	
Clubs	
Around town (Set B only)	
Leisure centre (Set B only)	
Speaking and writing	
Hobbies/activities	Module 2 Unit 1, Module 2 Unit 2, Module 2 Unit 4
Preferences	
Going out	Module 5 Unit 4
Pocket money	

Unit 5 – Healthy lifestyle

Sub-topics	Where in ¡Viva! 1
Reading and listening	
Healthy living	
Food/drink (Set B only)	Module 3 Unit 4, Module 5 Unit 3
Healthy/unhealthy eating (Set A only)	
Fast food (Set A only)	
Exercise (Set A only)	
Life as a footballer (Set B only)	
Sports	Module 2 Unit 4
Leisure centres (Set A only)	
Alcohol	
Smoking	
Illness	
Chemist's (Set B only)	
Stress (Set A only)	
Exam pressure	
Health farms (Set A only)	
Speaking and writing	
State of health	
Activities	Module 2 Unit 4
Eating and drinking	
Opinions	

© Pearson Education Ltd 2013. Copying permitted for purchasing institution only. This material is not copyright free.

Unit 6 – Food and drink

Sub-topics	Where in ¡Viva! 1
Reading and listening	
Food/drink vocabulary items	Module 3 Unit 4, Module 5 Unit 3
Eating out	Module 5 Unit 3
Opinions about food and drink	
Shopping for food	
Unhealthy/healthy food choices	
Speaking and writing	
Food and drink habits	
Eating out	Module 5 Unit 3
Opinions about food and drink	

Unit 7 – Local area and environment

Sub-topics	Where in ¡Viva! 1
Reading and listening	
Facilities	Module 5 Unit 1
Locations	Module 4 Unit 4
Preferences	
Environment	
Recycling	
Weather	Module 2 Unit 3
Speaking and writing	
Local area	Module 5 Unit 1
Activities	Module 5 Unit 2
Environment	

Unit 8 – Celebrations

Sub-topics	Where in ¡Viva! 1
Reading and listening	
Birthdays	Module 1 Unit 4
Various festivals	Module 2 Zona Proyecto 1, Module 2 Zona Proyecto 2, Module 5 Zona Proyecto 1, Module 5 Zona Proyecto 2
Parties	
Celebrating *(Set A only)*	
Engagements and weddings	
Celebrating success *(Set A only)*	
Carnival	Module 4 Unit 5
End of exams	
Speaking and writing	
Parties	
Opinions	
Special celebrations	Module 2 Zona Proyecto 1, Module 2 Zona Proyecto 2, Module 5 Zona Proyecto 1, Module 5 Zona Proyecto 2

© Pearson Education Ltd 2013. Copying permitted for purchasing institution only. This material is not copyright free.

Games and other teaching suggestions
Reading aloud
There are many reading activities in the Pupil Book which give scope for further activities.

1. You can use the texts to practise reading aloud. As an incentive, award five points to a pupil who can read a text without any errors. Points could also be given to teams, depending on seating arrangements – tables, rows, sides of the room.
2. Set a challenge – 'I bet no one can read this without a single mistake' or ask a volunteer pupil to predict how many mistakes he/she will make before having a go, then seeing if he/she can do better than predicted.
3. Texts could be read round the class with pupils simply reading up to a full stop and then passing it on to someone else in the room. They enjoy this activity if it is fast. Alternatively, pupils can read as much or as little as they want before passing it on.
4. You can also read a text, pause and have the pupils say the next word.

Reading follow-up
Motivation and participation can be enhanced by dividing the class into two teams and awarding points. Once they know a text very well, pupils should be able to complete a sentence from memory, hearing just the beginning. Move from a word to a phrase to a sentence: i.e. you say a word, the pupils give the word in a short context and then in a longer context.

1. You read aloud and stop (or insert the word 'beep') for pupils to complete the word or sentence.
2. You read aloud and make a deliberate mistake (either pronunciation or saying the wrong word). Pupils put up their hand as soon as they spot a mistake.
3. *Hot potato*: Pupils read a bit and pass it on quickly to someone who may not be expecting it.
4. *Marathon*: A pupil reads aloud until he/she makes a mistake. Pupils have to put up their hand as soon as they hear a mistake. A second pupil then takes over, starting at the beginning again and trying to get further than the previous pupil.
5. *Random reading*: You read a phrase at random and the pupils have to say the next bit.
6. You can play music and get the pupils to pass an object round the class. When the music stops, the person with the object has a turn. Let a pupil control the music, facing away from the class.

Mime activities
Mimes are a motivating way to help pupils to learn words.

1. You say a word, for example a job, sport or hobby, or an adjective, and the pupils mime it. This can be done silently with the whole class responding. Alternatively, it can be done as a knock-out game starting with six volunteers at the front who mime to the class as you say each word. Any pupil who does the wrong mime or who is slow to react is knocked out. Impose a two-minute time limit.
2. Pupils say a word or phrase and you mime it – but only if the pupils say it correctly. This really puts you on the spot and gets the pupils trying very hard. You could also insist that the pupils say it from memory.
3. You mime and pupils say the word or phrase.
4. Send five or six pupils out of the room. They each have to decide on an adjective which sums up their character. They return to the room individually or together, each one miming their character adjective. The remaining pupils then guess the adjective. Get them to use a sentence, e.g. *Daniel es tranquilo*.
5. *Un voluntario/Una voluntaria)*: One person goes out of the room. The rest of the class decides on a character adjective to mime. The volunteer comes back into the room and has to guess the adjective that the class is miming. Again, encourage the use of whole sentences.
6. *Class knock-down*: As above, but this time everyone in the class can choose different qualities to mime. The volunteer returns to the room with everyone doing his/her own mime. The volunteer points to each pupil and names the character adjective. If the volunteer is correct, the pupil sits down. This works well as a timed or team activity. The aim is to sit your team down as quickly as possible.
7. A version of charades is a good activity at the end of the lesson. Organise two teams, A and B. Have all the adjectives written down on separate cards, masculine forms only. Put the cards in a pile at the front. A volunteer from Team A comes to the front, picks up the first card and mimes it. The rest of the team must not see the word on the card. Anyone from Team A can put up his/her hand and is then invited by the volunteer to say the word. If correct, the volunteer picks up the next card and mimes it. The aim is to get through the whole list as quickly as possible. Note down the time for Team A. Team B then tries to beat that time.

Exploiting the songs
1. Pupils sing along. Fade out certain bits while they continue. When most of them know the song quite well you can pause the audio to let them give you the next line by heart. Then try the whole chorus, followed by a few verses completely from memory.
2. You could try the 'pick up a song' game: you fade the song after a few lines, the pupils

continue singing, and then you fade the song up again towards the end and they see whether they have kept pace with the recording.

Translation follow-up

Motivation and participation can be enhanced by dividing the class into two teams and awarding points. Once they know the text very well, you should be able to say any word, phrase or sentence from the text at random for the pupils to translate into English without viewing the text.

1 You translate the text and stop (or insert the word 'beep') for pupils to complete the word or sentence.
2 You translate, making a deliberate mistake. Pupils put up their hand as soon as they spot a mistake.
3 *Hot potato*: A pupil translates a bit and passes it on quickly to someone who may not be expecting it.
4 *Marathon*: A pupil translates until he/she makes a mistake. Pupils have to put up their hand as soon as they hear a mistake. A second pupil then takes over, starting from the beginning again and trying to get further than the previous pupil.
5 *Random translation*: You read a phrase in Spanish at random and the pupils have to translate it.
6 One half of the class has their books open, the other half has them closed. The half with their books open reads a sentence in Spanish at random. The other side has to translate. Do about five then swap round.
7 You can play music and get the pupils to pass an object round. When the music stops, the person with the object has a turn. Let a pupil control the music, facing away from the class.

Writing follow-up (text dissection)

Whiteboards are a useful tool. They do not need to be issued to every pupil. Pupils can work in pairs or groups or they can pass the whiteboards on. You could also divide the class into teams, with one whiteboard per team.

After reading a text in some detail:

1 Display some anagrams of key words from the text and ask pupils to write them correctly. You will need to prepare these in advance and check carefully. Award points for correct answers on each board.
2 Display some jumbled phrases from the text, e.g. *baloncesto el sábado juego al*. Pupils rewrite the phrase correctly in their exercise books or on the board. They could work in teams, producing one answer per team on paper.
3 Display an incorrect word or phrase in Spanish and ask pupils to spot the mistake and correct it. This can also be done as 'spot the missing word' or 'spot the word that is in the wrong place'.
4 Ask pupils to spell certain words from memory. Differentiate by first reading out a few words in Spanish and then giving a few in English for them also to write out in Spanish.
5 *Mini-dictado*: Read four or five short sentences in Spanish for pupils to write out. Again, this could be a group exercise.
6 Give pupils phrases in English to write out in Spanish.

Comprehension follow-up

1 Ask questions in English about the text.
2 Ask questions in Spanish about the text.
3 True or false?
4 Who… ?

Vocabulary treasure hunt

1 Find the word for…
2 Find (three) opinions.

Grammar treasure hunt

1 Find (three) adjectives.
2 Find (two) feminine adjectives.
3 Find a verb in the nous form.
4 Find a plural noun.
5 Find a negative.

A variation on pairwork

Musical pass the mobile phone: One pupil controls the music, facing away from the class. While the music is playing, a toy or old mobile phone is passed from pupil to pupil. As soon as the music stops, the music operator (who is ideally also equipped with a phone) says the first statement of a dialogue. The other pupil who has ended up with the phone replies. They can, if they like, disguise their voice. The music operator tries to guess who is speaking. The game then continues.

MODULE 1: Mi vida

Unit & Learning objectives	PoS references	Key language	Grammar and other language features
1 ¿Cómo te llamas? (pp. 8–9) Getting used to Spanish pronunciation Introducing yourself	**GV1** Tenses (present) **GV2** Grammatical structures (definite articles) **LC5** Accurate pronunciation and intonation	¡Hola! ¿Qué tal? Fenomenal. Bien, gracias. Regular. Fatal. ¿Cómo te llamas? Me llamo… ¿Dónde vives? Vivo en… Adiós. Hasta luego.	**G** definite articles (*el/la/los/las*) **G** verb endings – introduction to Spanish pronunciation
2 ¿Qué tipo de persona eres? (pp. 10–11) Talking about your personality Using adjectives that end in *-o/-a*	**GV2** Grammatical structures (adjectival endings) **LC6** Translation into English **LC8** Writing creatively	¿Qué tipo de persona eres? Soy sincero/a. Soy tímido/a. Soy tranquilo/a. Soy divertido/a. Soy serio/a. Soy simpático/a. Soy tonto/a. Soy listo/a. Soy generoso/a. Mi pasión es… Mi héroe es…	**G** adjectives that end in *-o* or *-a* **G** making sentences negative **G** *ser* (present, singular) – connectives: *y, también, pero* – pronunciation (stress on next to last syllable, accented words)
3 ¿Tienes hermanos? (pp. 12–13) Talking about age, brothers and sisters Using the verb *tener* (to have)	**GV2** Grammatical structures (indefinite articles) **LC5** Speaking coherently and confidently **LC6** Reading comprehension	¿Cuántos años tienes? Tengo… años. Numbers: *uno* to *quince* (and *cero*) ¿Tienes hermanos? Tengo un hermano. Tengo una hermana. Tengo un hermanastro Tengo una hermanastra Tengo dos hermanos. Tengo dos hermanas. No tengo hermanos. Soy hijo único. Soy hija única.	**G** *tener* (present, singular) **G** indefinite articles (*un/una*) – pronunciation of *n* and *ñ*

© Pearson Education Ltd 2013. Copying permitted for purchasing institution only. This material is not copyright free.

Mi vida 1

Unit & Learning objectives	PoS references	Key language	Grammar and other language features
4 ¿Cuándo es tu cumpleaños? (pp. 14–15) Saying when your birthday is Using numbers and the alphabet	**LC2** Transcription **LC5** Speaking coherently and confidently **LC7** Literary texts	¿Cuándo es tu cumpleaños? Mi cumpleaños es el… de… enero febrero marzo abril mayo junio julio agosto septiembre octubre noviembre diciembre Numbers: dieciséis to treinta y uno ¿Cómo se escribe? Se escribe… The alphabet in Spanish	– pronunciation of b and v – reading strategies: using patterns
5 ¿Tienes mascotas? (pp. 16–17) Talking about your pets Making adjectives agree with nouns	**GV2** Grammatical structures (adjectival agreement) **GV3** Developing vocabulary	¿Tienes mascotas? No tengo mascotas. Tengo… un perro, un gato, un conejo, un caballo un pez, un ratón, una serpiente, una cobaya blanco/a amarillo/a negro/a rojo/a verde gris marrón azul rosa naranja	**G** adjective forms (masculine and feminine, singular and plural) – pronunciation of r and rr – intensifiers: muy, un poco, bastante
6 Cómo soy… (pp. 18–19) Writing a text for a time capsule Adding variety to your writing	**GV3** Opinions and discussions **LC4** Expressing ideas (writing) **LC6** Writing creatively	Review of language from Units 1–5.	– developing writing skills – making your writing interesting – high-frequency words

© Pearson Education Ltd 2013. Copying permitted for purchasing institution only. This material is not copyright free.

Mi vida 1

Unit & Learning objectives	PoS references	Key language	Grammar and other language features
Resumen y Prepárate (pp. 20–21) Pupils' checklist and practice exercises			
Gramática (pp. 22–23) Detailed grammar summary and practice exercises			G the indefinite article (*un/una*) G the definite article (*el/la/los/las*) G regular verbs (*hablar, vivir* – present, singular) G irregular verbs (*ser, tener* – present, singular) G adjectives (masculine and feminine, singular and plural) G making verbs negative
Zona Proyecto: Los animales (pp. 26–27) Finding out about endangered animals Producing a set of animal cards to trade	**GV3** Developing vocabulary **LC3** Conversation		– saying new words – developing writing skills – using a dictionary to find new words
Te toca a ti (pp. 120–121) Self-access reading and writing at two levels			

© Pearson Education Ltd 2013. Copying permitted for purchasing institution only. This material is not copyright free.

1. ¿Cómo te llamas?

Mi vida 1.1

Pupil Book pages
Pages 6–9

Learning objectives
- Getting used to Spanish pronunciation
- Introducing yourself

Programme of Study
GV1 Tenses (present)
GV2 Grammatical structures (definite articles)
LC5 Accurate pronunciation and intonation

Grammar
- definite articles (*el/la/los/las*)
- verb endings

Key language
¡Hola!
¿Qué tal?
Fenomenal.
Bien, gracias.
Regular.
Fatal.
¿Cómo te llamas?
Me llamo…
¿Dónde vives?
Vivo en…
Adiós.
Hasta luego.

PLTS
T Team workers

Cross-curricular
Geography: Spanish-speaking countries
English: the definite article

Resources
Audio files:
01_Module1_Unit1_Ex1
02_Module1_Unit1_Ex4
03_Module1_Unit1_Ex5
Workbooks:
Cuaderno 1A & 1B, page 2
ActiveTeach:
p.008 Exercise 1 video
p.008 Class game
p.009 Grammar presentation
Starter 1 resource
ActiveLearn:
Listening A, Listening B
Reading A, Reading B
Grammar, Vocabulary

Module 1 Quiz (pp. 6–7)

Answers
1 b 2 b 3 b 4 g 5 b 6: 1 c 2 a 3 b

Starter 1

Aim

To practise Spanish pronunciation.

Give pupils the following list of Spanish towns: Oviedo, Barcelona, Cartagena, Valladolid, Jerez, Zaragoza, Huelva, Badajoz, Gijón, Sevilla (Starter 1 resource). Ask them to discuss in pairs how they think each one is pronounced. Check pupils' answers, asking them to explain their choices.

1 Escucha, mira y haz los gestos. (L1)

Listening. Pupils watch and listen to the videos on ActiveTeach and do the gestures. If you don't have ActiveTeach, students can listen to the audio and make up actions for the words to help them memorise them.

Audioscript Track 01

- *panda*, panda
- *elefante*, elefante
- *tigre*, tigre
- *oso*, oso
- *búfalo*, búfalo
- *cebra*, cebra
- *camello*, camello
- *gorila*, gorila
- *hipopótamo*, hipopótamo
- *jirafa*, jirafa
- *vaca*, vaca
- *zorro*, zorro

2 Con tu compañero/a, una persona dice una palabra, la otra persona hace el gesto. (L1)

Speaking. Pupils work in pairs. One pupil chooses an animal from exercise 1 and says the word, the other pupil does the appropriate gesture. Again, if you do not have ActiveTeach, pupils can use the gestures that they made up in the previous exercise.

Gramática

Use the *Gramática* box to introduce the concept of Spanish nouns having genders and the four words for 'the' in Spanish. See p.22 for more information and further practice.

3 Escribe el, la, los o las. (L1)

Writing. Pupils write the appropriate definite article for each of the given words.

Mi vida 1.1

Answers		
1 el búfalo	2 la cebra	3 los camellos
4 las vacas	5 el zorro	6 las jirafas

Reinforcement

For further practice of definite articles, pupils write the correct definite article for the following words revisited from exercise 1:

___ *panda* (m)   ___ *osas* (f)

___ *elefantes* (m)   ___ *tigre* (m)

___ *gorilas* (m)   ___ *hipopótamo* (m)

Starter 2

Aim

To revise the key sound-spelling links before introducing the greetings language.

Dictate the following sounds and ask pupils to write them down. They write the vowel sound, NOT the whole word:

'a' como 'p**a**nda'   'e' como '**e**lefante'

'i' como 't**i**gre'   'o' como '**o**so'

'ce' como '**ce**bra'   'ú' como 'b**ú**falo'

'j' como '**j**irafa'   'z' como '**z**orro'

Alternative Starter 2:

Use ActiveTeach p.008 Class Game to revise the pronunciation words.

4 Escucha y haz el rap. (L2)

Listening. Pupils listen to the rap in which people ask and answer the question *¿Qué tal?*, following the text at the same time. Play the song again and encourage pupils to rap at the same time. Split the class into two groups, and get one group to rap along to the questions, and the other to the answers, then swap.

Audioscript Track 02

– ¡Hola! ¿Qué tal?
– Fenomenal.
– ¡Hola! ¿Qué tal?
– Bien, gracias.
– ¡Hola! ¿Qué tal?
– Regular.
– ¡Hola! ¿Qué tal?
– Fatal. Fatal.

5 Escucha y lee. (L3)

Listening. Pupils listen to the dialogue, following it in the book. Draw their attention to the question *¿Dónde vives?* and how to answer it.

Audioscript Track 03

– ¡Hola! ¿Cómo te llamas?
– Me llamo Javier.
– ¿Qué tal, Javier?
– Bien, gracias.
– ¿Dónde vives?
– Vivo en Valencia.
– Adiós.
– Hasta luego.

Gramática

Use the *Gramática* box and the previous exercise to draw pupils' attention to the way verbs change in Spanish. At this stage, pupils do not need to learn the endings but just be aware that they change.

6 Con tu compañero/a, haz tres diálogos utilizando el diálogo del ejercicio 4 como modelo. (L3)

Speaking. Using exercise 4 as a model, pupils make up four dialogues – three using the details given in the book and one about themselves.

7 Elige tres famosos. Escribe dos frases para cada uno. (L2)

Writing. Pupils choose three celebrities and write two sentences about each, giving their name and where they live.

Extension

Encourage pupils to write a longer dialogue between two of the celebrities chosen in exercise 7. The conversation could include greetings, asking each other's names, where they live, how they feel and goodbyes.

Plenary

Put one pupil in the 'hot seat' as an expert on the lesson – the other pupils ask him or her questions on what they have learned in the unit so far. If the pupil answers them correctly, he or she gets to nominate another pupil to take the hot seat.

Mi vida 1.1

Workbook 1A, page 2

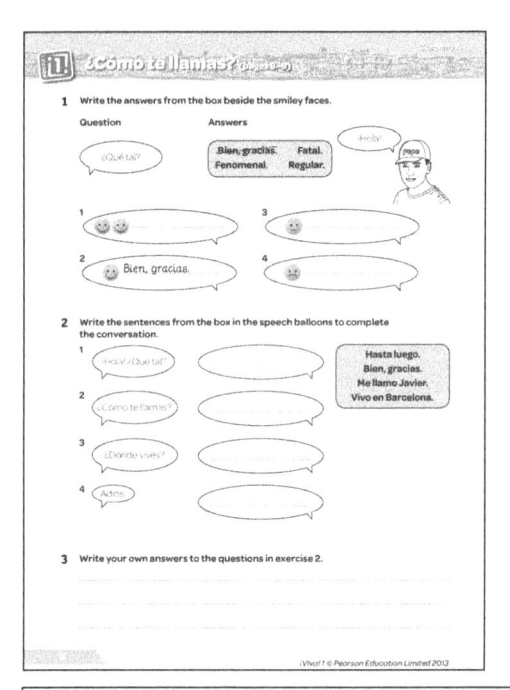

Answers

1. 1 Fenomenal.   2 *Bien, gracias.*
   3 Regular.   4 Fatal.
2. 1 *Bien, gracias.*
   2 Me llamo Javier.
   3 Vivo en Barcelona.
   4 Hasta luego.
3. Own answers.

Workbook 1B, page 2

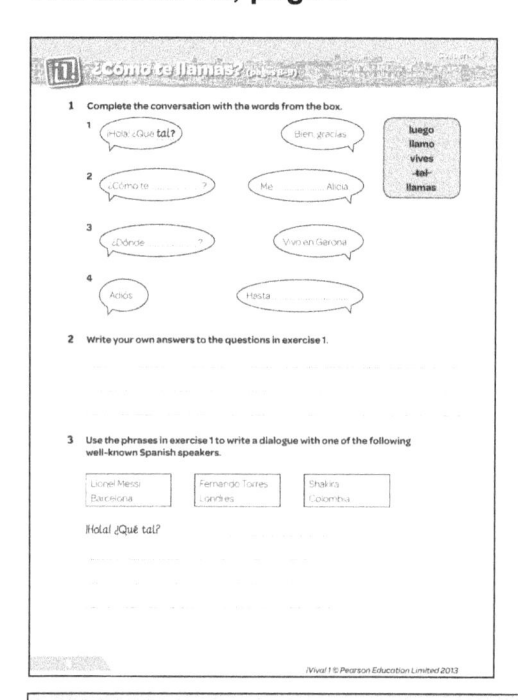

Answers

1. 1 *tal*   2 llamas, llamo
   3 vives   4 luego
2. Own answers
3. Own answers

¿Qué tipo de persona eres? — Mi vida 1.2

Pupil Book pages
Pages 10–11

Learning objectives
- Talking about your personality
- Using adjectives that end in -o/-a

Programme of Study
GV2 Grammatical structures (adjectival endings)
LC6 Translation into English
LC8 Writing creatively

FCSE links
Unit 1: Relationships, family and friends (Personal details, Descriptions)

Grammar
- adjectives that end in -o/-a
- making sentences negative
- ser (present, singular)

Key language
¿Qué tipo de persona eres?
Soy sincero/a.
Soy tímido/a.
Soy tranquilo/a.
Soy divertido/a.
Soy serio/a.
Soy simpático/a.
Soy tonto/a.
Soy listo/a.
Soy generoso/a.
Mi pasión es...
Mi héroe es...

PLTS
C Creative thinkers

Resources
Audio files:
04_Module1_Unit2_Ex1
05_Module1_Unit2_Ex3
06_Module1_Unit2_Ex6
Workbooks:
Cuaderno 1A & 1B, page 3
ActiveTeach:
p.010 Flashcards
p.010 Grammar presentation
p.010 Grammar presentation
p.010 Grammar presentation
p.011 Grammar worksheet
ActiveLearn:
Listening A, Listening B
Reading A, Reading B
Grammar, Vocabulary

Starter 1

Aim

To review the language of greetings.

Jumble the lines of the following conversation from Unit 1 and write it up on the board. Without opening their books, invite pupils to come up and put it back in the correct order.

¡Hola! ¿Cómo te llamas?

Me llamo Javier

¿Qué tal, Javier?

Bien, gracias.

¿Dónde vives?

Vivo en Valencia.

Adiós.

Hasta luego.

1 Escucha. ¿Quién habla? (1–9) (L1)

Listening. Pupils listen to the exchanges and decide which person is speaking each time.

Audioscript Track 04

1 – ¿Qué tipo de persona eres?
– Soy tímido.
2 – ¿Qué tipo de persona eres?
– Soy simpática.
3 – ¿Qué tipo de persona eres?
– Soy sincero.
4 – ¿Qué tipo de persona eres?
– Soy lista.
5 – ¿Qué tipo de persona eres?
– Soy tranquilo.
6 – ¿Qué tipo de persona eres?
– Soy divertido.
7 – ¿Qué tipo de persona eres?
– Soy serio.
8 – ¿Qué tipo de persona eres?
– Soy generosa.
9 – ¿Qué tipo de persona eres?
– Soy tonta.

Answers

1 Antonio	2 Claudia	3 Daniel
4 Carmen	5 Pablo	6 Miguel
7 Gabriel	8 Andrea	9 Laura

Gramática

Use the *Gramática* box to teach pupils that adjectives in Spanish have masculine and feminine forms. The box lists both forms of the adjectives taught in this unit. There is more information and further practice on p. 23.

Mi vida 1.2

> **Reinforcement**
>
> Pupils follow the adjective patterns in the *Gramática* box to work out the feminine forms of the following cognate adjectives: *honesto* (honest), *positivo* (positive), *negativo* (negative), *extrovertido* (extrovert), *delicioso* (delicious), *silencioso* (silent), *estúpido* (stupid), *moderno* (modern), *antiguo* (old), *nuevo* (new), *favorito* (favourite). Ask pupils to guess the English meanings.

2 Escribe estas frases correctamente. Traduce las frases al inglés. (L2)

Writing. Pupils unjumble the words given to write out the sentences correctly. Next, ask them to translate the sentences into English and write an M or an F to indicate whether each sentence was written by someone male or female.

> **Answers**
>
> 1 Soy divertido y simpático. I am funny and nice. (M)
> 2 Soy lista y tranquila. I am clever and calm. (F)
> 3 Soy sincero y generoso. I am sincere and generous. (M)
> 4 Soy seria y simpática. I am serious and nice. (F)
> 5 No soy tonta. I am not silly. (F)
> 6 No soy tímido. I am not shy. (M)

3 Escucha. Elige los adjetivos que entiendes y anota si es verdadero (V) o falso (F). (1–5) (L3)

Listening. Pupils listen and choose the adjectives the five people use to describe themselves to their friends. They then write whether that description is true (V) or false (F) according to the friend.

> **Audioscript Track 05**
>
> 1 – ¿Qué tipo de persona eres?
> – Soy simpático y generoso.
> – Sí, es verdad. Eres simpático y generoso.
> 2 – ¿Qué tipo de persona eres?
> – Soy lista y divertida.
> – Sí, es verdad.
> 3 – ¿Qué tipo de persona eres?
> – Soy serio y listo.
> – ¡No, no es verdad! No eres serio y listo.
> 4 – ¿Qué tipo de persona eres?
> – Soy sincera y tranquila.
> – Sí, es verdad.
> 5 – ¿Qué tipo de persona eres?
> – Soy tímido y soy tonto.
> – ¡No, no es verdad!
>
> **Answers**
>
> 1 b, c, V   2 a, c, V   3 b, c, F
> 4 a, b, V   5 a, b, F

> **Gramática**
>
> Pupils have seen examples of negative sentences in this unit but here is an opportunity to point them out and ensure that all pupils understand how to make a sentence negative.
>
> Use the *Gramática* box to teach pupils the singular paradigm of *ser*. They have seen all three parts in the unit but this is a chance for them to learn it formally. Stress that this is an important irregular verb and needs to be learned.
>
> There is more information and further practice exercise on Pupil Book p. 23.

4 ¿Qué tipo de persona eres? Trabaja en un grupo de cuatro personas, haz cuatro diálogos. (L2)

Speaking. In groups of four, pupils make up four dialogues in which they ask each person what type of person they are and then either agree or disagree using the phrases *Sí, es verdad* and *¡No, no es verdad!*

> **Starter 2**
>
> **Aim**
>
> To help pupils to learn the adjectives presented in this unit.
>
> Ask pupils to rank the adjectives from this unit in order of importance for themselves, starting with the adjective they would say describes them best. Then ask them to compare with their neighbour and discuss if they agree.
>
> **Alternative Starter 2:**
>
> Use ActiveTeach p. 010 Flashcards to review and practise personality adjectives.

5 Lee los textos. Copia y completa la tabla. (L3)

Reading. Pupils read the four texts and complete the table. Some vocabulary is glossed for support.

Mi vida 1.2

Answers

name	personality	passion	hero
Ana	serious, sincere	music	Shakira
Sergio	shy, but not silly	football	Cesc Fàbregas
Iker	calm, generous	tennis	Rafael Nadal
Pablo	nice, amusing	sport	Marc Gasol

6 Escucha. Copia y completa la ficha de identidad. (L3)

Listening. Pupils listen and then complete the identity card with the details given.

Audioscript Track 06

¡Hola! ¿Qué tal? Me llamo Ana.

Vivo en Sevilla. Soy divertida y también soy generosa.

Mi pasión es la música y mi héroe es Rihanna. ¡Es fenomenal!

Answers
Nombre: Ana
Carácter: divertida, generosa
Pasión: la música
Héroe: Rihanna

Extension

Pupils write up a short paragraph for the following imaginary person:

Nombre: Tomás
Carácter: sincero, tímido
Pasión: la televisión
Héroe: Gandhi

Pronunciación

Use the *Pronunciación* box to explain to pupils about how the stress in Spanish words normally falls on the penultimate syllable. Ask pupils to suggest some words they know that have an accent to show you which letter to stress.

7 ¿Qué tipo de persona eres? Haz un póster. (L3)

Writing. Pupils make a poster about themselves using all the personal description language they have learned so far. Draw pupils' attention to the Skills box and encourage them to use connectives to vary the structure of their sentences and add variety using negatives and *y*.

Plenary

Write up some pairs of sentences and discuss with pupils what connectives could be used to join them.

Workbook 1A, page 3

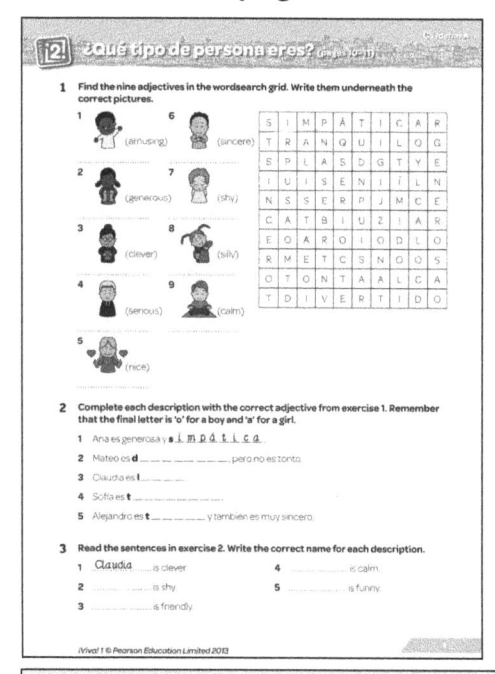

Answers

1
1 divertido 2 generosa 3 lista
4 serio 5 simpática 6 sincero
7 tímido 8 tonta 9 tranquilo

2
1 simpática 2 divertido 3 lista
4 tranquila 5 tímido

3
1 Claudia 2 Alejandro 3 Ana
4 Sofía 5 Mateo

Mi vida 1.2

Workbook 1B, page 3

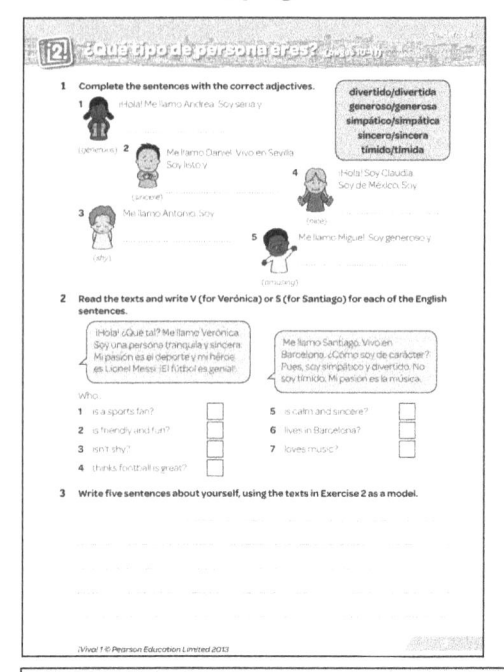

Answers

1. 1 generosa 2 sincero 3 tímido
   4 simpática 5 divertido
2. 1 V 2 S 3 S 4 V 5 V 6 S 7 S
3. Own answers

Worksheet 1.2 Personality adjectives

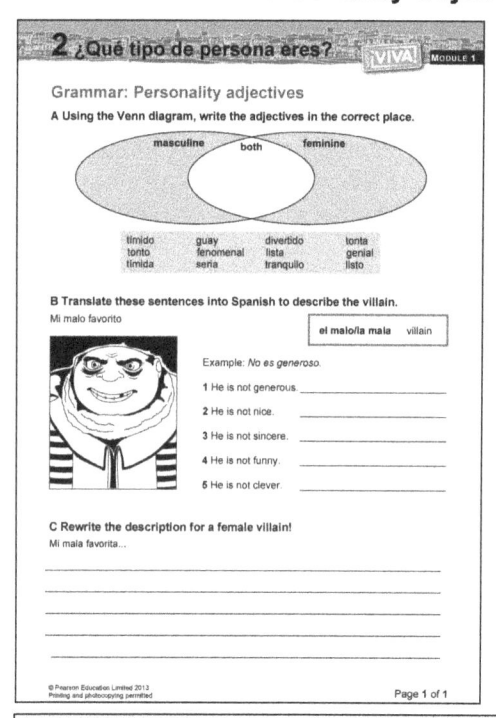

Answers

A **masculine:** tímido, tonto, listo, divertido, tranquilo

  feminine: tímida, tonta, lista, seria

  both: genial, guay, fenomenal

B 1 No es generoso. 2 No es simpático.
  3 No es sincero. 4 No es divertido.
  5 No es listo.

C 1 No es generosa. 2 No es simpática.
  3 No es sincera. 4 No es divertida.
  5 No es lista.

© Pearson Education Ltd 2013. Copying permitted for purchasing institution only. This material is not copyright free.

¿Tienes hermanos?

Mi vida 1.3

Pupil Book pages
Pages 12–13

Learning objectives
- Talking about age, brothers and sisters
- Using the verb *tener* (to have)

Programme of Study
GV2 Grammatical structures (indefinite articles)
LC5 Speaking coherently and confidently
LC6 Reading comprehension

FCSE links
Unit 1: Relationships, family and friends (Family and step-family, Personal details about family, Numbers)

Grammar
- *tener* (present, singular)
- indefinite articles (*un/una*)

Key language
¿Cuántos años tienes?
Tengo… años.
Numbers: *uno* to *quince* (and *cero*)
¿Tienes hermanos?
Tengo un hermano.
Tengo una hermana.
Tengo un hermanastro.
Tengo una hermanastra.
Tengo dos hermanos.
Tengo dos hermanas.
No tengo hermanos.
Soy hijo único.
Soy hija única.

PLTS
T Team workers

Cross-curricular
English: the indefinite article

Resources
Audio files:
07_Module1_Unit3_Ex1
08_Module1_Unit3_Ex2
09_Module1_Unit3_Ex5
Workbooks:
Cuaderno 1A & 1B, page 4
ActiveTeach:
p.012 Flashcards
p.012 Grammar presentation
p.012 Grammar practice
p.012 Video 1
p.012 Video 1 transcript
p.012 Video worksheet 1
p.012 Flashcards
p.013 Flashcards
Plenary resource
ActiveLearn:
Listening A, Listening B
Reading A, Reading B
Grammar, Vocabulary

Starter 1

Aim

To identify parts of speech in a sentence.

Write up the following sentences on the board. Give pupils three minutes to identify the adjectives (A), nouns (N), verbs (V) and connectives (C). Pupils can put a square around adjectives, a circle around nouns, a triangle around verbs, and a star around connectives.

1 *Me llamo* (V) *Ana. Soy* (V) *seria* (A) *y también* (C) *soy* (V) *generosa* (A).
2 *Mi pasión* (N) *es* (V) *el fútbol* (N). *¡Es* (V) *estupendo!* (A).
3 *Vivo* (V) *en Sevilla. Soy* (V) *tímido* (A), *pero* (C) *no soy* (V) *tonto* (A).
4 *Mi héroe* (N) *es* (V) *Beyoncé. ¡Es* (V) *genial!* (A).

Check the answers and ask pupils to translate the sentences into English.

Alternative Starter 1:
Use ActiveTeach p.012 Flashcards to introduce numbers 1-15.

1 Escucha. Hay tres números que no se mencionan. ¿Cuáles son? (L1)

Listening. Pupils listen to a list of consecutive numbers and note the three that are left out.

Audioscript Track 07
- uno
- dos
- tres
- cinco
- seis
- ocho
- nueve
- diez
- once
- doce
- trece
- quince

Answers
cuatro, siete, catorce

2 Escucha. Pon los dibujos en el orden correcto. (1–6) (L2)

Listening. Pupils listen to six people say how old they are and identify each speaker from the pictures. Key vocabulary is glossed for support.

© Pearson Education Ltd 2013. Copying permitted for purchasing institution only. This material is not copyright free.

Mi vida 1.3

Audioscript Track 08

1 – ¿Cuántos años tienes?
– Tengo quince años.

2 – ¿Cuántos años tienes?
– Tengo diez años.

3 – ¿Cuántos años tienes?
– Tengo once años.

4 – ¿Cuántos años tienes?
– Tengo doce años.

5 – ¿Cuántos años tienes?
– Tengo catorce años.

6 – ¿Cuántos años tienes?
– Tengo seis años.

Answers
c, f, a, e, b, d

Gramática

Use the *Gramática* box to teach pupils the present tense singular forms of *tener*. Stress that *tener* is a particularly useful verb that needs to be learned. Once pupils have worked out that *Tengo doce años* literally means 'I have twelve years', ask them to translate the question ¿*Cuántos años tienes?* literally too. There is more information and further practice on Pupil Book p. 23.

3 Con tu compañero/a, pregunta y contesta por las personas del ejercicio 2. (L3)

Speaking. In pairs, pupils practise the dialogue using the picture prompts supplied in question 2. A sample exchange is given. Draw pupils' attention to the *Pronunciación* box to encourage them to stress the *ny* sound in *años*. They can then make up their own dialogues by substituting their own names and birthdays.

4 ¿Qué números faltan? (L1)

Writing. Pupils fill in the gaps by choosing the missing numbers in each sequence.

Answers
1 dos, cuatro, **seis**, ocho, **diez**, doce, **catorce**
2 uno, **tres**, cinco, **siete**, nueve, **once**, trece
3 quince, **doce**, nueve, **seis**, tres
4 catorce, **doce**, diez, **ocho**, seis, **cuatro**

Reinforcement
Pupils create three number sequences of their own for their partner to complete.

Starter 2

Aim

To introduce the months of the year.

Write up the months of the year in random order on the board. Give pupils three minutes to list them in the correct order, encouraging them to identify the cognates first. To reinforce, with books closed, ask pupils to say the months going around the class.

Alternative Starter 2:

Use ActiveTeach p.012 Grammar practice to review the verb *tener*.

5 Escucha y escribe la letra correcta. (1–8). (L2)

Listening. Pupils listen to eight people answer the question ¿*Tienes hermanos?* and identify each speaker from the pictures. Point out the Tip box, which explains the two meanings of *hermanastro* and *hermanastra*.

Audioscript Track 09

1 – ¿Tienes hermanos?
– Sí, tengo un hermano.

2 – ¿Tienes hermanos?
– Tengo una hermanastra.

3 – ¿Tienes hermanos?
– Sí, tengo una hermana.

4 – ¿Tienes hermanos?
– Sí, tengo un hermanastro.

5 – ¿Tienes hermanos?
– Sí, tengo dos hermanos.

6 – ¿Tienes hermanos?
– No. No tengo hermanos. Soy hija única.

7 – ¿Tienes hermanos?
– Sí, tengo un hermano y dos hermanas.

8 – ¿Tienes hermanos?
– No. No tengo hermanos. Soy hijo único.

Answers
1 a   2 d   3 b   4 c   5 e   6 h   7 f   8 g

© Pearson Education Ltd 2013. Copying permitted for purchasing institution only. This material is not copyright free.

Mi vida 1.3

Gramática

Use the *Gramática* box to introduce the indefinite article in Spanish. In Unit 1, pupils will have already learned that the word 'the' in Spanish changes according to whether the noun is masculine or feminine. Here, they will learn that the same rule applies to the Spanish word for 'a'. There is more information and further practice on Pupil Book p. 22.

6 Haz un sondeo en tu clase. Pregunta a diez personas. (L2)

Speaking. Pupils carry out a survey of ten people in the class to find out whether they have brothers or sisters. A sample exchange is given for support.

7 Lee los textos y completa las frases. (L3)

Reading. Pupils read the texts and complete the sentences summarising them in English.

Answers

1 **Óscar** lives in Ecuador.
2 Carmen lives in **Santiago de Chile**.
3 **Hugo** is twelve years old.
4 Carmen has two **brothers** and one **sister**.
5 **Hugo** has no brothers or sisters.
6 Oscar has two **sisters** and one **stepbrother/half-brother**.

Extension

Using the model framework below, pupils write a short description of themselves, including their name, where they live, how old they are and how many brothers and sisters they have. They could then write a similar description for a friend or a famous celebrity.

¡Hola! Me llamo Robert Pattinson y vivo en… Tengo… años y tengo dos hermanas. Hasta luego.

Plenary

Put the class into two teams. Have a pre-prepared list of number sequences ready for the teams to complete (Plenary resource). Teams nominate one person to race for them. Following team discussion, the person chosen has to race to the board to write the next number(s) in a sequence before the opposing team. Award two points for a completely correct answer, one point for an answer with an error. The team with the most points wins.

Note: You many want to set up permanent teams at the start of term to save time. You could keep a running total of points scored and award a prize to the winning team at the end of each term.

Workbook 1A, page 4

Answers

C	A	T	O	R	C	E		Q
U		R		I				U
A		E		U	N	O		I
T		S		C				N
R				D	O	S		C
O	C	H	O			I		E
					S	E	I	S
		D		O		T		
		O		N	U	E	V	E
		C		C				
T	R	E	C	E		D	I	E	Z

© Pearson Education Ltd 2013. Copying permitted for purchasing institution only. This material is not copyright free.

Mi vida 1.3

1 horizontales	verticales
1 catorce	1 cuatro
5 uno	2 tres
6 dos	3 cinco
8 ocho	4 quince
9 seis	7 siete
12 nueve	10 doce
13 trece	11 once
14 diez	

2 1 Tengo trece años.
    2 No tengo hermanos.
    3 Me llamo Luisa.
    4 Tengo una hermanastra.
    5 Tiene cinco años.

Workbook 1B, page 4

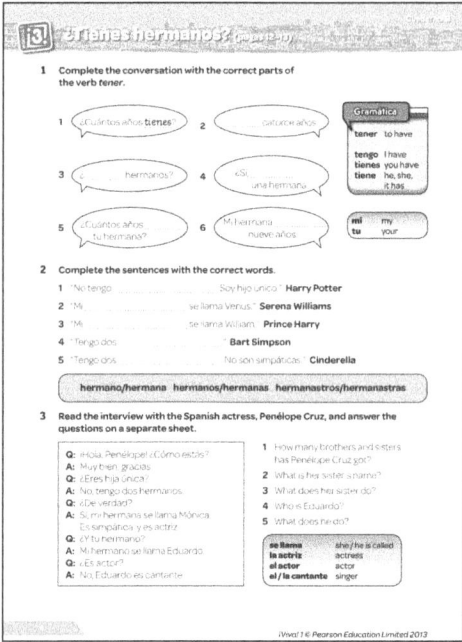

Answers

1 *1 tienes* 2 Tengo 3 ¿Tienes
   4 tengo 5 tiene 6 tiene
2 1 hermanos 2 hermana
   3 hermano 4 hermanas
   5 hermanastras
3 1 two, a brother and a sister
   2 Mónica
   3 She's an actress.
   4 her brother
   5 He's a singer.

Video

The video component provides opportunities for speaking activities in a plausible and stimulating context. The ¡TeleViva! team – Samuel, Estela, Marco, José, Laura, Aroa and Ramona – report from their studio in Oviedo, Asturias. They are making video reports about the town to answer emails they have received from viewers in the UK. Each video is around three minutes long.

Episode 1: ¡Bienvenidos a TeleViva!

The ¡TeleViva! team introduce themselves from their studio in Oviedo, Asturias. Video worksheet 1 can be used in conjunction with this episode.

Answers to video worksheet (ActiveTeach)

A

1 Answers given are likely to be:
   Me llamo …   Tengo … años.
   Vivo en …   ¿Cómo te llamas?
   ¿Cuántos años tienes?   ¿Dónde vives?

2 Answers will vary and may include the nine adjectives introduced in unit 2 of the Pupil Book.

B

1 It is the city where they live.
2 a) Laura
   b) Samuel
   c) Ramona

C

1 an email (from Lily in Brighton)
2 nice/kind and generous
3 a) José is <u>14</u> years old.
   b) Aroa describes herself as amusing and <u>nice / kind</u>.
   c) <u>Ramona</u> says that her passion is technology (*'la tecnología'*).

D

1 Welcome to *TeleViva*.
2 Because she asks him his name but she already knows it!
3 Because she is shy./Because she doesn't want to appear in the video.
4 Answers will vary.
5 Answers will vary.

E

Pupils will produce their own dialogues in small groups.

© Pearson Education Ltd 2013. Copying permitted for purchasing institution only. This material is not copyright free.

¿Cuándo es tu cumpleaños?

Mi vida 1.4

Pupil Book pages
Pages 14–15

Learning objectives
- Saying when your birthday is
- Using numbers and the alphabet

Programme of Study
LC2 Transcription
LC5 Speaking coherently and confidently
LC7 Literary texts

FCSE links
Unit 1: Relationships, family and friends (Personal details, Family celebrations, Numbers)
Unit 2: Education and future plans (Alphabet, Numbers)

Key language
¿Cuándo es tu cumpleaños?
Mi cumpleaños es el… de…
enero
febrero
marzo
abril
mayo
junio
julio
agosto
septiembre
octubre
noviembre
diciembre
Numbers: *dieciséis* to *treinta y uno*
¿Cómo se escribe?
Se escribe…
The alphabet in Spanish

PLTS
C Creative thinkers

Resources
Audio files:
10_Module1_Unit4_Ex4
11_Module1_Unit4_Ex5
12_Module1_Unit4_Ex8
13_Module1_Unit4_Ex9
Workbooks:
Cuaderno 1A & 1B, page 5
ActiveTeach:
p.014 Class game
p.015 Thinking skills worksheet
ActiveLearn:
Listening A, Listening B
Reading A, Reading B
Vocabulary

Starter 1

Aim

To review numbers 0–15.

Give pupils two minutes to create three bingo *Número* cards of 16 squares (4 rows of 4) on a piece of paper for three games of quick-fire bingo. Instruct pupils to fill in each card in a random order using all 16 numbers (including zero). Starting with the first bingo card, call out numbers, which pupils cross out on their card. When a pupil has marked off an entire row vertically, horizontally or diagonally, he or she calls ¡Número! The pupil then reads those four numbers out loud. He or she can have a go at being the caller for bingo card number two.

1 Mira el póster. Pon los meses en el orden correcto. (L1)

Reading. Pupils read the poster and put the months of the year in the correct order. This exercise helps pupils practise using cognates as a reading strategy.

Answers
enero, febrero, marzo, abril, mayo, junio, julio, agosto, septiembre, octubre, noviembre, diciembre

2 Con tu compañero/a, lee los meses en voz alta, en el orden correcto. (L1)

Speaking. In pairs, pupils take it in turns to read the months out loud in the correct order. Draw pupils' attention to the *Pronunciación* box and encourage them to practise their pronunciation of the letters *b* and *v* in Spanish (when found at the beginning of a word or following a consonant, they are both pronounced like the English letter *b*).

3 Completa los números. (L1)

Writing. Pupils complete the gaps in the list of numbers. Check answers as a class. Point out the usefulness of reading strategies such as recognising patterns and using logic. In this case, *dieciséis* is actually a contraction of *diez y seis* (or '10 and 6'), *veintiuno* is a contraction of *veinte y uno*, and so on.

Answers	
diec**iséis**	**veinticuatro**
dieci**siete**	**veinticinco**
dieci**ocho**	veintiséis
diecinueve	**veintisiete**
veinte	**veintiocho**
veintiuno	**veintinueve**
veintidós	treinta
veinti**trés**	treinta y **uno**

Mi vida 1.4

4 Escucha y comprueba tus respuestas. (L1)

Listening. Pupils listen and check their answers to exercise 3. Check pupils' understanding of the saying in the *Zona Cultura* box. Point out that when reading for gist, they should look for key words and cognates, leaving words that they don't know to be looked up in a dictionary.

Audioscript Track 10

dieciséis, diecisiete, dieciocho, diecinueve
veinte, veintiuno, veintidós, veintitrés
veinticuatro, veinticinco, veintiséis, veintisiete
veintiocho, veintinueve, treinta, treinta y uno

5 Escucha. Copia y completa los cumpleaños. (1–6). (L2)

Listening. Pupils listen to six people answering the question *¿Cuándo es tu cumpleaños?* and fill in the gaps with the correct number and/or month.

Audioscript Track 11

1 – ¿Cuándo es tu cumpleaños?
 – Mi cumpleaños es el veintisiete de mayo.

2 – ¿Cuándo es tu cumpleaños?
 – Mi cumpleaños es el veinticuatro de octubre.

3 – ¿Cuándo es tu cumpleaños?
 – Mi cumpleaños es el dieciocho de marzo.

4 – ¿Cuándo es tu cumpleaños?
 – Mi cumpleaños es el treinta y uno de agosto.

5 – ¿Cuándo es tu cumpleaños?
 – Mi cumpleaños es el veintidós de diciembre.

6 – ¿Cuándo es tu cumpleaños?
 – Mi cumpleaños es el diecisiete de enero.

Answers

1 27th **May**
2 24th **October**
3 18th **March**
4 31st **August**
5 22nd **December**
6 17th **January**

Extension

Ask pupils to translate the following dates into Spanish:
1 15th June
2 30th April
3 12th February
4 5th July
5 18th December
6 8th September

Starter 2
Aim

To review months and numbers.

Play Kim's game using months and/or number sequences. Display the full list of vocabulary on the board (projected on a PowerPoint slide) to pupils for 20 seconds, then cover it. Remove one item, then reveal them all again. Pupils must name the item that has been removed.

6 Con tu compañero/a, pregunta y contesta. (L3)

Speaking. In pairs, pupils take it in turns to ask and answer two questions about the names and birthdays of four celebrities. A framework is provided and *mi* and *tu* are glossed for support.

Reinforcement

As a follow-up, ask the whole class to write their own birthday in Spanish on a piece of paper. Collect and re-distribute all the papers. Pupils then read out the date on their piece of paper for the others to guess who wrote it (this activity is suitable for groups or the whole class).

7 Lee los textos. Escribe la edad y el cumpleaños de cada persona. (L2)

Reading. Pupils read the texts and note the name, age and birthday of the three people.

Answers

a Marta – 12 years old, 25/12, Christmas
b Javi – 13 years old, 19/9
c Irene – 14 years old, 14/2, Valentine's day

Mi vida 1.4

8 Escucha y canta la canción del alfabeto. (L1)

Listening. Pupils listen to the song, following the text at the same time. Play the song again and encourage pupils to sing along. A pronunciation guide is provided for the pupils and in the audioscript below – note this is not the official phonetic spelling of the Spanish alphabet.

Audioscript Track 12

A ah, B beh, C theh, D deh, E eh, F efeh, G heh

H acheh, I ee, J hota

K kah, L eleh, M emeh, N eneh, Ñ enyeh

O oh, P peh, Q koo, R ereh, S eseh

T teh, U oo, V ooveh, W ooveh dobleh

X ekis, Y ee gri-ehga, Z theta

Z es la última letra

Canto el alfabeto.

9 ¿Cómo se escribe? Escucha y escribe los nombres. (1–6) (L2)

Listening. Pupils listen to six conversations and note down the spellings of the names that are mentioned. When checking the answers, ask pupils to spell the names out loud.

Audioscript Track 13

1 – ¡Hola! Me llamo Alejandro.
 – ¿Cómo se escribe?
 – Se escribe A–L–E–J–A–N–D–R–O.

2 – ¡Hola! Me llamo Laila.
 – Laila… ¿Cómo se escribe?
 – Se escribe L-A-I-L-A.

3 – ¡Hola! Me llamo Iñaki.
 – ¿Cómo se escribe?
 – Se escribe I-Ñ-A-K-I.

4 – ¡Hola! Me llamo Valeria.
 – ¿Cómo se escribe?
 – Se escribe V-A-L-E-R-I-A.

5 – ¡Hola! Me llamo Mohamed.
 – ¿Cómo se escribe?
 – Se escribe M-O-H-A-M-E-D.

6 – ¡Hola! Me llamo Mercedes.
 – ¿Cómo se escribe?
 – Se escribe M-E-R-C-E-D-E-S.

Answers

1 Alejandro 2 Laila 3 Iñaki
4 Valeria 5 Mohamed 6 Mercedes

10 Haz una presentación. (L3)

Speaking. Pupils prepare a detailed presentation of themselves following the framework supplied, to present to their partner, a small group or the whole class.

Plenary

To review the letters of the alphabet, do a mini spelling bee, asking pupils to spell certain words from memory. Differentiate by first reading out a few words in Spanish and then giving a few in English for them also to write out in Spanish. When checking the answers, ask pupils to spell the words out loud.

Workbook 1A, page 5

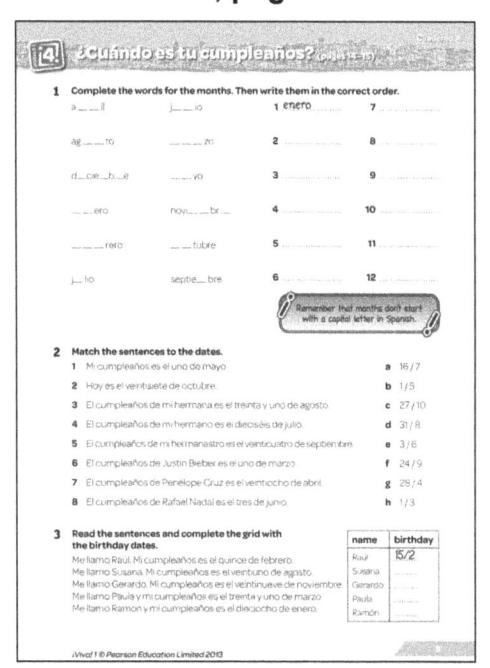

Answers

1 1 enero 2 febrero 3 marzo
   4 abril   5 mayo   6 junio
   7 julio   8 agosto 9 septiembre
   10 octubre 11 noviembre 12 diciembre

2 1b 2c 3d 4a 5f 6h 7g 8e

3 Raúl 15 / 2   Susana 21 / 8
   Gerardo 29 / 11   Paula 31 / 3
   Ramón 18 / 1

© Pearson Education Ltd 2013. Copying permitted for purchasing institution only. This material is not copyright free.

Workbook 1B, page 5

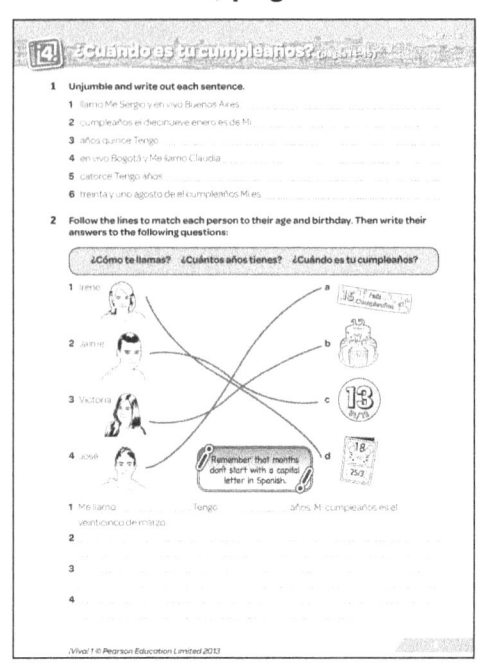

Answers

1.
   1. Me llamo Sergio y vivo en Buenos Aires.
   2. Mi cumpleaños es el diecinueve de enero.
   3. Tengo quince años.
   4. Me llamo Claudia y vivo en Bogotá.
   5. Tengo catorce años.
   6. Mi cumpleaños es el treinta y uno de agosto.

2.
   1. *Me llamo* Irene. *Tengo* 18 *años. Mi cumpleaños es el veinticinco de marzo.*
   2. Me llamo Jaime. Tengo 13 años. Mi cumpleaños es el treinta y uno de diciembre.
   3. Me llamo Victoria. Tengo 12 años. Mi cumpleaños es el veintiuno de julio.
   4. Me llamo José. Tengo 15 años. Mi cumpleaños es el veintisiete de septiembre.

Worksheet 1.4 Number crunching!

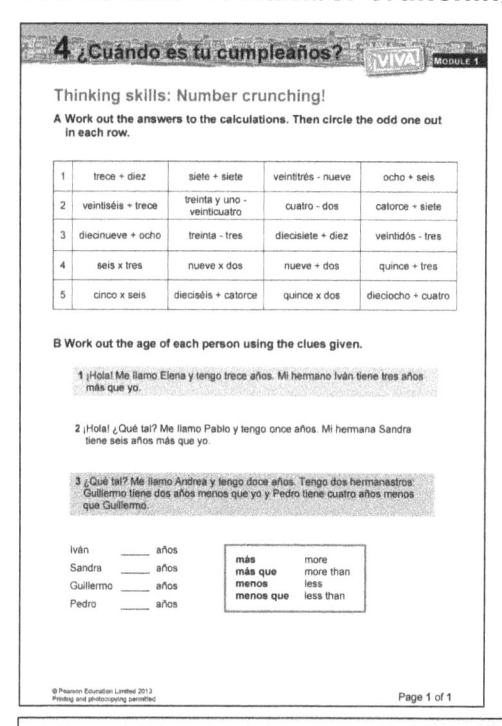

Answers

A
1. 13, 14, 14, 14
   Odd one out: trece + diez= 13
2. 2, 7, 2, 2,
   Odd one out: treinta y uno – veinticuatro= 7
3. 27, 27, 27, 19
   Odd one out: veintidós – tres= 19
4. 18, 18, 11, 18
   Odd one out: nueve + dos = 11
5. 30, 30, 30, 22
   Odd one out: dieciocho + cuatro = 22

B **Iván:** 16 años
Sandra: 17 años
Guillermo: 10 años
Pedro: 6 años

5 ¿Tienes mascotas?

Mi vida 1.5

Pupil Book pages
Pages 16–17

Learning objectives
- Talking about your pets
- Making adjectives agree with nouns

Programme of Study
GV2 Grammatical structures (adjectival agreement)
GV3 Developing vocabulary

FCSE links
Unit 1: Relationships, family and friends (Pets)

Grammar
- adjective forms (masculine and feminine, singular and plural)

Key language
¿Tienes mascotas?
No tengo mascotas.
Tengo…
un perro, un gato, un conejo
un caballo, un pez, un ratón
una serpiente, una cobaya
blanco/a
amarillo/a
negro/a
rojo/a
verde
gris
marrón
azul
rosa
naranja

PLTS
C Creative thinkers

Cross-curricular
English: grammatical terms

Resources
Audio files:
14_Module1_Unit5_Ex1
15_Module1_Unit5_Ex3
Workbooks:
Cuaderno 1A & 1B, page 6
ActiveTeach:
p.016 Flashcards: pets
p.016 Flashcards: colours
p.016 Video 2
p.016 Video 2 transcript
p.016 Video worksheet 2
p.017 Grammar presentation
p.017 Class game
p.017 Extension reading activity
p.017 Grammar worksheet
Starter 2 resource
ActiveLearn:
Listening A, Listening B
Reading A, Reading B
Grammar, Vocabulary

Starter 1

Aim

To introduce vocabulary for pets.

Present the following gapped words on the board next to visuals of the pets to show their meanings (use ActiveTeach flashcards). Read out the words for each pet and ask pupils to use their sound-spelling knowledge to predict the missing letters.

1 perr_	2 _ato
3 pe_	4 cone_o
5 caba_ _o	6 r_tón
7 _obaya	8 _erpiente

1 Escucha. Pon las mascotas en el orden correcto. (1–9) (L2)

Listening. Pupils listen to the nine exchanges while referring to the photos on p. 16 of the Pupil Book. They note the numbers of the animals in the order that they hear them mentioned.

Audioscript Track 14

– ¿Tienes mascotas?
– Sí. Tengo un gato.

– ¿Tienes mascotas?
– Sí. Tengo una serpiente.

– ¿Tienes mascotas?
– Sí. Tengo una cobaya.

– ¿Tienes mascotas?
– No. No tengo mascotas.

– ¿Tienes mascotas?
– Sí. Tengo un caballo.

– ¿Tienes mascotas?
– Sí. Tengo un pez.

– ¿Tienes mascotas?
– Sí. Tengo un ratón.

– ¿Tienes mascotas?
– Sí. Tengo un perro.

– ¿Tienes mascotas?
– Sí. Tengo un conejo.

© Pearson Education Ltd 2013. Copying permitted for purchasing institution only. This material is not copyright free.

Mi vida 1.5

Answers

2, 7, 8, 9, 4, 5, 6, 1, 3

Pronunciación

Use the *Pronunciación* box to encourage pupils to practise rolling their tongues to produce the *r* and *rr* sounds in Spanish. Once they've mastered this, they can practise this popular *trabalenguas* (tongue twister):

El perro de Rosa y Roque no tiene rabo, porque Ramón Ramírez se lo ha cortado.

Rosa and Roque's dog doesn't have a tail, because Ramón Ramírez cut it off.

2 Con tu compañero/a, haz cálculos con los números del ejercicio 1. (L2)

Speaking. In pairs, pupils take it in turns to make up simple maths sums using the numbers from exercise 1. A framework is supplied and *más*, *menos* and *igual a* are glossed for support.

3 Escucha. Copia y completa la tabla. (1–5) (L3)

Listening. Pupils listen to five conversations and fill in the grid by noting which pet(s) each person has and what colour it is/they are. Some vocabulary is glossed for support.

Audioscript Track 15

1 – ¿Tienes mascotas?
– Sí. Tengo un ratón.
– ¿Cómo es?
– Es gris.

2 – ¿Tienes mascotas?
– Sí. Tengo un conejo.
– ¿Cómo es?
– Es marrón.

3 – ¿Tienes mascotas?
– Sí. Tengo un gato.
– ¿Cómo es?
– Es blanco y negro.

4 – ¿Tienes mascotas?
– Sí. Tengo una serpiente.
– ¿Cómo es?
– Es roja y amarilla.

5 – ¿Tienes mascotas?
– Sí, tengo tres peces.
– ¿Cómo son?
– Son azules.

Answers

	animal	colour
1	mouse	grey
2	rabbit	brown
3	cat	black and white
4	snake	red and yellow
5	three fish	blue

Reinforcement

Ask pupils to translate the following colour combinations into Spanish:

1. black + white = grey
(negro más blanco igual a gris)

2. red + white = pink
(rojo más blanco igual a rosa)

3. blue + yellow = green
(azul más amarillo igual a verde)

4. yellow + red = orange
(amarillo más rojo igual a naranja)

5. red + green = brown
(rojo más verde igual a marrón)

Gramática

Use the *Gramática* box on p. 17 to review masculine and feminine forms for adjectives (first introduced in Unit 2) and introduce the concept of singular and plural forms. Stress to pupils that whereas in English, adjectives are always found in front of a noun, Spanish adjectives usually follow the noun that they modify. There is more information and further practice on Pupil Book p. 23.

Starter 2

Aim

To review adjectival agreement.

Write up the following on the board (Starter 2 resource). Give pupils two minutes to choose the correct adjectival endings.

1 *Tengo un perro negro/negra.*
2 *Mi serpiente es amarillo/amarilla.*
3 *Tengo dos gatos blancos/blanco.*
4 *Mis cobayas son bastante tímidos/tímidas.*
5 *Mi pez, que se llama Coco, es blanco y rojo/blanca y roja.*

Mi vida 1.5

Check answers, asking pupils to explain their choices and to translate each completed sentence into English.

4 Con tu compañero/a, juega a las tres en raya. (L2)

Speaking. In pairs, pupils play noughts and crosses using the nine artworks on p. 17 of the Pupil's book as a backdrop for a grid. Each pupil takes it in turns to specify which square they will be going for, then they have to correctly say the sentence decoded by the picture when asked the question *¿Tienes mascotas?*, for example, top row left = *Sí. Tengo un pez azul.* The object of the game is to get three in a row.

5 ¿Verdadero o falso? Escribe V o F. (L3)

Reading. Pupils read the four short texts then decide whether the statements that follow are true (V) or false (F). Some vocabulary is glossed for support.

Answers

1 F 2 V 3 F 4 F 5 V 6 V 7 V 8 F

Extension

Write up the following sentences on the board, jumbling the order of the words. With books closed, pupils say the sentences in the correct order.

1 *Tengo dos peces que se llaman Flip y Flop.*
2 *Mi serpiente es bastante tranquila pero muy tonta.*
3 *Mi gato tiene diez años y se llama Butch.*
4 *Tengo un conejo que es tímido.*
5 *¿Y tú, tienes mascotas?*

6 Eres un/a fanático/a de los animales. Tienes muchas mascotas. Descríbelas. (L3)

Writing. Pupils imagine that they are crazy about animals. They write an imaginative description of their numerous pets, adding as much detail as possible. Draw pupils' attention to the Skills box and encourage them to use intensifiers to extend their sentences. When they have finished, pupils swap with a partner to check each other's work: they identify errors but don't correct them. Pupils then write a second draft.

Plenary

Ask pupils to explain how adjectival agreement works to their partner. Ask them to write a couple of multiple choice questions for their partner, giving two options, for example:

How do you say 'black cat' in Spanish?

a un gato negro   b un gato negra

Workbook 1A, page 6

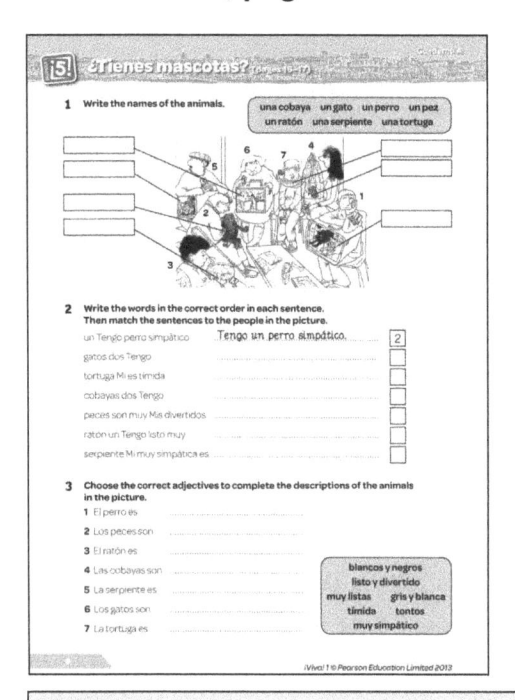

Answers

1 1 un gato   2 un perro   3 un pez
   4 un ratón 5 una tortuga 6 una cobaya
   7 una serpiente

2 Tengo un perro simpático. (2)
  Tengo dos gatos. (1)
  Mi tortuga es tímida. (5)
  Tengo dos cobayas. (6)
  Mis peces son muy divertidos. (3)
  Tengo un ratón muy listo. (4)
  Mi serpiente es muy simpática. (7)

3 1 El perro es muy simpático.
   2 Los peces son tontos.
   3 El ratón es listo y divertido.
   4 Las cobayas son muy listas.
   5 La serpiente es gris y blanca.
   6 Los gatos son blancos y negros.
   7 La tortuga es tímida.

© Pearson Education Ltd 2013. Copying permitted for purchasing institution only. This material is not copyright free.

Mi vida 1.5

Workbook 1B, page 6

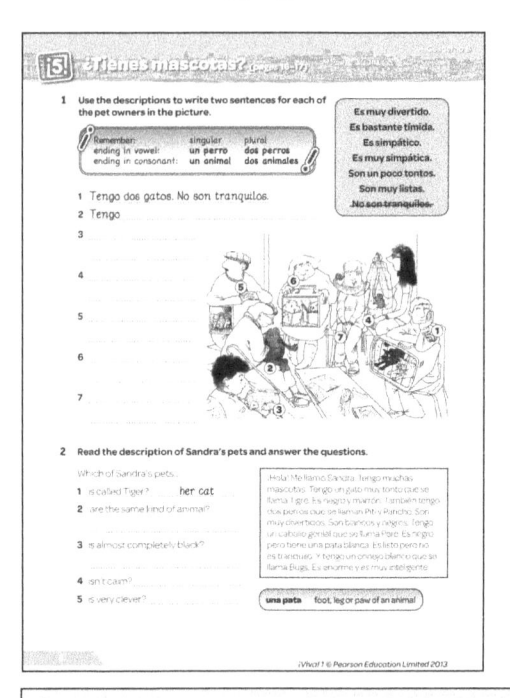

Answers

1 1 *Tengo dos gatos. No son tranquilos.*
   2 *Tengo* un perro. Es simpático.
   3 Tengo dos peces. Son un poco tontos.
   4 Tengo un ratón. Es muy divertido.
   5 Tengo una tortuga. Es bastante tímida.
   6 Tengo dos cobayas. Son muy listas.
   7 Tengo una serpiente. Es muy simpática.

2 1 *her cat*
   2 Piti and Pancho, her dogs
   3 her horse, Pere
   4 her horse
   5 her rabbit, Bugs

Worksheet 1.5 What a lot of animals!

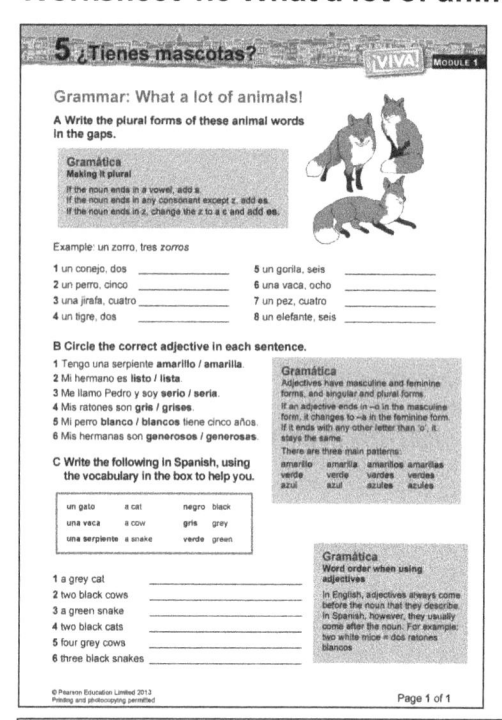

Answers

A 1 conejos   2 perros   3 jirafas
   4 tigres   5 gorilas   6 vacas
   7 peces   8 elefantes

B 1 amarilla   2 listo   3 serio
   4 grises   5 blanco   6 generosas

C 1 un gato gris
   2 dos vacas negras
   3 una serpiente verde
   4 dos gatos negros
   5 cuatro vacas grises
   6 tres serpientes negras

© Pearson Education Ltd 2013. Copying permitted for purchasing institution only. This material is not copyright free.

Mi vida 1.5

ActiveTeach, Extension Reading

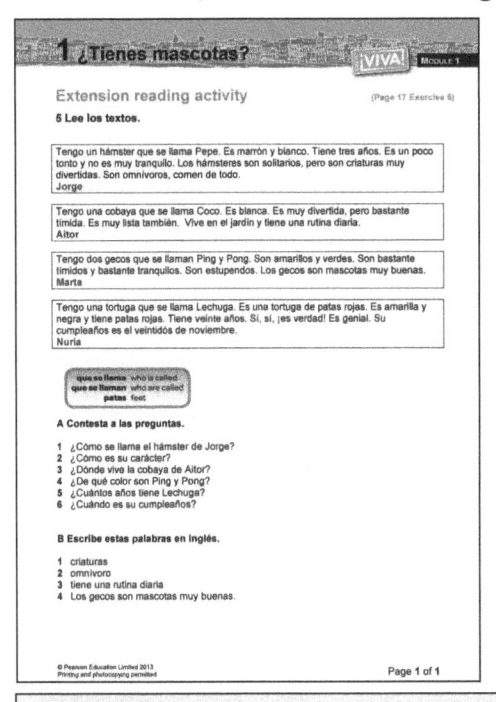

Answers (Question 5)

A

1. El hámster de Jorge se llama Pepe.
2. Es un poco tonto y no es muy tranquilo.
3. La cobaya de Aitor vive en el jardín.
4. Ping y Pong son amarillos y verdes.
5. Lechuga tiene veinte años.
6. Su cumpleaños es el veintidós de noviembre.

B

1. creatures
2. omnivore
3. (it) has its daily routine
4. Geckos are really/very good pets.

Video

Episode 2: Los osos de Asturias

Laura, Estela and Samuel are at the bear reserve in Asturias, paying a visit to some of their region's most unusual residents: Paca, Tola and Furaco. Video worksheet 2 can be used in conjunction with this episode.

Answers to video worksheet (ActiveTeach)

A

1. Answers will vary and may include the eight pets introduced in Unit 5 of the Pupil Book.
2. Answers will vary and may include the animals introduced in exercise 1 in Unit 1 of the Pupil Book.

B

1. perros, gatos, caballos, serpientes, ratones, elefantes, jirafas, camellos, hipopótamos
2. the Asturian bear ('*el oso de Asturias*', also called '*el oso pardo*')
3. He is the bearkeeper.

C

1. elephants, camels, hippos
2. a) true
   b) true
   c) false (Tola is active and nice/kind, not shy.)
3. **Name:** <u>FURACO</u>
   Age: <u>15</u>
   Character: <u>quiet</u>, <u>clever</u>

D

1. Estela is confident – because she says she is great *(fenomenal)*.
2. Laura, again, please.
3. Answers will vary.
4. What animals does your region have?
5. Answers will vary.

E

Pupils will produce their own dialogues in small groups.

Writing Skills: Cómo soy...

Mi vida 1.6

Pupil Book pages
Pages 18–19

Learning objectives
- Writing a text for a time capsule
- Adding variety to your writing

Programme of Study
GV3 Opinions and discussions
LC4 Expressing ideas (writing)
LC8 Writing creatively

Key language
Review of language from Units 1–5.

PLTS
R Reflective learners

Resources
Audio file:
16_Module1_Unit6_Ex1
Workbooks:
Cuaderno 1A & 1B, page 7
ActiveTeach:
p.019 Extension worksheet

Starter 1

Aim

To revise language met in the Module so far.

Give pupils three minutes to create four phrases using a word from the three columns below. Pupils can swap their work with their partners and translate their phrases into English.

1	2	3
soy	doce	años
tengo	en	cobayas
vivo	diez	gato
	dos	hermano
	una	mascotas
	un	España
		hermana

1 Escucha y lee el mensaje que escribe Antonio para su cápsula del tiempo. (L4)

Listening. Pupils listen to Antonio read out the message he has written for his time capsule and follow the text at the same time.

Read together through the first Skills box on p. 19 on making their writing interesting with connectives, intensifiers, range of verbs, adjectives and negatives. Encourage pupils to work these features into their own speech and writing wherever they can.

Audioscript Track 16

¡Hola! ¿Qué tal? Me llamo Antonio y vivo en Argentina, en Buenos Aires. Tengo trece años y mi cumpleaños es el quince de mayo.

Soy bastante sincero. También soy generoso pero no soy tímido. Tengo una hermana que se llama Rosa. Tiene catorce años. En mi opinión, es un poco tonta.

Tengo un ratón y dos peces. Mi ratón es blanco y muy divertido. Mis peces son azules y amarillos y son estupendos pero no son muy listos. Mi color favorito es el amarillo.

Mi pasión es el rugby y mi héroe es Felipe Contepomi. ¡Es genial! Mi cantante favorita es Beyoncé porque es fenomenal. Mi programa favorito es 'Factor X'.

¿Y tú? ¿Qué tipo de persona eres? ¿Tienes mascotas? ¿Tienes hermanos? ¿Cuándo es tu cumpleaños?

2 Lee el mensaje otra vez. Pon las fotos en el orden correcto según el texto. (L4)

Reading. Pupils read the text in exercise 1 again and put the pictures in the order that they are mentioned.

Answers
e, f, b, a, d, c

Reinforcement

Pupils identify all the adjectives in the text in exercise 1 and translate them into English.

3 Eres Antonio. Contesta a estas preguntas en español. (L3)

Reading. Pupils write answers to the questions in Spanish from Antonio's point of view. Draw pupils' attention to the Tip box, which highlights that usually in Spanish, nouns referring to a person's profession do not change according to gender but the adjective still does, e.g. *mi cantante favorito* (male singer), *mi cantante favorita* (female singer). *¿Cuál?* is glossed for support.

Answers
1 Me llamo Antonio.
2 Vivo en Argentina, en Buenos Aires.
3 Tengo trece años.
4 Mi cumpleaños es el quince de mayo.
5 Soy bastante sincero. También soy generoso pero no soy tímido.

© Pearson Education Ltd 2013. Copying permitted for purchasing institution only. This material is not copyright free.

Mi vida 1.6

6 Sí. Tengo una hermana (que se llama Rosa).
7 Sí. Tengo un ratón y dos peces.
8 Mi programa favorito es 'Factor X'.

Extension

Pupils read aloud Antonio's email in Spanish round the class, a sentence at a time, translating it into English.

Starter 2

Aim

To practise *Mi... favorito/a es...*

Go round the class. The first pupil makes a statement about one of his or her favourite things from the categories used in exercise 1, (e.g. favourite colour, singer or television programme). The next pupil then makes a statement about himself/herself, and so on round the class.

4 ¿Y tú? Con tu compañero/a, haz un diálogo. Utiliza las preguntas y las respuestas del ejercicio 3 como modelo. (L4)

Speaking. In pairs, pupils take it in turns to practise a dialogue, using the questions and answers from exercise 3 as a model. A Skills box containing high-frequency words is supplied for additional support.

5 Escribe tu mensaje para una cápsula del tiempo. (L4)

Writing. Pupils now write their own message for the time capsule, bearing in mind the advice given in the Skills box on making their writing interesting. A list of features to include in their own writing is supplied. This work could be done on a computer.

6 Lee el mensaje de tu compañero/a y comprueba el uso de: (L4)

Reading. Pupils swap texts from exercise 5 with a partner, then read through and assess the other's work. A list of language to focus on is supplied: connectives, intensifiers, verbs, adjectives and negatives.

7 Comenta el trabajo de tu compañero/a. (L2)

Writing. Before asking pupils to comment on their partner's work, check that they understand the meanings of the three Spanish feedback comments. Point out an unusual aspect of Spanish punctuation: the Spanish use upside-down exclamation marks to precede exclamatory sentences so that the reader knows to say the sentence with emotion (as well as using an upside-down question mark to precede a question).

Plenary

Ask pupils to write three quiz questions to test one another on three things from the Module.

For example:

How do you make the phrase *Soy sincero* negative?
(a) put *no* before the verb?
(b) put *no* after the verb?

Workbook 1A, page 7

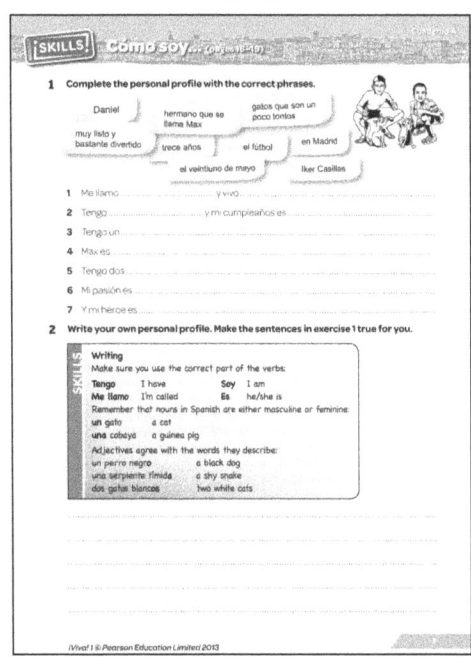

Answers

1   1 Me llamo Daniel y vivo en Madrid.
    2 Tengo trece años y mi cumpleaños es el veintiuno de mayo.
    3 Tengo un hermano que se llama Max.
    4 Max es muy listo y bastante divertido.
    5 Tengo dos gatos que son un poco tontos.
    6 Mi pasión es el fútbol.
    7 Y mi héroe es Iker Casillas.

2   Own answers.

© Pearson Education Ltd 2013. Copying permitted for purchasing institution only. This material is not copyright free.

Mi vida 1.6

Workbook 1B, page 7

Answers

1 1 S 2 J 3 J 4 S 5 J 6 S 7 J 8 S
   9 J 10 S 11 S 12 J

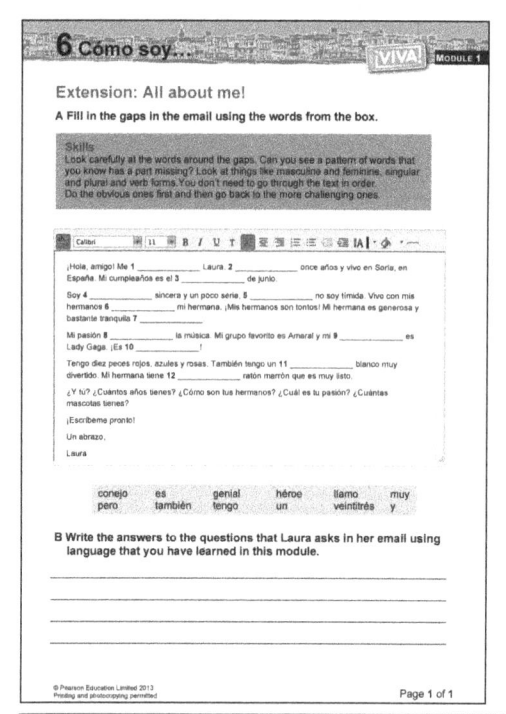

2 Own answers

Worksheet 1.6 All about me!

Answers

A 1 llamo   2 tengo   3 veintitrés
   4 muy   5 pero   6 y
   7 también 8 es   9 héroe
   10 genial 11 conejo 12 un

B Own answers.

© Pearson Education Ltd 2013. Copying permitted for purchasing institution only. This material is not copyright free.

40

RESUMEN Y PREPÁRATE

Mi vida 1

Pupil Book pages
Pages 20–21

Resumen
Pupils use the checklist to review language covered in the module, working on it in pairs in class or on their own at home. Encourage them to follow up any areas of weakness they identify. There are Target Setting Sheets included in the Assessment Pack and an opportunity for pupils to record their own levels and targets on the Self-assessment pages in the Workbooks, p. 11. You can also use the *Resumen* checklist (available in the ActiveTeach) as an end-of-module plenary option.

Prepárate
These revision exercises can be used for assessment purposes or for pupils to practise before tackling the assessment tasks in the Assessment Pack.

Resources
Audio file:
17_Module1_Prep_Ex1
Workbooks:
Cuaderno 1A & 1B, pages 8 & 9
ActiveTeach:
p.020 *Resumen* checklist

1 Escucha. Copia y completa la tabla. (1–4) (L2)

Listening. Pupils copy out the table. They listen to four conversations and complete the table – for each conversation they note the age and birthday of the speaker.

Answers

	age	birthday
Antonio	16	9/10
Lucía	11	30/8
Marcos	15	22/6
Alba	12	18/11

Audioscript Track 17

1 – ¿Cuántos años tienes, Antonio?
  – Tengo dieciséis años.
  – ¿Cuándo es tu cumpleaños?
  – Mi cumpleaños es el nueve de octubre.

2 – ¿Cuántos años tienes, Lucía?
  – Tengo once años.
  – ¿Cuándo es tu cumpleaños?
  – Mi cumpleaños es el treinta de agosto.

3 – ¿Cuántos años tienes, Marcos?
  – Tengo quince años.
  – ¿Cuándo es tu cumpleaños?
  – Mi cumpleaños es el veintidós de junio.

4 – ¿Cuántos años tienes, Alba?
  – Tengo doce años.
  – ¿Cuándo es tu cumpleaños?
  – Mi cumpleaños es el dieciocho de noviembre.

2 Con tu compañero/a, pregunta y contesta. (L2)

Speaking. In pairs, pupils take it in turns to ask and answer questions about the pets they have. A sample dialogue is given. More able pupils could also be asked to say what colour each animal is.

3 Lee los textos y completa las frases en inglés. (L3)

Reading. Pupils read the texts and complete the sentences that summarise them in English.

Answers
1 Carlos is funny and quite **nice**.
2 His passion is **football**.
3 His **brother** is called Rodrigo.
4 Carmen is not very **calm**.
5 Her **sisters** are called Juana and Catalina.
6 Juana is very **clever**, but Catalina is a bit **silly**.

4 ¿Cómo eres? Escribe un texto. (L3)

Writing. Pupils write a short text about themselves, including their name, where they live, their age, brothers and sisters and personality traits. A writing frame is supplied for each topic. Stretch more able pupils by encouraging them to add extra details, writing from memory.

© Pearson Education Ltd 2013. Copying permitted for purchasing institution only. This material is not copyright free.

Mi vida 1

Workbook 1A, page 8

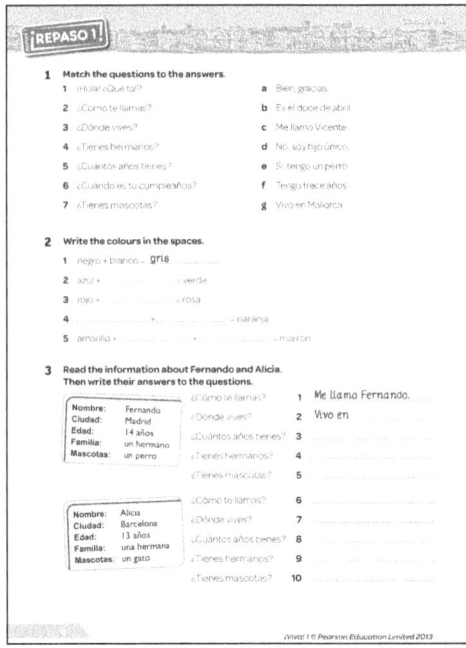

Answers

1 1 a 2 c 3 g 4 d 5 f 6 b 7 e

2 1 *gris* 2 amarillo 3 blanco
   4 rojo, amarillo 5 rojo, azul

3 1 *Me llamo Fernando.*
   2 *Vivo en* Madrid.
   3 Tengo catorce años.
   4 Sí, tengo un hermano.
   5 Sí, tengo un perro.
   6 Me llamo Alicia.
   7 Vivo en Barcelona.
   8 Tengo trece años.
   9 Sí, tengo una hermana.
   10 Sí, tengo un gato.

Workbook 1A, page 9

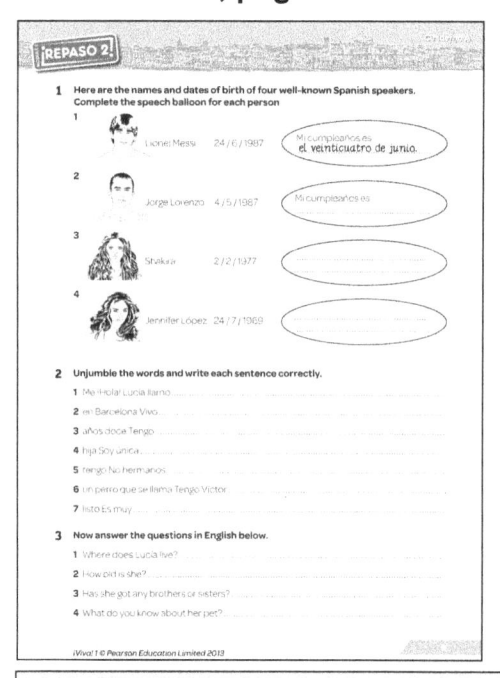

Answers

1 1 Mi cumpleaños es *el veinticuatro de junio*.
   2 Mi cumpleaños es el cuatro de mayo.
   3 Mi cumpleaños es el dos de febrero.
   4 Mi cumpleaños es el veinticuatro de julio.

2 1 ¡Hola! Me llamo Lucía.
   2 Vivo en Barcelona.
   3 Tengo doce años.
   4 Soy hija única.
   5 No tengo hermanos.
   6 Tengo un perro que se llama Víctor.
   7 Es muy listo.

3 1 Lucía lives in Barcelona.
   2 She's 12 years old.
   3 No, she's an only child.
   4 She's got a dog called Víctor.

Mi vida 1

Workbook 1B, page 8

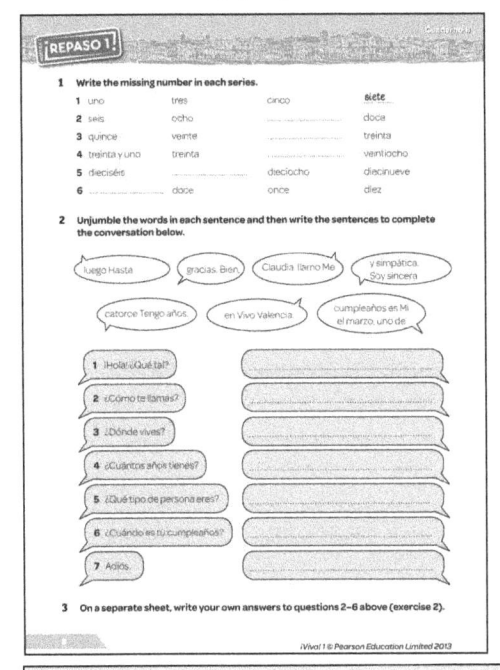

Workbook 1B, page 9

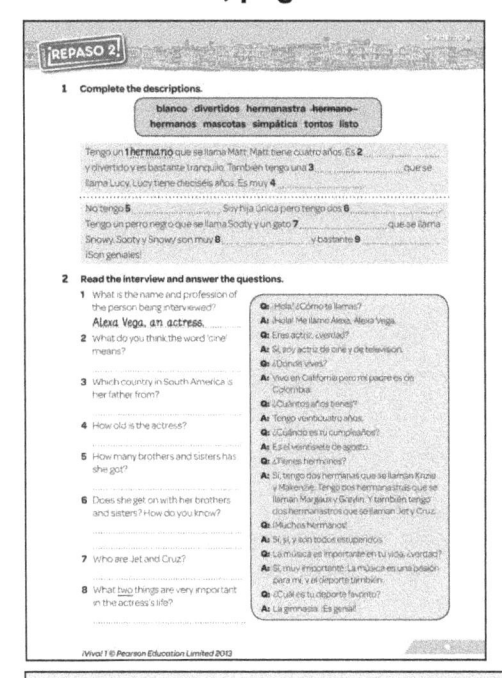

Answers

1 1 *siete* 2 diez 3 veinticinco
   4 veintinueve 5 diecisiete 6 trece

2 1 Bien, gracias.
   2 Me llamo Claudia.
   3 Vivo en Valencia.
   4 Tengo catorce años.
   5 Soy sincera y simpática.
   6 Mi cumpleaños es el uno de marzo.
   7 Hasta luego.

3 Own answers

Answers

1 1 *hermano* 2 listo
   3 hermanastra 4 simpática
   5 hermanos 6 mascotas
   7 blanco 8 divertidos/tontos
   9 divertidos/tontos.

2 1 *Alexa Vega, an actress*
   2 cinema, film
   3 Colombia
   4 24
   5 six in total: two sisters, two stepsisters and two stepbrothers
   6 Yes, she gets on well with her brothers and sisters. She says: 'They're all great!'
   7 They're her stepbrothers.
   8 Music and sport.

© Pearson Education Ltd 2013. Copying permitted for purchasing institution only. This material is not copyright free.

¡GRAMÁTICA!

Mi vida 1

Pupil Book pages
Pages 22–23

The *Gramática* section provides a more detailed summary of the key grammar covered in the module, along with further exercises to practise these points.

Grammar topics
- the indefinite article (*un/una*)
- the definite article (*el/la/los/las*)
- regular verbs (*hablar*, *vivir* – present, singular)
- irregular verbs (*ser*, *tener* – present, singular)
- adjectives (masculine and feminine, singular and plural)
- making verbs negative

Resources
Workbooks:
Cuaderno 1A & 1B, page 10
ActiveTeach:
p.022 Grammar practice
p.022 Grammar presentation
p.023 Grammar presentation
p.023 Grammar presentation
p.023 Grammar practice
p.023 Grammar presentation
p.023 Grammar presentation

The indefinite article

1 Copy the sentences and put in the correct word for 'a'.

Pupils complete the gap-fill text with the correct form of the indefinite article.

Answers
1 Tengo **un** gato.
2 ¿Tienes **una** cobaya?
3 Tengo **una** hermana.
4 ¿Tienes **un** pez?
5 Tengo **un** hermanastro.
6 Tiene **una** serpiente.

The definite article

2 Choose the correct article each time.

Pupils write out the sentences, choosing the correct definite article from the four options given.

Answers
1 **El** gato es negro.
2 **La** cobaya es tímida.
3 **Los** peces son rojos.
4 **Los** caballos son blancos.
5 **El** perro es tonto.
6 **La** serpiente es verde.

Regular verbs

3 Decode these verbs, then translate them into English.

Pupils use the symbols key to decode the Spanish verbs, then translate them into English.

Answers
1 vivo / I live
2 hablas / you speak
3 vive / he/she lives
4 hablo / I speak
5 vives / you live
6 habla / he/she speaks

Irregular verbs

4 Unjumble the verb forms. Translate the sentences into English.

Pupils work out the verb anagrams then translate the sentences into English.

Answers
1 **Soy** simpático.	I am nice.
2 **Eres** tranquila.	You are calm.
3 **Es** sincero y generoso.	He is sincere and generous.
4 **Tengo** dos hermanas pero no tengo animales.	I have two sisters but I don't have any pets.
5 ¿**Tienes** hermanos?	Do you have any brothers and sisters?
6 **Tiene** tres ratones y un perro.	He/she has three mice and a dog.

5 Translate these sentences into Spanish.

Pupils translate the English sentences into Spanish using *tener* and *ser*.

Answers
1 Soy sincero.
2 Es simpático.
3 Eres generosa.
4 Tengo un conejo.
5 ¿Tienes mascotas?
6 Tiene una serpiente.

Mi vida 1

Adjectives

6 Translate these sentences into Spanish.

Pupils use the picture and word prompts to write five sentences in Spanish, paying attention to the agreement of adjectives.

Answers
1 Es seria y sincera.
2 Es listo y tímido.
3 Es tranquilo y generoso.
4 Es simpática y divertida.

Making verbs negative

7 Make these sentences negative.

Pupils convert the positive sentences into negative ones. A framework is provided for support.

Answers
1 No soy seria.
2 No vivo en Sevilla.
3 Mi hermano no es tonto.
4 Mi hermanastra no es divertida.

Workbook 1A, page 10

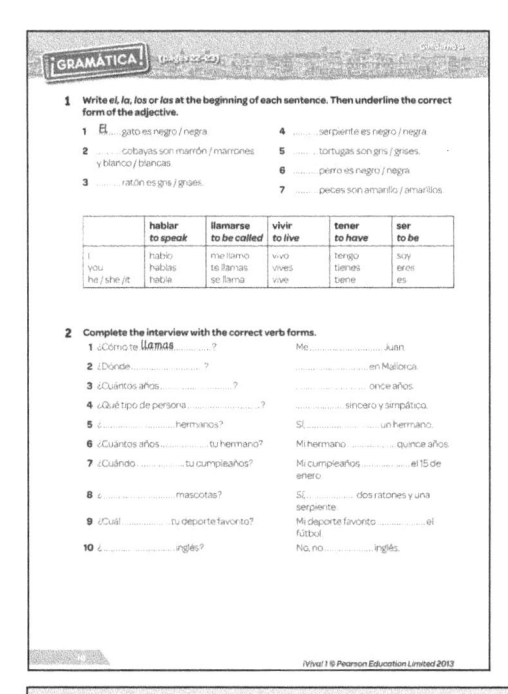

Answers
1 1 *El* gato es negro.
   2 *Las* cobayas son marrones y blancas.
   3 *El* ratón es gris.
   4 *La* serpiente es negra.
   5 *Las* tortugas son grises.
   6 *El* perro es negro.
   7 *Los* peces son amarillos.

2 1 *llamas*, llamo   2 vives, Vivo
   3 tienes, Tengo   4 eres, Soy
   5 Tienes, tengo   6 tiene, tiene
   7 es, es   8 Tienes, tengo
   9 es, es   10 Hablas, hablo
   (also possible: Eres, soy)

Workbook 1B, page 10

Answers
1 1 *llamas*   2 vives   3 tienes
   4 Tienes   5 es   6 Tienes
   Own answers.

2 1 *Me llamo*, Tengo   2 tiene, vive
   3 es, Habla   4 vive
   5 tiene, se llama

3 1 ¡Hola! Me llamo Sofía. Vivo en Barcelona y tengo 13 (trece) años.
   2 Mi cumpleaños es el 21 (veintiuno) de abril.
   3 ¿Dónde vive tu hermanastro?
   4 Mi hermana tiene un gato negro que se llama Negrito.
   5 Es muy divertido y un poco tonto.

© Pearson Education Ltd 2013. Copying permitted for purchasing institution only. This material is not copyright free.

¡Zona Proyecto! Los animales

Mi vida 1

Pupil Book pages
Pages 26–27

Learning objectives
- Finding out about endangered animals
- Producing a set of animal cards to trade

Programme of Study
GV3 Developing vocabulary
LC3 Conversation

PLTS
I Independent enquirers

Cross-curricular
Biology: animal species and behaviour
Computing: internet research

Resources
Audio file:
18_Module1_ZP_Ex2
ActiveTeach:
Starter 1 resource

Starter 1

Aim

To review verb structures.

Write up the following on the board, mixing the order of the right-hand column (Starter 1 resource). Give pupils several minutes to match the sentence halves.

1	Soy bastante	a	sincero.
2	Mi pasión es	b	la música.
3	¿Cómo se	c	escribe?
4	Mi hermana tiene	d	doce años.
5	¿Cómo se llaman	e	los peces?

Check pupils' answers, asking them to explain how they worked them out. Ask pupils to translate the sentences into English.

1 Empareja las palabras con las definiciones. (L1)

Reading. Pupils match the words to the definitions. Remind them, if necessary, to look for cognates and patterns.

Answers
| 1 d | 2 h | 3 i | 4 j | 5 f |
| 6 a | 7 k | 8 b | 9 c | 10 g |

2 Escucha y lee. Rellena los espacios en blanco con las palabras del cuadro. (L4)

Listening. Pupils listen to the short extract, reading the text at the same time. They then complete the gap-fill version of the text using words from the box provided. *Come* is glossed for support.

Audioscript Track 18

El búho real vive en Europa y Asia. Es silencioso y omnívoro.

Come insectos, reptiles, anfibios, peces y aves. Es marrón y negro.

Vive aproximadamente veinte años.

Answers
| 1 Europa | 2 omnívoro | 3 reptiles |
| 4 y | 5 negro | 6 veinte |

3 Lee el texto otra vez y completa las frases en inglés. (L4)

Reading. Pupils read the text again, then copy and complete the English sentences. When they have finished, they can practise the tongue twister in the *Zona Cultura* box with their partner.

Answers
1 The eagle owl lives in **Europe and Asia**.
2 It eats **insects, reptiles, amphibians, fish and birds**.
3 Its colours are **brown and black**.
4 It lives for **about 20 years**.

Starter 2

Aim

To review language for talking about animals.

Write up the following headings on the board: country of habitat, diet, lifespan, personality, physical appearance. Give pupils three minutes working in pairs to remember as many of the facts as they can for the eagle owl. Pupils can answer in Spanish or English, depending on the level of the class.

Mi vida 1

4 Lee las cartas. Contesta a las preguntas en inglés. (L4)

Reading. Pupils read the Trump cards on three endangered animals. Each card lists information on the animal's country of habitat, colour, characteristics, personality traits, diet and lifespan. Pupils answer the questions in English. Some vocabulary is glossed for support.

Answers	
1 The bear	2 The wolf
3 The lynx	4 The lynx
5 The bear and the wolf	6 The bear

5 Haz unas cartas. Elige cinco animales. Busca información. Dibuja las cartas. (L4)

Writing. Pupils do some Internet research on five animals of their choice in order to design their own eye-catching Trump cards with the help of a dictionary. A list of features to include on their cards is given. This work could be carried out on a computer, either individually or in groups.

6 Con tus compañeros/as, intercambia las cartas. (L3)

Speaking. In groups of four, pupils play 'Trumps' using the cards that they designed and made. A model dialogue is supplied and vocabulary for 'do you want to trade… for…' is provided for support.

Plenary

Create a mini-presentation on an imaginary animal in class, using the topics outlined in exercise 5 (animal name, country, habitat, diet, character, physical appearance, lifespan). Encourage the class to be as creative as possible. Note the details on the board, then ask pupils to say a sentence each about the 'animal'.

Pupil Book pages Self-access reading and writing
Pages 120–121

A Reinforcement

1 Empareja los dibujos con las frases correctas. (L2)

Reading. Pupils match the pictures to the correct sentences.

Answers
1 c 2 d 3 e 4 b 5 f 6 a

2 Completa el diálogo con palabras del cuadro. (L2)

Reading. Pupils complete the gap-fill dialogue using words from the box.

Answers		
1 Cómo	2 llamo	3 tal
4 gracias	5 Vivo	6 Adiós

3 Escribe cuatro diálogos utilizando estos datos. Utiliza el diálogo del ejercicio 2 como modelo. (L3)

Writing. Pupils write four dialogues using the visual prompts provided and the conversation from the previous exercise as a model. The Tip box gives support in answering the question ¿Qué tal?

B Extension

1 Mira los dibujos y lee las frases. ¿Verdadero (V) o falso (F)? (L3)

Reading. Pupils look at the drawings and read the sentences. They decide whether the sentences are true (V) or false (F).

Answers
1 V 2 F 3 F 4 F 5 V 6 V

2 Corrige las frases falsas del ejercicio 1. (L3)

Writing. In Spanish, pupils rewrite the three false sentences from exercise 1 so that they are correct.

Answers
2 Óscar tiene **tres ratones** y un perro.
3 Leo tiene una cobaya y **dos** conejos.
4 Alba tiene **cuatro** perros.

3 Lee los textos. Copia y completa la ficha de identidad de Ariana y Omar en inglés. (L4)

Reading. Pupils read the texts, then copy and complete the identity cards for Ariana and Omar.

Answers	
Name	Ariana
Lives in	Malaga
Personality	serious and generous
Age	13
Birthday	9/12
Brothers/sisters	3 brothers
Pets	none
Passion	music
Hero	Rihanna

Name	Omar
Lives in	Las Palmas
Personality	shy, sincere, nice
Age	14
Birthday	17/4
Brothers/sisters	1 sister
Pets	1 dog, 1 cat
Passion	football
Hero	Lionel Messi

4 Eres Elena o Ernesto. Descríbete utilizando los textos del ejercicio 3 como modelo. (L4)

Writing. Pupils write two short paragraphs about Elena and Ernesto based on the identity cards supplied. The texts for Ariana and Omar in exercise 3 can be used as writing frameworks.

MODULE 2: Mi tiempo libre

Unit & Learning objectives	PoS references	Key language	Grammar and other language features
1 ¿Qué te gusta hacer? (pp. 30–31) Saying what you like to do Giving opinions using *me gusta* + infinitive	**GV2** Grammatical structures (the infinitive) **GV3** Opinions and discussions **LC4** Expressing ideas (writing)	¿Qué te gusta hacer? Me gusta… Me gusta mucho… No me gusta… No me gusta nada… navegar por Internet chatear escuchar música jugar a los videojuegos mandar SMS ver la televisión leer escribir correos salir con mis amigos porque (no) es… interesante guay divertido/a estúpido/a aburrido/a	**G** the infinitive – pronunciation of *j* and *d* – using *porque* to give a reason – non-literal translations
2 ¿Cantas karaoke? (pp. 32–33) Saying what you do in your spare time Using *-ar* verbs in the present tense	**GV1** Tenses (present) **LC6** Translation into English	¿Qué haces en tu tiempo libre? bailo toco la guitarra saco fotos hablo con mis amigos monto en bici canto karaoke todos los días a veces nunca de vez en cuando	**G** present tense of regular *-ar* verbs (full paradigm) – expressions of frequency: *todos los días, a veces, nunca, de vez en cuando*
3 ¿Qué haces cuando llueve? (pp. 34–35) Talking about the weather Using *cuando* (when)	**LC6** Reading comprehension **LC8** Writing creatively	¿Qué tiempo hace? hace calor hace frío hace sol hace buen tiempo llueve nieva en primavera en verano en otoño en invierno	– pronunciation of *ll* – *cuando* as a connective

© Pearson Education Ltd 2013. Copying permitted for purchasing institution only. This material is not copyright free.

Mi tiempo libre 2

Unit & Learning objectives	PoS references	Key language	Grammar and other language features
4 ¿Qué deportes haces? (pp. 36–37) Saying what sports you do Using *hacer* (to do) and *jugar* (to play)	**GV2** Grammatical structures (irregular verbs) **GV3** Opinions and discussions **LC1** Listening and responding	¿Qué deportes haces? Hago gimnasia. Hago artes marciales. Hago equitación. Hago atletismo. Hago natación. Juego al fútbol. Juego al tenis. Juego al voleibol. Juego al baloncesto. lunes martes miércoles jueves viernes sábado domingo	**G** present tense of *hacer* (irregular verb, full paradigm) **G** present tense of *jugar* (stem-changing verb, full paradigm) – giving opinions – pronunciation of *c* before *e* and *i* (soft)
5 ¿Eres fanático? (pp. 38–39) Reading about someone's favourite things Understanding more challenging texts	**GV3** Developing vocabulary **LC6** Reading comprehension	Review of language from Units 1–4.	– developing reading skills – recognising cognates and near-cognates – using context to work out the meaning of new words
6 ¿Qué haces en tu tiempo libre? (pp. 40–41) Taking part in a longer conversation Using question words	**LC3** Conversation **LC5** Speaking coherently and confidently	Review of language from Units 1–4.	– developing speaking skills – using question words – making sentences more interesting
Resumen y Prepárate (pp. 42–43) Pupils' checklist and practice exercises			
Gramática (pp. 44–45) Detailed grammar summary and practice exercises			**G** the infinitive and the three verb endings (*-ar*, *-er*, *-ir*) **G** present tense *-ar* verbs (*hablar*) **G** stem-changing verbs (*jugar*) **G** irregular verbs (*hacer*) **G** verbs with the infinitive

© Pearson Education Ltd 2013. Copying permitted for purchasing institution only. This material is not copyright free.

Mi tiempo libre 2

Unit & Learning objectives	PoS references	Key language	Grammar and other language features
Zona Proyecto I: Navidad en España (pp. 48–49) Learning about Christmas in Spain Writing an acrostic about Christmas	**GV3** Opinions and discussions **LC4** Expressing ideas (speaking)		– *me gusta (mucho) / no me gusta (nada)* + infinitive
Zona Proyecto II: Los Reyes Magos (pp. 50–51) Learning about the Day of the Three Kings Creating a Spanish Christmas calendar	**GV3** Developing vocabulary **LC6** Reading comprehension		
Te toca a ti (pp. 122–123) Self-access reading and writing at two levels			

¿Qué te gusta hacer?

Mi tiempo libre 2.1

Pupil Book pages
Pages 28–31

Learning objectives
- Saying what you like to do
- Giving opinions using *me gusta* + infinitive

Programme of Study
GV2 Grammatical structures (the infinitive)
GV3 Opinions and discussions
LC4 Expressing ideas (writing)

FCSE links
Unit 1: Relationships, family and friends (Hobbies/free time activities)
Unit 4: Leisure (Hobbies, Free time)

Grammar
- the infinitive

Key language
¿Qué te gusta hacer?
Me gusta…
Me gusta mucho…
No me gusta…
No me gusta nada…
navegar por Internet
chatear
escuchar música
jugar a los videojuegos
mandar SMS
ver la televisión
leer
escribir correos
salir con mis amigos
porque (no) es…
interesante
guay
divertido/a
estúpido/a
aburrido/a

PLTS
S Self-managers

Resources
Audio files:
19_Module2_Unit1_Ex1
20_Module2_Unit1_Ex4
Workbooks:
Cuaderno 1A & 1B, page 14
ActiveTeach:
p.030 Flashcards
p.030 Grammar presentation
ActiveLearn:
Listening A, Listening B
Reading A, Reading B
Grammar, Vocabulary

Module 2 Quiz (pp. 28–29)

Answers
1 a En Gran Bretaña
   b En España
   c En los dos
   d En los dos
2 b   3 b   4 a, b   5 a, c   6 c

Starter 1

Aim
To introduce language for talking about leisure activities.

Provide the vocabulary that pupils will meet in exercise 1 on the board. Ask pupils to sort it into three categories: words they can definitely understand the meaning of (cognates / near-cognates such as *Internet*, *música*, *televisión*); words they can make a guess at (*videojuegos*, *chatear*) and words that they definitely cannot work out (*leer*, *correos*).

Alternative starter 1:
Use ActiveTeach p.030 Flashcards to introduce language for talking about leisure activities.

1 Escucha y escribe el nombre correcto. (1–9) (L2)

Listening. Pupils listen and look at the photos on p.30 of the Pupil Book. They write the name of the person speaking each time.

Audioscript Track 19

1 – ¿Qué te gusta hacer?
   – Me gusta escuchar música.
2 – ¿Qué te gusta hacer?
   – Me gusta escribir correos.
3 – ¿Qué te gusta hacer?
   – Me gusta mandar SMS.
4 – ¿Qué te gusta hacer?
   – Me gusta chatear.
5 – ¿Qué te gusta hacer?
   – Me gusta navegar por Internet.
6 – ¿Qué te gusta hacer?
   – Me gusta ver la televisión.
7 – ¿Qué te gusta hacer?
   – Me gusta salir con mis amigos.
8 – ¿Qué te gusta hacer?
   – Me gusta jugar a los videojuegos.
9 – ¿Qué te gusta hacer?
   – Me gusta leer.

© Pearson Education Ltd 2013. Copying permitted for purchasing institution only. This material is not copyright free.

Mi tiempo libre 2.1

Answers		
1 Nuria	2 David	3 Laura
4 Antonio	5 Martina	6 Lucas
7 Alba	8 Javier	9 Sofía

Gramática

Use the *Gramática* box to introduce the concept of the infinitive to pupils. Point out that infinitives always end in -*ar*, -*er* or -*ir*. Ask pupils how many infinitives of each group they can find in exercise 1. Pupils can practise using infinitives in the following exercise. There is also more information and further practice on Pupil Book p. 44.

2 Con tu compañero/a, juega. Haz una raya horizontal o vertical. (L3)

Speaking. In pairs, using the Blockbusters grid, pupils take it in turns to ask and answer the question *¿Qué te gusta hacer?* using the picture prompts for their responses. The aim is to make a horizontal or vertical line. A framework is supplied for support.

Pronunciación

Draw pupils' attention to the *Pronunciación* box, which directs pupils back to page 8 for a reminder on how to pronounce the letter *j* in *jugar* and *videojuegos*.

3 Escribe estas frases. Traduce las frases al inglés. (L3)

Writing. Pupils write out full sentences in Spanish using the phrase *me gusta* with activities covered in exercise 1, by decoding single letter prompts. They then translate the sentences into English.

Answers

1 Me gusta navegar por Internet.
  I like surfing the net.
2 Me gusta chatear.
  I like chatting online.
3 Me gusta escuchar música.
  I like listening to music.
4 Me gusta jugar a los videojuegos.
  I like playing videogames.
5 Me gusta salir con mis amigos.
  I like going out with my friends.
6 Me gusta ver la televisión.
  I like watching TV.

Reinforcement

Pupils write four things that they like doing and four things that they dislike going, using *me gusta* and *no me gusta*.

Starter 2

Aim

To introduce adjectives for giving an opinion.

Provide the vocabulary that pupils will meet in exercise 4 on the board. They should be able to work out the meaning of the two cognates*. See whether pupils can guess the meanings of the other three words. Ask pupils to map the adjectives out on a line ranging from negative to positive, according to their own opinion. They can add intensifiers such as *muy*, *un poco* or *bastante* if they wish.

| aburrido | divertido | *estúpido |
| guay | *interesante | |

4 Escucha y escribe la opinión, la actividad y la razón. (1–5) (L3)

Listening. Pupils listen to the five conversations about what people like doing and identify the opinion, activity and reason given in each.

Audioscript Track 20

1 – ¿Qué te gusta hacer?
  – Me gusta navegar por Internet porque es interesante.
2 – ¿Qué te gusta hacer?
  – Me gusta mucho jugar a los videojuegos porque es divertido.
3 – ¿Qué no te gusta hacer?
  – No me gusta chatear porque es estúpido.
4 – ¿Qué no te gusta hacer?
  – No me gusta nada mandar SMS porque es aburrido.
5 – ¿Qué te gusta hacer?
  – Me gusta mucho ver la televisión porque es guay.

Answers

1 ♥ surf the net, interesting
2 ♥♥ videogames, fun
3 ♥ chat, stupid
4 ♥♥ texting, boring
5 ♥♥ TV, cool

© Pearson Education Ltd 2013. Copying permitted for purchasing institution only. This material is not copyright free.

Mi tiempo libre 2.1

5 Lee los textos y escribe el nombre correcto. (L3)

Reading. Pupils read the three texts and then identify who is being described in each of the questions that follow.

Answers					
1 Santiago	2 Lucía	3 Carlos
4 Carlos	5 Santiago	6 Lucía

Extension

Write up some sentences from exercise 5 on the board (e.g. *no me gusta nada leer porque no es interestante*), jumbling the order of the words. With books closed, pupils write out the sentences in the correct order.

6 ¿Qué te gusta hacer? Prepara una presentación. (L4)

Speaking. Pupils prepare and deliver a short presentation on their leisure activities, giving details of what they like and dislike doing and including opinions and reasons. Encourage them to take the advice of the Tip box to use connectives such as *y*, *pero* and *porque* to extend their sentences. A writing framework is given.

7 Eres famoso/a. ¿Qué te gusta hacer? ¿Qué no te gusta hacer? Escribe una entrada para un blog. (L4)

Writing. Pupils write a blog entry for a celebrity of their choice, describing what they like and dislike doing. A sample starter is given. Remind pupils to use connectives and intensifiers to extend their sentences. Draw their attention also to the Skills box on phrases such as *me gusta* that cannot be translated word for word.

Plenary

Split the class into two teams. Have a pre-prepared list of *(no) me gusta* + activity phrases from the unit on the board, in Spanish. Teams nominate one person each time to play 'Splat' for them. Ask two pupils to come to the front, you say a phrase in English and the pupils 'splat' the equivalent phrase in Spanish with their hands.

Award two points to the pupil who splats correctly first. The team with most points wins.

Workbook 1A, page 14

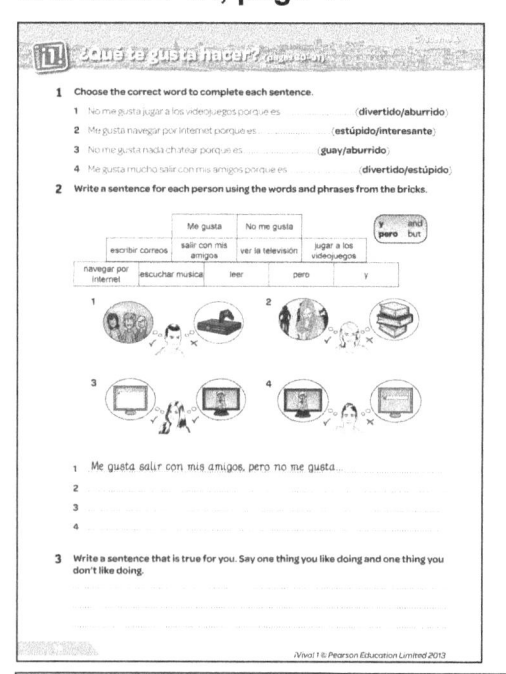

Answers

1
 1 aburrido 2 interesante 3 aburrido
 4 divertido

2
 1 *Me gusta salir con mis amigos pero no me gusta jugar a los videojuegos.*
 2 Me gusta escuchar música pero no me gusta leer.
 3 Me gusta escribir correos y me gusta ver la televisión.
 4 No me gusta ver la televisión pero me gusta navegar por Internet.

3 Own answers.

Mi tiempo libre 2.1

Workbook 1B, page 14

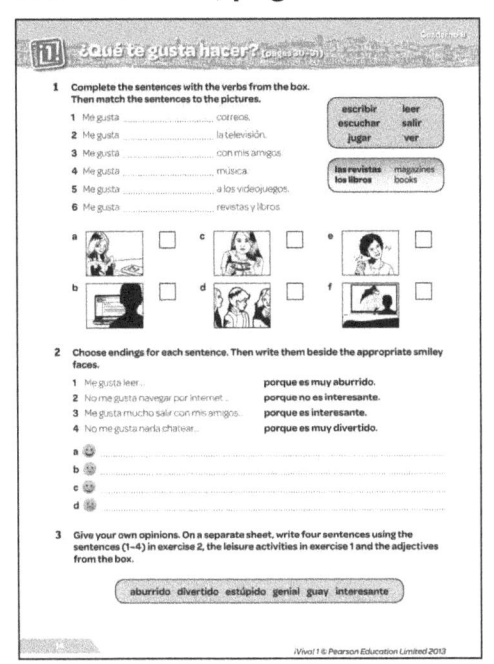

Answers

1.
   1 escribir, b   2 ver, f   3 salir, d
   4 escuchar, e   5 jugar, c   6 leer, a

2.
   1 Me gusta leer porque es interesante. c
   2 No me gusta navegar por Internet porque no es interesante. b
   3 Me gusta mucho salir con mis amigos porque es muy divertido. a
   4 No me gusta nada chatear porque es muy aburrido. d

3. Own answers

2 ¿Cantas karaoke?

Mi tiempo libre 2.2

Pupil Book pages
Pages 32–33

Learning objectives
- Saying what you do in your spare time
- Using -ar verbs in the present tense

Programme of Study
GV1 Tenses (present)
LC6 Translation into English

FCSE links
Unit 1: Relationships, family and friends (Hobbies/free time activities)
Unit 4: Leisure (Hobbies, Free time)

Grammar
- present tense of regular -ar verbs (full paradigm)

Key language
¿Qué haces en tu tiempo libre?
bailo
toco la guitarra
monto en bici
saco fotos
hablo con mis amigos
canto karaoke
todos los días
a veces
nunca
de vez en cuando

PLTS
T Team workers

Resources
Audio files:
21_Module2_Unit2_Ex2
22_Module2_Unit2_Ex5
Workbooks:
Cuaderno 1A & 1B, page 15
ActiveTeach:
p.032 Video 3
p.032 Video 3 transcript
p.032 Video worksheet 3
p.032 Flashcards
p.032 Grammar presentation
p.032 Grammar worksheet
p.033 Extension reading
ActiveLearn:
Listening A, Listening B
Reading A, Reading B
Grammar, Vocabulary

Starter 1

Aim

To introduce the first person forms of the verbs for talking about activities.

Have a pre-prepared list of a variety of verb forms from exercise 1 presented randomly on the board (e.g. *saco, sacamos, sacas, toca, toco, tocan*, etc.). Ask pupils to identify the 'I' forms of verbs from the list.

1 Empareja las frases con los dibujos. (L2)

Reading. Pupils match the pictures and the sentences. Point out the Tip box, which offers advice on tackling texts with new words.

Answers
1 f 2 b 3 e 4 a 5 c 6 d

2 Escucha y comprueba tus respuestas. (1–6) (L2)

Listening. Pupils listen and check their answers to exercise 1.

Audioscript Track 21

¿Qué haces en tu tiempo libre?
1 – Canto karaoke.
2 – Toco la guitarra.
3 – Hablo con mis amigos.
4 – Bailo.
5 – Monto en bici.
6 – Saco fotos.

Gramática

Use the *Gramática* box to teach the full paradigm of *hablar*, a regular -ar verb. Once pupils know the pattern it follows, they can apply the rules to other -ar verbs they come across. Point out the subject pronouns, which are listed in brackets. Explain that these are often omitted in Spanish, and are used primarily for clarity or emphasis because the verb endings make it clear who is speaking. There is more information and further practice of -ar verbs on Pupil Book p. 44.

3 Con tu compañero/a, haz mímica de las actividades del ejercicio 1. Tu compañero/a adivina. (L3)

Speaking. In pairs, one pupil mimes activities from exercise 1, while the other guesses what they are. A sample exchange is given for support.

Reinforcement

Practise conjugating the first person of regular -ar verbs with books closed. Prompt with an opinion on any activity from exercise 1, e.g. *Me gusta mucho sacar fotos*. Pupils respond with the first person singular form: *Saco fotos*.

© Pearson Education Ltd 2013. Copying permitted for purchasing institution only. This material is not copyright free.

Mi tiempo libre 2.2

4 Traduce estas frases al inglés. (L2)

Writing. Pupils translate the sentences into English, paying particular attention to the verb endings to work out which subject pronoun to use.

Answers
1 You play the guitar.   2 I talk to my friends.
3 You take photos.   4 They sing karaoke.
5 We dance.   6 He/she rides a bike.

Starter 2

Aim

To review the spellings of regular -ar verb forms.

Read out the following six verb forms and ask pupils to transcribe them in Spanish using their sound-spelling knowledge.

bailo   tocas   monta
saco   hablas   canta

Pupils can then translate each verb into English.

Alternative starter 2:

Use ActiveTeach p.032 Flashcards to review and practice spare time vocabulary.

5 Escucha y escribe las letras correctas. (1–4) (L3)

Listening. Pupils listen to two teenagers doing the multiple-choice magazine quiz. They note the letter (a–c) of the answer given to each survey question. Some vocabulary is glossed for support.

Audioscript Track 22

– Hacemos esta encuesta "¿Eres una persona activa?"
– Vale. Tú preguntas, y yo contesto.
– Bueno. Uno. ¿Cantas karaoke de vez en cuando?
– Sí, todos los días canto karaoke.
– Dos. ¿Escuchas música de vez en cuando?
– Sí, a veces escucho música.
– Tres. ¿Tocas la guitarra de vez en cuando?
– Nunca toco la guitarra.
– ¿Navegas por Internet de vez en cuando?
– Sí, todos los días navego por Internet.
– A ver... Tienes mayoría de la letra a. ¡Tranquilo! Eres muy, muy activo. Relájate de vez en cuando.
– Ja, ja, ja. Sí, ¡es verdad!

Answers
1 a   2 b   3 c   4 a

6 Con tu compañero/a, haz la encuesta del ejercicio 5. (L3)

Speaking. Working in pairs, pupils take it in turns to ask and answer the four questions from the multiple-choice quiz in exercise 5. *Relájate* and *nada* are glossed for support.

Extension

To challenge the more able, suggest that pupils give their partner a reason for why they do or don't do the activities. When pupils have finished the quiz, they can write some more questions either individually or in pairs.

7 ¿Cómo son los amigos de Ana? Copia y rellena la tabla. (L4)

Reading. Pupils copy out the table. They read the two texts about Luz and Sergio and complete the table – for each person they note what activities they do and how often. *No le gusta* and *o* are glossed for support.

Answers

name	every day	sometimes	never
Luz	plays guitar, listens to music	dances, rides bike	takes photos
Sergio	surfs the Internet, talks to friends	sends texts	sings karaoke

8 ¿Qué haces en tu tiempo libre? Escribe un texto. (L4)

Writing. Pupils write a short text about what they do in their spare time and how often, using the text in exercise 7 as a model. A sample answer is also supplied.

Plenary

Ask pupils to tell you how to conjugate -ar verbs in the present tense. Then prompt in English using verbs from the unit (e.g. we dance, they play, I ride, we send, you speak, they listen, he surfs, you take, she sings) for pupils to respond to with the Spanish. You could increase the level of challenge by including some negative forms and expressions of frequency.

Mi tiempo libre 2.2

Workbook 1A, page 15

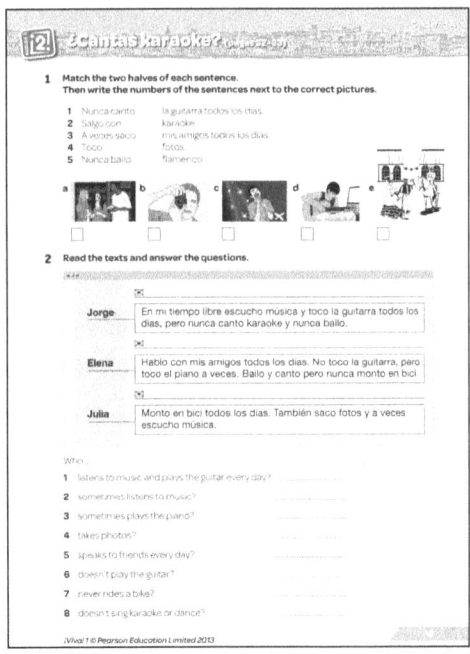

Answers

1. 1 Nunca canto karaoke.
   2 Salgo con mis amigos todos los días.
   3 A veces saco fotos.
   4 Toco la guitarra todos los días.
   5 Nunca bailo salsa.
   a 2 b 3 c 1 d 4 e 5

2. 1 Jorge   2 Julia   3 Elena
   4 Julia   5 Elena   6 Elena
   7 Elena   8 Jorge

Workbook 1B, page 15

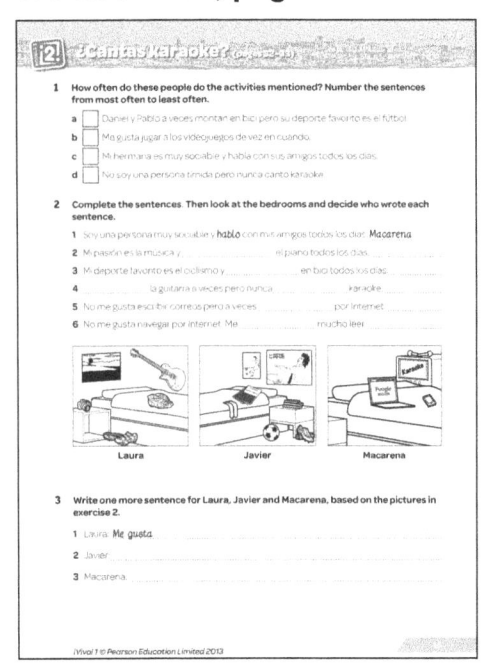

Answers

1. a 2 b 3 c 1 d 4
2. 1 hablo, Macarena   2 toco, Javier
   3 monto, Laura   4 Toco, canto, Laura
   5 navego, Macarena   6 gusta, Javier
3. Own answers

Worksheet 2.2 Find the endings!

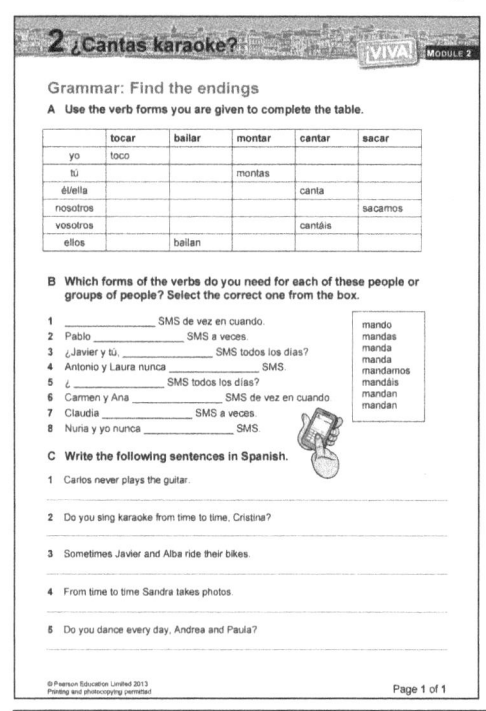

Answers

A

	tocar	bailar	montar
(yo)	*toco*	bailo	monto
(tú)	tocas	bailas	*montas*
(él/ella)	toca	baila	monta
(nosotros)	tocamos	bailamos	montamos
(vosotros)	tocáis	bailáis	montáis
(ellos)	tocan	*bailan*	montan

	cantar	sacar
(yo)	canto	saco
(tú)	cantas	sacas
(él/ella)	*canta*	saca
(nosotros)	cantamos	*sacamos*
(vosotros)	*cantáis*	sacáis
(ellos)	cantan	sacan

Mi tiempo libre 2.2

B
1 Mando	2 manda	3 mandáis
4 mandan	5 Mandas	6 mandan
7 manda	8 mandamos	

C
1. Carlos nunca toca la guitarra.
2. Cristina, ¿cantas karaoke de vez en cuando?
3. A veces Javier y Alba montan en bici.
4. De vez en cuando Sandra saca fotos.
5. Andrea y Paula, ¿bailáis todos los días?

ActiveTeach, Extension Reading

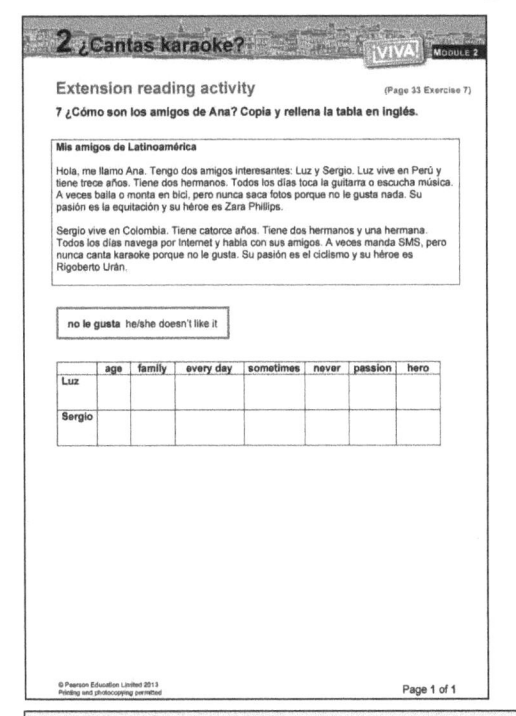

Answers (Question 7)

	Luz	Sergio
age	13	14
family	2 sisters	2 brothers and 1 sister
every day	plays guitar, listens to music	surfs the net, talks to his friends
sometimes	dances, rides her bike	sends text messages
never	takes photos	sings karaoke
passion	horseriding	cycling
hero	Zara Phillips	Rigoberto Urán

Video

Episode 3: El tiempo libre

Aroa is in Oviedo's San Francisco park, finding out what the ¡TeleViva! team like – or don't like – to do in their free time. Video worksheet 3 can be used in conjunction with this episode.

Answers to video worksheet (ActiveTeach)

A
1. What do you like to do in your spare time?
2. Answers given are likely to be:
   Me gusta (mucho) …
   No me gusta (nada) …
3. Answers will vary and may include the nine adjectives introduced in Unit 1 of the Pupil Book.

B
1. a cool – 4 (one of these in the phrase '*superguay*')
   b boring – 2 (one of these in the phrase '*superaburrido*')
   c stupid – 1
2. tenis

C
1. take photos (of her friends)
2. Because it's fun.
3. a) Laura likes to play <u>ping pong</u> because it's <u>fun</u>.
   b) Estela likes to <u>surf the net</u> and send text messages.
   c) Samuel likes to watch television and <u>listen to music</u>.
   d) Marco likes to <u>play football</u> because it's <u>really fun</u>.

D
1. José is not a good loser because he says that he likes an activity (e.g. basketball, ping pong, football) until he loses, when he changes his mind!
2. go skateboarding
3. Answers will vary.
4. Answers will vary.

E
Pupils will produce their own dialogues in small groups.

3. ¿Qué haces cuando llueve?

Mi tiempo libre 2.3

Pupil Book pages
Pages 34–35

Learning objectives
- Talking about the weather
- Using *cuando* (when)

Programme of Study
LC6 Reading comprehension
LC8 Writing creatively

FCSE links
Unit 7: Local area and environment (Weather)

Key language
¿Qué tiempo hace?
hace calor
hace frío
hace sol
hace buen tiempo
llueve
nieva
en primavera
en verano
en otoño
en invierno

PLTS
C Creative thinkers

Cross-curricular
Geography: weather, climate, maps

Resources
Audio files:
23_Module2_Unit3_Ex1
24_Module2_Unit3_Ex5
25_Module2_Unit3_Ex6
Workbooks:
Cuaderno 1A & 1B, page 16
ActiveTeach:
p.034 Flashcards
Starter 1 resource
Plenary resource
ActiveLearn:
Listening A, Listening B
Reading A, Reading B
Vocabulary

Starter 1

Aim

To review all forms of regular *-ar* verbs.

Put the following wordsnake up on the board (Starter 1 Resource).

cantamostocoescuchasnaveganbailáissaca mandohablasescuchamos

Allow pupils four minutes to unravel it to identify nine *-ar* verbs. Ask them to write two sentences in Spanish and offer the English translation.

1 Escucha y escribe la letra correcta. (1–6) (L2)

Listening. Pupils listen and look at the pictures of the weather conditions. They write the letter (a–f) of the weather being mentioned each time.

Audioscript Track 23

1 – *Hace frío.*
2 – *Hace buen tiempo.*
3 – *Llueve.*
4 – *Hace sol.*
5 – *Hace calor.*
6 – *Nieva.*

Answers
1 a 2 d 3 e 4 b 5 c 6 f

Reinforcement

With books closed, and working in pairs, pupils take turns to quickly draw a sketch of a weather condition for their partner to name.

2 Con tu compañero/a juega a un juego de memoria. Una persona cierra el libro, la otra dice una letra. (L2)

Speaking. In pairs, pupils play a memory game using the six weather phrases from exercise 1. One person says a letter, while the other (whose book is closed) tries to remember the phrase from memory. A sample dialogue is supplied. The *Pronunciación* box reminds pupils that they will need to tackle pronunciation of the *ll* sound in Spanish, which is similar to the 'y' sound in yellow.

3 Lee las frases. Escribe las dos letras correctas. (L3)

Reading. Pupils read the sentences and identify the weather and activity, writing down the letters for each. Draw their attention to the Skills box and encourage them to use the connective *cuando* as often as possible to extend their sentences.

Answers
1 b, h 2 f, i 3 d, g 4 c, l 5 a, j 6 e, k

Starter 2

Aim

To practise extending and joining sentences.

Write up some short sentences on the board. Ask pupils to use the connectives they have learned such as *y*, *pero* and *porque* to extend and join each sentence.

© Pearson Education Ltd 2013. Copying permitted for purchasing institution only. This material is not copyright free.

Mi tiempo libre 2.3

4 Con tu compañero/a, haz un diálogo. (L3)

Speaking. In pairs, pupils practise asking and answering the question *¿Qué haces cuando…?* with all the weather phrases they have learned. A framework is supplied for support.

5 Escucha y lee los textos. Copia y completa la tabla en inglés. (L4)

Listening. Read through the *Zona Cultura* box together before starting this exercise. Pupils copy out the table. They listen to four people talking about the weather in their country, reading the texts at the same time. Their task is to fill in the table, noting where each person lives and what the weather is like during each season.

Audioscript Track 24

- Hola, me llamo Marcos. Vivo en Esquel, en Argentina. En invierno nieva mucho, pero en verano hace sol.
- Hola, me llamo Martina y vivo en Punta Arenas, en Chile. Generalmente en verano hace buen tiempo, pero a veces llueve.
- Me llamo Samuel y vivo en Nasca, en Perú. Hace sol en primavera, en verano, en otoño y en invierno. Nunca llueve. ¡Qué bien!
- Me llamo Rosa y vivo en La Paz, en Bolivia. En verano hace calor, pero llueve a veces. En otoño y en invierno hace frío. No me gusta cuando hace frío. ¡Uy!

Answers

	Marcos	Martina	Samuel	Rosa
town	Esquel	Punta Arenas	Nasca	La Paz
coun.	Argentina	Chile	Perú	Bolivia
spring			sunny, no rain	
sum.	sunny	nice weather, sometimes rains	sunny, no rain	hot, sometimes rains
aut.			sunny, no rain	cold
winter	snow		sunny, no rain	cold

Extension

Ask pupils to write descriptions of the seasons, stating two common weather conditions, e.g. *En verano, hace sol y hace calor*. Encourage them to include connectives such as *pero* and *y* and/or expressions of frequency such as *a veces*.

6 Escucha y apunta en inglés la estación y el tiempo. (L3)

Listening. Pupils listen to Alonso talk about the weather where he lives. They make notes in English of the weather in each season.

Audioscript Track 25

Me llamo Alonso y vivo en Oviedo, en España. En primavera hace buen tiempo pero a veces llueve.

En verano en Oviedo hace calor pero llueve de vez en cuando.

En otoño llueve mucho y en invierno hace frío y nieva a veces.

Answers

Spring: good weather, sometimes rains
Summer: hot, sometimes rains
Autumn: rains (a lot)
Winter: cold, sometimes snows

7 ¿Dónde vives? ¿Cómo es el clima allí? ¿Qué haces cuando llueve? Escribe una entrada para un blog. (L3)

Writing. Pupils write a short blog entry to include details on where they live, how the weather changes over the seasons and what they do in different types of weather. A writing frame is supplied for support.

Plenary

Play 'Odd-one-out' using the following lists (Plenary resource):

invierno, otoño, enero, verano

bailo, tocan, mando, canto

todos los días, nunca, de vez en cuando, pero

guay, fenomenal, divertido, aburrido

chatear, leer, salir, escribir, juego

Ask pupils to create their own odd-one-out list on any theme: weather, verbs, connectives.

Mi tiempo libre 2.3

Workbook 1A, page 16

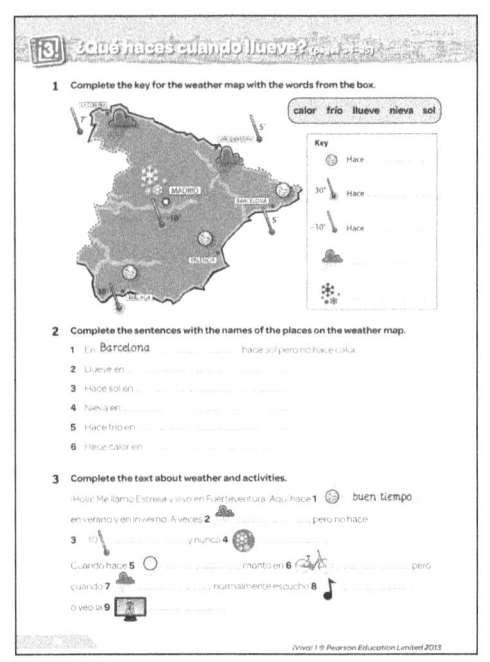

Answers

1 (sunny) *Hace* sol. (hot) *Hace* calor.
  (cold) *Hace* frío. (rain) Llueve.
  (snow) Nieva.

2 **1** *Barcelona*
  2 San Sebastián, La Coruña
  3 Barcelona, Málaga, Valencia
  4 Madrid   **5** Madrid   **6** Málaga

3 **1** *buen tiempo*   **2** llueve   **3** frío
  4 nieva   **5** sol   **6** bici
  7 llueve   **8** música
  9 televisión

Workbook 1B, page 16

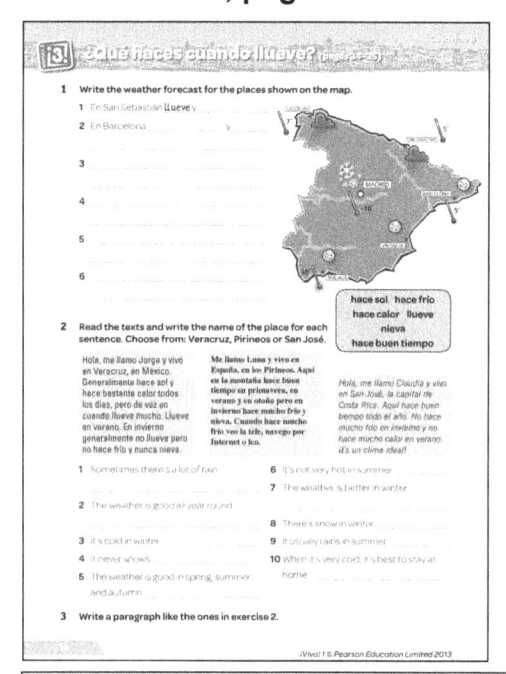

Answers

1 **1** *En San Sebastián llueve y hace frío.*
  2 *En Barcelona hace sol y hace frio.*
  3 En Madrid nieva y hace mucho frío.
  4 En Málaga hace sol y hace calor.
  5 En Valencia hace sol.
  6 En La Coruña llueve y hace frío.

2 **1** Veracruz   **2** San José   **3** Pirineos
  4 Veracruz   **5** Pirineos   **6** San José
  7 Veracruz   **8** Pirineos   **9** Veracruz
  10 Pirineos

3 Own answers

¿Qué deportes haces?

Mi tiempo libre 2.4

Pupil Book pages
Pages 36–37

Learning objectives
- Saying what sports you do
- Using *hacer* (to do) and *jugar* (to play)

Programme of Study
GV2 Grammatical structures (irregular verbs)
GV3 Opinions and discussions
LC1 Listening and responding

FCSE links
Unit 4: Leisure (Hobbies, Free time)
Unit 5: Healthy lifestyle (Sports, Activities)

Grammar
- present tense of *hacer* (irregular verb, full paradigm)
- present tense of *jugar* (stem-changing verb, full paradigm)

Key language
¿Qué deportes haces?
Hago gimnasia.
Hago artes marciales.
Hago equitación.
Hago atletismo.
Hago natación.
Juego al fútbol.
Juego al tenis.
Juego al voleibol.
Juego al baloncesto.
lunes
martes
miércoles
jueves
viernes
sábado
domingo

PLTS
E Effective participators

Resources
Audio files:
26_Module2_Unit4_Ex1
27_Module2_Unit4_Ex2
28_Module2_Unit4_Ex4
29_Module2_Unit4_Ex5
Workbooks:
Cuaderno 1A & 1B, page 17
ActiveTeach:
p.036 Flashcards
p.036 Grammar presentation
p.036 Grammar worksheet
p.037 Video 4
p.037 Video 4 transcript
p.037 Video worksheet 4
p.037 Grammar presentation
ActiveLearn:
Listening A, Listening B
Reading A, Reading B
Grammar, Vocabulary

Starter 1

Aim

To revise key sound-spelling links with sports vocabulary.

Present the following gapped words on the board next to visuals of the sports activities to show their meanings (use ActiveTeach flashcards). Read out the words for each sport and ask pupils to use their sound-spelling knowledge to predict the missing letters.

1 fút_ol   2 t_nis
3 v_leibol   4 gi_nasi_
5 _tletismo   6 b_lonc_st_
7 nata_ión   8 _quitación

1 Escucha y escribe la letra correcta. (1–9) (L2)

Listening. Pupils listen and look at the pictures of young people playing sport. They write the letter of the activity being described each time.

Audioscript Track 26

1 – ¿Qué deportes haces, Ana?
  – Hago natación.

2 – ¿Qué deportes haces, Álvaro?
  – Hago artes marciales.

3 – ¿Qué deportes haces, Jorge?
  – Juego al tenis.

4 – Y tú, Ainhoa, ¿qué deportes haces?
  – Hago equitación.

5 – ¿Qué deportes haces, David?
  – Yo juego al fútbol.

6 – Noelia, ¿qué deportes haces?
  – Hago gimnasia.

7 – ¿Qué deportes haces, Paula?
  – Juego al voleibol.

8 – Y tú, Marcos. ¿Qué deportes haces?
  – Juego al baloncesto.

9 – ¿Qué deportes haces, Carla?
  – Hago atletismo.

Answers
1 e 2 b 3 g 4 c 5 f 6 a 7 h 8 i 9 d

Mi tiempo libre 2.4

Reinforcement

Discuss with pupils the options for learning the new vocabulary for playing/doing sports. They could list items alphabetically, or grammatically (e.g. all the *hago* and *juego* items together, etc.), or draw pictures to help the words stick in their mind. When trying to remember which sports take *hacer* and which take *jugar*, they can look for links between the sports in each category, or links with the English, and also use different colours to note them.

Gramática

Use the *Gramática* box to teach the full paradigm of *hacer*, an important irregular -*er* verb that they will need to learn by heart. The key 'irregularity' is that the *c* changes to a *g* in the 'I' form. There is more information and further practice of *hacer* on Pupil Book p. 45.

2 Escucha. Escribe las letras correctas del ejercicio 1 y dibuja el símbolo correcto. (1–5) (L3)

Listening. Allow pupils to listen to the five conversations twice. First, they identify which three activities each of the speakers enjoys, writing the correct letters from exercise 1 on p. 36. Pupils listen again, drawing the correct symbol for the opinion that they hear as shown in the Skills box.

Audioscript Track 27

1 – Adrián ¿Qué deportes haces?
– Hago atletismo y juego al voleibol. También hago natación. Me gusta mucho.

2 – ¿Qué deportes haces, Marta?
– Hago gimnasia y también juego al baloncesto. Hago equitación y me gusta mucho porque es fenomenal.

3 – ¿Qué deportes haces, Claudia?
– A ver… juego al tenis y juego al voleibol. También hago artes marciales. Me encanta.

4 – ¿Qué deportes haces, Hugo?
– Pues… hago natación todos los días, hago gimnasia también y juego al fútbol. Me gusta porque es divertido.

5 – ¡Hola, Samuel! ¿Cómo estás? ¿Qué deportes haces?
– Juego al fútbol y juego al tenis. Hago artes marciales también. Me gusta muchísimo.

Answers

1 Adrián d, h, e (♥♥)
2 Marta a, i, c (♥♥)
3 Claudia g, h, b (♥♥♥♥)
4 Hugo e, a, f (♥)
5 Samuel f, g, b (♥♥♥)

3 Con tu compañero/a, haz cuatro diálogos. (L3)

Speaking. In pairs, pupils take it in turns to make up four dialogues that mention the sports that they play and why they like them. A sample exchange is provided.

Pronunciación

Use the *Pronunciación* box to explain to pupils that the Spanish letter *c* has a soft sound when it comes before *e* and *i*. Ask pupils to suggest some more words they know that have a soft *c*.

Extension

Ask pupils to translate the following sentences into Spanish.

1 He goes swimming.
2 She plays tennis.
3 Do you do gymnastics?
4 They play volleyball.
5 We go horseriding.
6 He does athletics.

Starter 2

Aim

To review how to say what sports you do.

Write up the following on the board

Hagoatletismoyavecesjuegoalvoleibol.Tambiénhagonatación.Megustamuchoporqueesdivertido.

Ask pupils to separate the wordsnake to reveal the three sentences. Then ask them to create a different text, by changing the nouns and opinions.

Alternative starter 2:

Use ActiveTeach p.037 Grammar practice to review and practice the verbs *hacer* and *jugar*.

© Pearson Education Ltd 2013. Copying permitted for purchasing institution only. This material is not copyright free.

Mi tiempo libre 2.4

4 Escucha. ¿Quién dice los días en el orden correcto? ¿Juan o Ana? (L1)

Listening. Pupils hear two people recite the days of the week. Who says them in the correct order?

Audioscript Track 28

- (Juan) lunes, martes, miércoles, jueves, viernes, sábado, domingo
- (Ana) lunes, martes, jueves, miércoles, sábado, viernes, domingo

Answer Juan

Gramática

Use the *Gramática* box on p. 37 to teach the full paradigm of *jugar*, a stem-changing verb. *Jugar* does not include the sense of playing music or an instrument. In order to say that you play the guitar, you will need to use the verb *tocar*, as in, *toco la guitarra*. There is more information and further practice on Pupil Book p. 45.

5 Escucha y lee el rap. Contesta a las preguntas en inglés. (L3)

Listening. Pupils listen to the rap song, following the text at the same time. Play the song again and encourage pupils to rap along. They then answer the questions that follow in English. Some vocabulary is glossed for support. Draw their attention to the Tip box, which highlights the phrase *los lunes*, meaning 'on Mondays'.

Audioscript Track 29

¿Qué haces en tu tiempo libre? ¿Qué deportes haces tú?

¿Qué haces en tu tiempo libre? ¿Qué deportes haces tú?

Los lunes hago atletismo, a mí me gusta muchísimo.

Los martes hago artes marciales. Es divertido, ¡muy divertido!

Los miércoles juego al baloncesto, porque a mí me gusta mucho.

Los jueves juego al tenis cuando hace sol y buen tiempo.

Los viernes juego al fútbol normalmente con mi equipo.

Los sábados hago natación o a veces equitación.

Y los domingos, no hago nada. ¡Yo veo la televisión!

No, los domingos, no hago nada. ¡Yo veo la televisión!

¿Qué haces en tu tiempo libre? ¿Qué deportes haces tú?

Answers
a 8 **b** 3

6 Lee el rap otra vez y completa las frases en inglés. (L4)

Reading. Pupils read the text of the rap in exercise 5 then complete the gap-fill sentences in English.

Answers
1 On Mondays, Isham does **athletics**.
2 Isham thinks martial arts are **fun**.
3 On Wednesdays, he plays basketball because **he likes it a lot**.
4 When it's nice weather, Isham plays **tennis**.
5 He plays in a **football** team.
6 On Saturdays, he goes **swimming** or sometimes **horseriding**.

7 Cambia un elemento en cada línea del rap. (L4)

Writing. Pupils rewrite the rap, changing one element in each line. An example is given.

8 Haz tu rap para la clase. (L4)

Speaking. Pupils rap the verses they have written in exercise 7 to the rest of the class. You could make a recording of everyone's efforts.

Plenary

Ask pupils to write three multiple-choice verb questions for their partner, giving four options.

For example:

How do you say 'they play' in Spanish?
(a) *juega*
(b) *juegan*
(c) *jugamos*
(d) *juego*

© Pearson Education Ltd 2013. Copying permitted for purchasing institution only. This material is not copyright free.

Mi tiempo libre 2.4

Workbook 1A, page 17

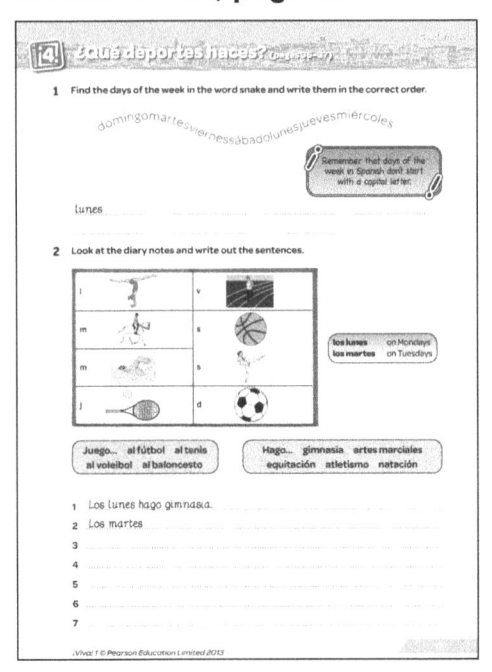

Answers

1. Days of the week: lunes, martes, miércoles, jueves, viernes, sábado, domingo
2. 1 *Los lunes hago gimnasia.*
   2 *Los martes* hago equitación.
   3 Los miércoles hago natación
   4 Los jueves juego al tenis.
   5 Los viernes hago atletismo.
   6 Los sábados juego al baloncesto y hago artes marciales.
   7 Los domingos juego al fútbol.

Workbook 1B, page 17

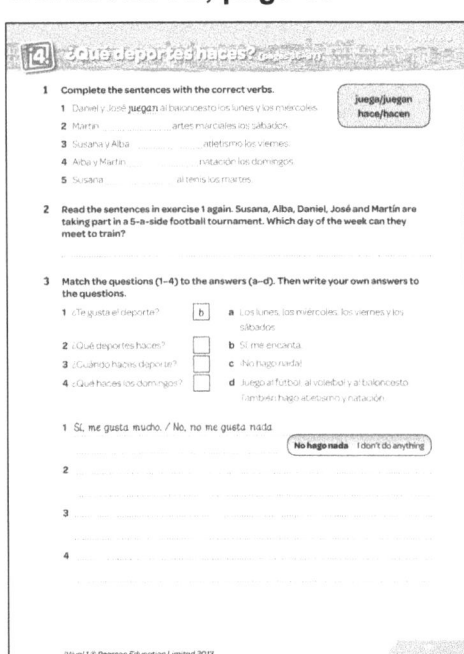

Answers

1. 1 *juegan* 2 hace 3 hacen 4 hacen
   5 juega
2. Thursdays
3. 1 b 2 d 3 a 4 c

Students write own answers to questions.

Worksheet 2.4 All muddled up!

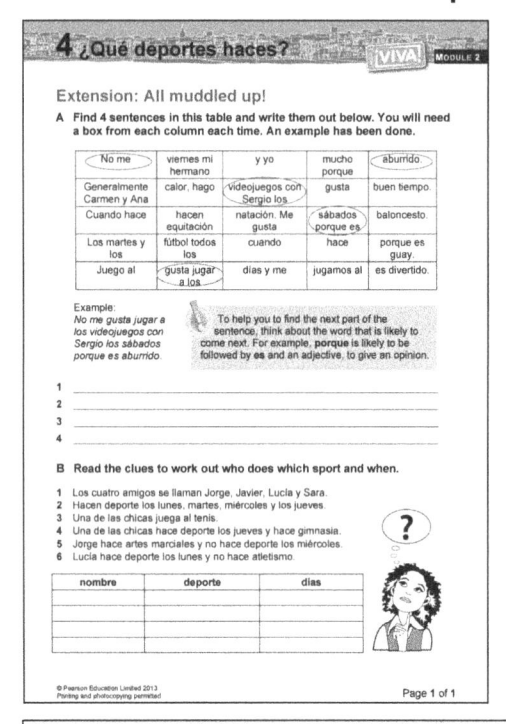

Answers

A

1. Generalmente Carmen y Ana hacen equitación cuando hace buen tiempo.
2. Cuando hace calor, hago natación. Me gusta mucho porque es divertido.
3. Los martes y los viernes mi hermano y yo jugamos al baloncesto.
4. Juego al fútbol todos los días y me gusta porque es guay.

B

nombre	deporte	días
Jorge	artes marciales	martes
Javier	atletismo	miércoles
Lucía	tenis	lunes
Sara	gimnasia	jueves

Mi tiempo libre 2.4

Video

Episode 4: Los deportes

The ¡TeleViva! team discuss the sports and activities that they practise in Asturias at different times of the year, and José takes them mountain-biking. Video worksheet 4 can be used in conjunction with this episode.

Answers to video worksheet (ActiveTeach)

A

1 primavera   verano   otoño   invierno

2 a) a veces – sometimes
   b) de vez en cuando – from time to time
   c) nunca – never
   d) todos los días – every day

3 Answers will vary and may include the nine sports introduced on page 36 of the Pupil Book, plus '*montar en bici*' from Unit 2.

B

1 atletismo, fútbol, baloncesto, natación, montar en bici/ciclismo/bicicleta de montaña

2 in all four seasons

3 sing karaoke

C

1
Season	Sport
summer	athletics
autumn	football
winter	basketball
spring	swimming

2 from time to time

3 snowy

D

1 It means 'in the gym(nasium)'. You can distinguish it from the word for 'gymnastics' ('*gimnasia*') by the gender of the word (shown by the article) and by the last letter – gymnasium is masculine and gymnastics is feminine.

2 No, because when she asks if he likes going cycling with her, he replies that he likes going with his friends, and then looks away.

3 He says that he loves it/that he does it every day of the week/that he does it in lots of different weather conditions.

4 Because he loses the race./Because it is raining.

5 Answers will vary.

E
Pupils will produce their own dialogues in small groups.

[5] Reading Skills: ¿Eres fanático? Mi tiempo libre 2.5

Pupil Book pages
Pages 38–39

Learning objectives
- Reading about someone's favourite things
- Understanding more challenging texts

Programme of Study
GV3 Developing vocabulary
LC6 Reading comprehension

Key language
Review of language from Units 1–4.

PLTS
C Creative thinkers

Resources
Audio files:
30_Module2_Unit5_Ex3
31_Module2_Unit5_Ex4
Workbooks:
Cuaderno 1A & 1B, page 18
ActiveTeach:
p.038 Grammar worksheet
Starter 2 resource

Starter 1

Aim

To review saying what sports you do.

Play a game of 'Loser has the last word'. Pupils work in groups of four and each choose a number between 2 and 5. They read the rap from exercise 5 in Unit 4 (p. 37) out loud, saying up to as many words as their chosen number. If their chosen number is four, for example, they can choose to read out 1, 2, 3 or 4 words. The object of the game is not to say the last word in each sentence.

---

1 Lee las frases. Busca un cognado en cada frase. (L4)

Reading. Pupils read the sentences and find the cognate in each one. Stress to pupils that although Spanish and English cognates look very similar, they may be pronounced differently.

Answers

1 capital	2 hockey	3 pizza
4 piano	5 actor	6 waterpolo

---

2 Eres Yasmina del ejercicio 1. Copia y rellena la ficha de identidad en inglés. (L4)

Reading. Students copy and fill in Yasmina's identity card in English, using information given in exercise 1.

Answers

Name: Yasmina
Lives in: Montevideo, Uruguay
Personality: quite funny
Likes: playing hockey, going out with friends, eating pizza
Dislikes: playing water polo
Other details: favourite actor is Rupert Grint; when weather is bad, sometimes plays piano

---

3 Escucha y lee los textos. Luego busca las palabras en los textos. (L4)

Listening. Pupils listen to the three young people introduce themselves, following the text at the same time. They then find the eight near-cognates in the text. This exercise helps pupils practise using cognates as a reading strategy.

Audioscript Track 30

– ¡Hola! Me llamo Carlos. Soy honesto y bastante paciente. En mi tiempo libre toco el saxofón o navego por Internet.

– Me llamo Juan. Soy optimista y muy positivo. Mi deporte favorito es el ciclismo y mi animal favorito es el tigre.

– Me llamo Valentina. Vivo en Buenos Aires en Argentina. En invierno hago esquí. Me encanta. ¡Es genial!

Answers

1 honesto	2 paciente	3 saxofón
4 optimista	5 positivo	6 ciclismo
7 tigre	8 esquí	

Starter 2

Aim

To review language from the module.

Play 'Odd-one-out' using the following lists (Starter 2 resource):

1 juego	juegas	canta
2 hablo	navegan	mando
3 escribir	hacer	chateo
4 haces	juega	hago
5 hablamos	mandamos	cantan

Ask pupils to create their own odd-one-out list on any theme: pets, intensifiers, leisure.

© Pearson Education Ltd 2013. Copying permitted for purchasing institution only. This material is not copyright free.

Mi tiempo libre 2.5

4 Escucha y lee el texto. Completa las frases. (L4)

Listening. Pupils listen to Felipe introduce himself, following the text at the same time. They then fill in the gap-fill sentences that summarise the text in English. Draw pupils' attention to the Skills box, which highlights using context to deduce the meaning of words as a useful reading strategy.

Audioscript Track 31

Me llamo Felipe y vivo en la Ciudad de México, que es la capital de México. Tengo dieciséis años. Soy bastante extrovertido. No soy nada pesimista. Juego al fútbol todos los días. Es mi pasión. Soy miembro del equipo nacional sub-17. Soy defensa. La camiseta de fútbol mexicana es verde y me gusta mucho. Llevo el número 5.

En mi tiempo libre me gusta montar en bici porque es divertido. Me gusta mucho navegar por Internet porque es interesante, también me gusta hacer alpinismo. Me encanta jugar a los videojuegos. Mi juego favorito es 'Football up!', por supuesto.

Answers
1 national under-17 team
2 defender (in defence)
3 football shirt
4 wears
5 climbing
6 favourite (video) game

Extension
Pupils read aloud Felipe's letter in Spanish round the class, a sentence at a time, translating it into English.

5 Lee el texto. Copia y completa la tabla. (L4)

Reading. Pupils copy out the table. They read the text about Marta and complete the table, noting how they worked out the meaning of any new words – whether cognates, near-cognates, or by looking at the context.

Answers (may vary)

cognates	near-cognates	context
península	futbolista	delantera
México	fanática	marcar (goles)
piano	rápida	películas
	talento, goles	tocar (el piano)
	ciencia ficción	subir fotos
	actriz	

Reinforcement
Pupils identify all the verbs in the first person in Marta's letter in exercise 5 and translate them into English.

6 Lee el texto otra vez. Apunta cinco detalles en inglés sobre la vida de Marta. (L4)

Reading. Pupils reread the text in exercise 5 and note down five details in English about Marta's life.

Answers (will vary)
She lives in Mérida, in the Yucatan Peninsula, in Mexico.

She is a footballer and is fanatical about it.

She is very fast and talented. She loves scoring goals. She is a forward/striker.

She watches science-fiction films or listens to music with her friends. Her favourite film is *Avatar*.

She likes dancing and playing the piano.

Her favourite actress is Jennifer Lawrence.

She doesn't like chatting online, because it's boring, but she likes uploading/posting photos and texting her family. She texts every day.

Plenary
Ask pupils to produce a quick acrostic based around a central word, 'near-cognate', using only near-cognates from Modules 1 and 2, as shown in the example below.

```
                    M
          H         Ú
          O         S
          N         I
          N  E  A  R  C  O  G  N  A  T  E
          E         S
          S         A
          T
          O
```

Mi tiempo libre 2.5

Workbook 1A, page 18

Answers

1 1 *Buenos Aires,* Argentina
   2 la flauta, el violín
   3 julio, agosto, diciembre, enero
   4 invierno, verano
   5 natación, surf, hockey, voleibol
   6 extrovertida, sociable
2 1 She lives in Buenos Aires.
   2 She's 13 years old.
   3 She plays the flute and the violin.
   4 The winter months in Buenos Aires are July and August.
   5 Summer is in December and January.
   6 In summer she swims and goes surfing.
   7 In winter she plays hockey and volleyball.
   8 She's outgoing. She says she's extroverted and sociable.

Workbook 1B, page 18

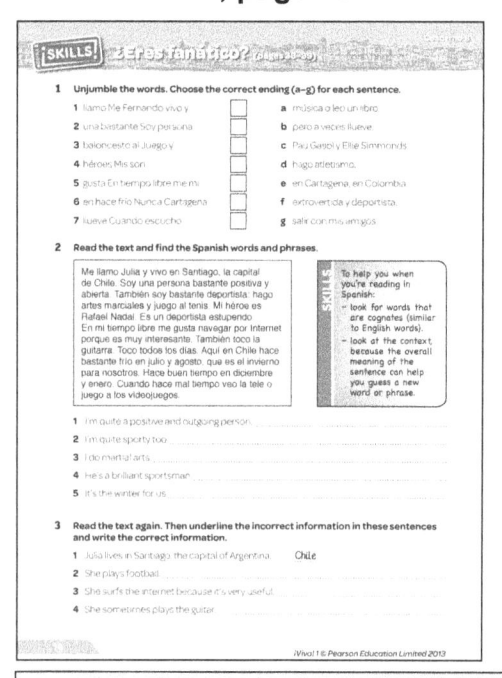

Answers

1 1 Me llamo Fernando y vivo, e
   2 Soy una persona bastante, f
   3 Juego al baloncesto y, d
   4 Mis héroes son, c
   5 En mi tiempo libre me gusta, g
   6 Nunca hace frío en Cartagena, b
   7 Cuando llueve escucho, a
2 1 Soy una persona bastante positiva y abierta.
   2 También soy bastante deportista.
   3 Hago artes marciales.
   4 Es un deportista estupendo.
   5 Es el invierno para nosotros.
3 1 Julia lives in Santiago, the capital of Argentina. *Chile*
   2 She plays football. tennis
   3 She surfs the internet because it's very useful. interesting
   4 She sometimes plays the guitar. every day

© Pearson Education Ltd 2013. Copying permitted for purchasing institution only. This material is not copyright free.

Mi tiempo libre 2.5

Worksheet 2.5 Recognising cognates

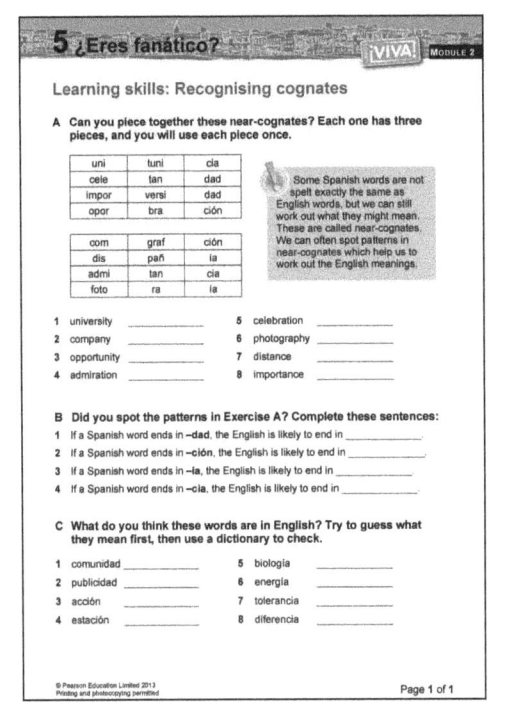

5 ¿Eres fanático? ¡VIVA! MODULE 2

Learning skills: Recognising cognates

A Can you piece together these near-cognates? Each one has three pieces, and you will use each piece once.

uni	tuni	cia
cele	tan	dad
impor	versi	dad
opor	bra	ción

com	graf	ción
dis	pañ	ia
admi	tan	cia
foto	ra	ia

Some Spanish words are not spelt exactly the same as English words, but we can still work out what they might mean. These are called near-cognates. We can often spot patterns in near-cognates which help us to work out the English meanings.

1 university _____   5 celebration _____
2 company _____   6 photography _____
3 opportunity _____   7 distance _____
4 admiration _____   8 importance _____

B Did you spot the patterns in Exercise A? Complete these sentences:
1 If a Spanish word ends in –dad, the English is likely to end in _____.
2 If a Spanish word ends in –ción, the English is likely to end in _____.
3 If a Spanish word ends in –ia, the English is likely to end in _____.
4 If a Spanish word ends in –cia, the English is likely to end in _____.

C What do you think these words are in English? Try to guess what they mean first, then use a dictionary to check.
1 comunidad _____   5 biología _____
2 publicidad _____   6 energía _____
3 acción _____   7 tolerancia _____
4 estación _____   8 diferencia _____

Answers

A
1 universidad   2 compañía
3 oportunidad   4 admiración
5 celebración   6 fotografía
7 distancia   8 importancia

B
1 –ity, –ty   2 –ion, –tion, –ation, –ition
3 –y   4 –ance

C
1 community   2 publicity
3 action   4 station
5 biology   6 energy
7 tolerance   8 difference

Speaking Skills: ¿Qué haces en tu tiempo libre?

Mi tiempo libre 2.6

Pupil Book pages
Pages 40–41

Learning objectives
- Taking part in a longer conversation
- Using question words

Programme of Study
LC3 Conversation
LC5 Speaking coherently and confidently

Key language
Review of language from Units 1–4.

PLTS
R Reflective learners

Resources
Audio files:
32_Module2_Unit6_Ex2
33_Module2_Unit6_Ex7
ActiveTeach:
Starter 1 resource

Starter 1

Aim

To review personal information from Module 1.

Write the following phrases up on the board, jumbling the order of the words in the right-hand column (Starter 1 resource). Give pupils three minutes to match up the sentence halves. Check pupils' answers, asking them to explain their choices and to translate the completed phrases into English.

¿Qué tipo de	persona eres?
Soy tímida y también	soy generosa.
Soy hija	única.
Mi cumpleaños es	el primero de mayo.
¿Dónde	vives?
Mi perro es	marrón y negro.
Mi nombre se escribe	S-A-R-A-H.

1 Completa las preguntas con la palabra correcta. (L2)

Reading. Firstly, draw pupils' attention to the *Skills* box to review the question words that they have met already. Discuss the concept of the upside-down question mark in front of interrogatives in Spanish, which pupils first came across in Unit 6 of Module 1. Explain that all the question words have accents on them to differentiate them from their non-question counterparts. Pupils complete the gap-fill sentences choosing the correct interrogative word each time.

Answers

1 Cuándo	2 Dónde	3 Qué
4 Qué	5 Cómo	6 Qué
7 Cuántos		

2 Escucha y comprueba tus respuestas. (1–7) (L2)

Listening. Pupils listen and check their answers to exercise 1.

Audioscript Track 32

1 – ¿Cuándo es tu cumpleaños?
2 – ¿Dónde vives?
3 – ¿Qué tipo de persona eres?
4 – ¿Qué te gusta hacer en tu tiempo libre?
5 – ¿Cómo te llamas?
6 – ¿Qué deportes haces?
7 – ¿Cuántos años tienes?

Reinforcement

Ask pupils to translate the following questions into Spanish:

1 How many brothers and sisters do you have?
   ¿Cuántos hermanos tienes?
2 How is it spelt?
   ¿Cómo se escribe?
3 What do you do when it rains?
   ¿Qué haces cuando llueve?
4 What is it like?
   ¿Cómo es?

3 Completa la conversación con las preguntas correctas. (L3)

Reading. Pupils read through the one-sided dialogue, then use their understanding of the answers to complete the gaps with the correct questions.

Answers

1 ¿Cuántos años tienes?
2 ¿Cuándo es tu cumpleaños?
3 ¿Dónde vives?
4 ¿Qué te gusta hacer en tu tiempo libre?
5 ¿Qué tipo de persona eres?
6 ¿Qué deportes haces?

© Pearson Education Ltd 2013. Copying permitted for purchasing institution only. This material is not copyright free.

Mi tiempo libre 2.6

4 Con tu compañero/a, practica el diálogo. (L4)

Speaking. In pairs, pupils take it in turns to ask and answer the questions in the dialogue that they completed in exercise 3.

Starter 2

Aim

To review free time phrases.

Give pupils three minutes to prepare a sentence about a famous celebrity that includes what they do in their free time. Ask pupils to read out their sentence for the class to guess who it is.

5 Lee el artículo. Busca en el texto: (L4)

Reading. Pupils read the magazine interview of a teenager called Carmen and are asked to find the following features in the text: five connectives, two intensifiers, two opinions with reasons and two expressions of frequency.

Before pupils start, read together through the Skills box on how to make sentences longer and more interesting. Review the connectives, intensifiers, reasons and frequency expressions that pupils have met so far in Modules 1 and 2.

Answers

Connectives: y, porque, o, cuando, pero

Intensifiers: muy, bastante

Opinions with reasons: me gusta bailar y cantar porque es guay/nunca mando SMS porque es aburrido.

Expressions of frequency: a veces, nunca

Extension

Pupils identify all verbs and adjectives in the text in exercise 5 and translate them into English.

6 Con tu compañero/a, ¿cómo se dicen las letras rojas del ejercicio 5? (L1)

Speaking. In pairs, pupils practise pronouncing the letters highlighted in red in the text in exercise 5. They will have learned how to pronounce these letters when encountered in previous units, but draw pupils' attention to the *Pronunciación* box, which advises them to go back to p. 8, as well as to refer to pronunciation tips in previous units.

7 Escucha y comprueba la pronunciación. (L4)

Listening. Pupils listen and check how well they pronounced the letters in exercise 6 (these are in bold in the audioscript below).

Audioscript Track 33

- ¿Cómo te **ll**amas?
- Me **ll**amo Carmen.
- ¿Dónde vives?
- **V**ivo en Toledo, en España. Me gus**t**a mu**ch**o.
- ¿Cuántos años tienes?
- Tengo tre**c**e años.
- ¿Cuándo es tu cumpleaños?
- Mi cumpleaños es el **c**inco de **j**ulio.
- ¿Qué **t**ipo de persona eres?
- Soy muy divertida y bastante simpática. No soy tímida.
- ¿Qué te gusta hacer en **t**u tiempo libre?
- **E**n mi tiempo libre me gusta **b**ailar y cantar porque es guay.
- ¿Qué **d**eportes ha**c**es?
- Cuando **h**ace sol, monto en bi**c**i o a **v**eces hago natación. Cuando ha**c**e frío, no hago deporte. Escucho música o navego por Internet, pero nunca mando SMS porque es aburrido.

8 Con tu compañero/a, haz una conversación, utilizando las preguntas del ejercicio 5. (L4)

Speaking. In pairs, pupils use the dialogue framework provided in exercise 5 to make up a conversation of their own, adapting Carmen's answers to suit themselves. They take it in turns to ask and answer the seven questions.

9 Trabaja con otra pareja. Escucha su conversación y comprueba el uso de: (L4)

Listening. Pupils work with another pair, taking it in turns to listen to the dialogues that each pair practised in exercise 8. They award marks out of 3, looking out in particular for use of connectives, intensifiers, opinions with reasons, and time phrases.

© Pearson Education Ltd 2013. Copying permitted for purchasing institution only. This material is not copyright free.

10 ¿Qué opinas de la pronunciación? (L2)

Speaking. Each pair now assesses the other pair's pronunciation, awarding marks out of 3. Before asking pupils to comment, check that they understand the meanings of the three Spanish feedback comments.

Plenary

Ask pupils to each come up with five pronunciation tips to share with the class.

RESUMEN Y PREPÁRATE

Mi tiempo libre 2

Pupil Book pages
Pages 42–43

Resumen

Pupils use the checklist to review language covered in the module, working on it in pairs in class or on their own at home. Encourage them to follow up any areas of weakness they identify. There are Target Setting Sheets included in the Assessment Pack and an opportunity for pupils to record their own levels and targets on the Self-assessment pages in the Workbooks, p. 22. You can also use the *Resumen* checklist (available in the ActiveTeach) as an end-of-module plenary option.

Prepárate

These revision exercises can be used for assessment purposes or for pupils to practise before tackling the assessment tasks in the Assessment Pack.

Resources

Audio file:
34_Module2_Prep_Ex1
Workbooks:
Cuaderno 1A & 1B, pages 19 & 20
ActiveTeach:
p.042 *Resumen* checklist

1 Escucha. Copia y completa la tabla. (1–5) (L2)

Listening. Pupils copy out the table. They listen to five sentences and complete the table – for each sentence, they note the correct letter for the weather and the activity.

Audioscript Track 34

1 – Cuando hace calor, hago natación.
2 – Cuando nieva, navego por Internet.
3 – Cuando hace sol, juego al voleibol.
4 – Cuando llueve, toco la guitarra.
5 – Cuando hace frío, mando SMS.

Answers

	tiempo	actividad
1	d	i
2	b	h
3	c	j
4	a	f
5	e	g

2 Con tu compañero/a, haz un diálogo. (L3/4)

Speaking. In pairs, pupils take it in turns to ask and answer questions on what activities they do, including sport. A sample dialogue is given. You could extend the level to 4 by asking pupils to add opinions and extra detail, such as when or how often they do things.

3 Lee el texto. ¿Verdadero o falso? Escribe V o F. (L3)

Reading. Pupils read the text and the six statements about it. They identify the statements that are correct and false.

Answers

1 V   2 V   3 V   4 F   5 V   6 F

4 Escribe las frases en el orden correcto. (L2)

Writing. Pupils write out the jumbled sentences in the correct order.

Answers

1 Los viernes juego al fútbol.
2 Los domingos juego al baloncesto.
3 Los martes canto karaoke.
4 Los sábados hago atletismo.
5 Todos los días mando SMS.
6 A veces escucho música.

5 Cambia la actividad o la expresión de tiempo en cada frase del ejercicio 4. (L3)

Writing. Pupils rewrite the sentences from exercise 4, changing the activity or the time expression in each sentence.

© Pearson Education Ltd 2013. Copying permitted for purchasing institution only. This material is not copyright free.

Mi tiempo libre 2

Workbook 1A, page 19

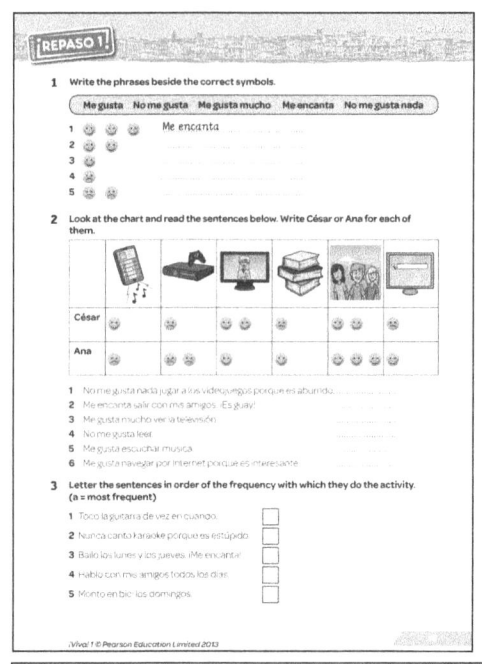

Answers

1 1 *Me encanta* 2 Me gusta mucho
   3 Me gusta 4 No me gusta
   5 No me gusta nada

2 1 Ana 2 Ana 3 César
   4 César 5 César 6 Ana

3 1 d 2 e 3 b 4 a 5 c

Workbook 1A, page 20

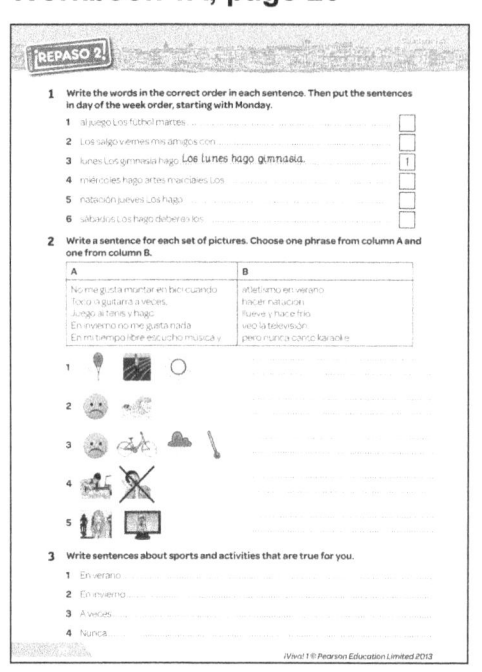

Answers

1 1 Los martes juego al fútbol. 2
   2 Los viernes salgo con mis amigos. 5
   3 *Los lunes hago gimnasia. 1*
   4 Los miércoles hago artes marciales. 3
   5 Los jueves hago natación. 4
   6 Los sábados hago los deberes. 6

2 1 Juego al tenis y hago atletismo en verano.
   2 En invierno no me gusta nada hacer natación.
   3 No me gusta montar en bici cuando llueve y hace frío.
   4 Toco la guitarra a veces, pero nunca canto karaoke.
   5 En mi tiempo libre escucho música y veo la televisión.

3 Own answers.

Workbook 1B, page 19

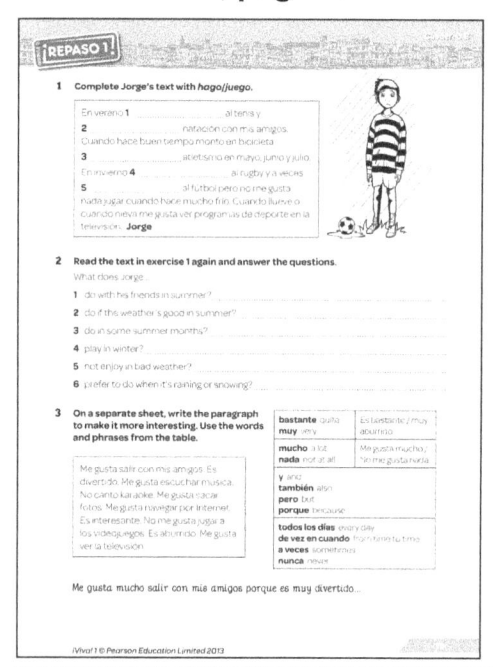

Answers

1 1 juego 2 hago 3 hago 4 juego 5 juego

2 1 He plays tennis and goes swimming.
   2 He rides his bike.
   3 He does athletics.
   4 He plays rugby and he sometimes plays football.
   5 He doesn't enjoy playing football.
   6 He prefers to watch sport on TV.

3 Own answers

© Pearson Education Ltd 2013. Copying permitted for purchasing institution only. This material is not copyright free.

Mi tiempo libre 2

Workbook 1B, page 20

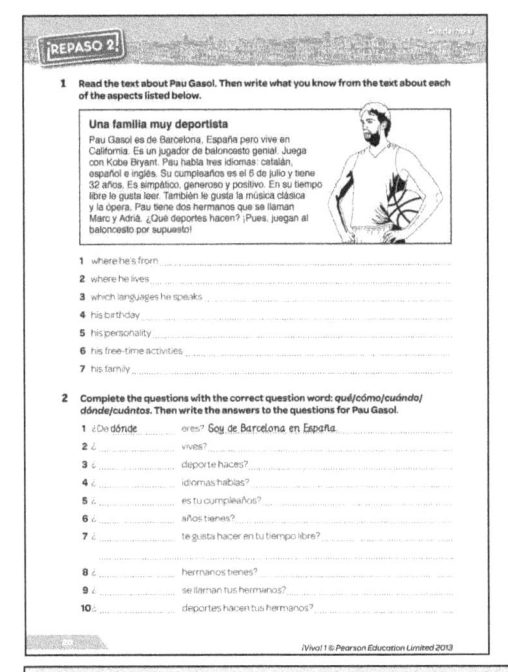

Answers

1 1 He's from Barcelona, Spain.

   2 He lives in California.

   3 He speaks Catalan, Spanish and English.

   4 His birthday is 6th July.

   5 He's friendly, generous and positive.

   6 He likes reading and he also likes classical music and opera.

   7 He's got two brothers, Marc and Adrià, who play basketball too.

2 1 dónde, Soy de Barcelona en España.

   2 Dónde, Vivo en California.

   3 Qué, Juego al baloncesto.

   4 Qué, Hablo catalán, español e inglés.

OR Cuántos, Hablo tres idiomas.

   5 Cuándo, Mi cumpleaños es el 6 de julio.

   6 Cuántos, Tengo 32 (treinta y dos) años.

   7 Qué, Me gusta leer y me gusta la música clásica y la ópera.

   8 Cuántos, Tengo dos hermanos.

   9 Cómo, Mis hermanos se llaman Marc y Adrià.

   10 Qué, Juegan al baloncesto.

© Pearson Education Ltd 2013. Copying permitted for purchasing institution only. This material is not copyright free.

¡GRAMÁTICA!

Mi tiempo libre 2

Pupil Book pages	Grammar topics	Resources
Pages 44–45	• the infinitive and the three verb endings (-ar, -er, -ir)	Workbooks: Cuaderno 1A & 1B, page 21
The *Gramática* section provides a more detailed summary of the key grammar covered in the module, along with further exercises to practise these points.	• present tense -ar verbs (*hablar*)	ActiveTeach:
	• stem-changing verbs (*jugar*)	p.044 Grammar presentation
	• irregular verbs (*hacer*)	p.045 Grammar presentation
	• verbs with the infinitive	p.045 Grammar presentation
		p.045 Grammar presentation

The infinitive

1 Match up the halves of these infinitives. Find the correct English translation.

Pupils match up the two halves of the Spanish infinitives, then find the equivalent verbs in English.

Answers
1	jugar	to play
2	hacer	to do
3	chatear	to chat online
4	leer	to read
5	escribir	to write
6	vivir	to live
7	cantar	to sing
8	hablar	to talk / speak

Present tense -ar verbs

2 Play a dice game with your partner. Throw the dice twice and make a sentence.

Pupils look at the summary of the present tense of regular *-ar* verb *hablar* on p. 44 before playing the dice game. In pairs, each person takes turns to throw the dice twice and makes up a sentence using the key provided (the first throw determines which subject pronoun to use and the second throw decides which form of the verb to conjugate).

3 Translate these sentences into Spanish.

This exercise provides further practice of regular *-ar* verbs. Pupils translate the sentences into Spanish, referring to the model paradigm as necessary.

Answers
1 Mandamos SMS.
2 Toca la guitarra.
3 Hablo con mis amigos/amigas.
4 Cantas karaoke.
5 Bailan.
6 Escucháis.

Stem-changing verbs

4 Unjumble the verbs, then translate the sentences into English.

Pupils work out the verb anagrams, then translate the full sentences into English.

Answers
1 Todos los días **juego** al baloncesto.
   Every day I play basketball.
2 De vez en cuando **juega** al fútbol.
   From time to time he/she plays football.
3 A veces **juegan** al tenis.
   Sometimes they play tennis.
4 ¿**Juegas** al voleibol?
   Do you play volleyball?
5 **Jugamos** al rugby.
   We play rugby.

Irregular verbs

5 Hannah has spilt tea all over her verb tables. Can you write out the verb *hacer* for her?

Pupils fill in the gaps to write out the full paradigm of the verb *hacer*.

© Pearson Education Ltd 2013. Copying permitted for purchasing institution only. This material is not copyright free.

Mi tiempo libre 2

Answers	
hacer	to do
ha**go**	I do
haces	**you** (singular) do
hace	**he/she** does
hac**emos**	we do
hacéis	**you** (plural) do
hac**en**	they do

6 Write six sentences each containing one element from each circle and a different form of the verb *hacer*.

Pupils write six sentences in Spanish, choosing a time phrase, an activity and a different form of the verb *hacer* each time.

Verbs with the infinitive

7 Choose the correct form of the verb to complete each sentence.

Pupils write out the completed sentences, choosing the correct verb form from the three options given each time.

Answers
1 No me gusta **hacer** atletismo.
2 Me encanta **jugar** al fútbol.
3 Me gusta **mandar** SMS.
4 ¿Te gusta **escuchar** música?
5 No me gusta nada **leer**.

Workbook 1A, page 21

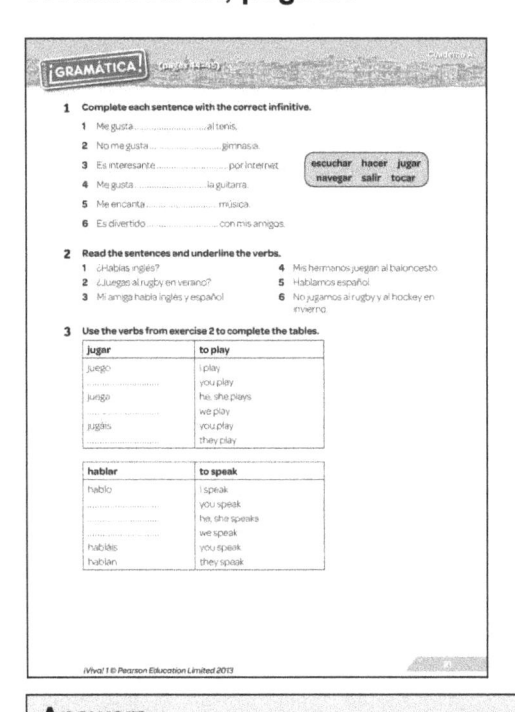

Answers					
1 1 jugar		2 hacer		3 navegar	
4 tocar		5 escuchar		6 salir	
2 1 Hablas		2 Juegas		3 habla	
4 juegan		5 Hablamos		6 jugamos	

3 Jugar (to play)

juego	I play
juegas	you play
juega	he, she plays
jugamos	we play
jugáis	you play
juegan	they play

Hablar (to speak)

hablo	I speak
hablas	you speak
habla	he, she speaks
hablamos	we speak
habláis	you speak
hablan	they speak

© Pearson Education Ltd 2013. Copying permitted for purchasing institution only. This material is not copyright free.

Mi tiempo libre 2

Workbook 1B, page 21

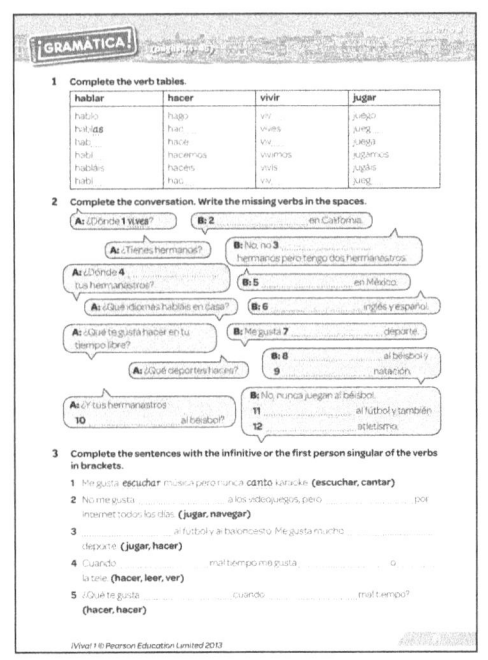

Answers

1

hablar	hacer	vivir	jugar
hablo	hago	vivo	juego
hablas	haces	vives	juegas
habla	hace	vive	juega
hablamos	hacemos	vivimos	jugamos
habláis	hacéis	vivís	jugáis
hablan	hacen	viven	juegan

2 1 vives 2 Vivo 3 tengo
4 viven 5 Viven 6 Hablamos
7 hacer 8 Juego 9 hago
10 juegan 11 Juegan 12 hacen

3 1 escuchar, canto 2 jugar, navego
3 Juego, hacer 4 hace, leer, ver
5 hacer, hace

¡PROYECTO! Navidad en España — Mi tiempo libre 2

Pupil Book pages
Pages 48–49

Learning objectives
- Learning about Christmas in Spain
- Writing an acrostic about Christmas

Programme of Study
GV3 Opinions and discussions
LC4 Expressing ideas (speaking)

FCSE links
Unit 8: Celebrations (Various festivals, Special celebrations)

PLTS
C Creative thinkers

Cross-curricular
Religious Studies: Christian festivals

Resources
Audio files:
35_Module2_ZP1_Ex1
36_Module2_ZP1_Ex2
37_Module2_ZP1_Ex4

Starter 1

Aim

To introduce Christmas vocabulary.

Allow pupils a few minutes to write out in Spanish the six aspects of celebrating Christmas depicted in the photos in exercise 1, in order of personal preference. When the time is up, do a quick class survey via a show of hands to see how similar the class's preferences are.

1 ¿Quién habla? Escucha y escribe el nombre correcto. (1–6) (L2)

Listening. Before you start, read together through the *Zona Cultura* feature, which explains how Christmas is celebrated in Spain. Pupils listen to six short exchanges about what people like doing at Christmas and note the name of the person whose reply matches each of the photos.

Audioscript Track 35

1 – ¿Qué te gusta hacer en Navidad?
 – En Navidad me gusta decorar el árbol.

2 – ¿Qué te gusta hacer en Navidad?
 – En Navidad me gusta ir a la Misa del Gallo.

3 – ¿Qué te gusta hacer en Navidad?
 – En Navidad me gusta cantar villancicos.

4 – ¿Qué te gusta hacer en Navidad?
 – En Navidad me gusta mandar postales navideñas.

5 – ¿Qué te gusta hacer en Navidad?
 – En Navidad me gusta estar de vacaciones.

6 – ¿Qué te gusta hacer en Navidad?
 – En Navidad me gusta hacer una cena especial.

Answers

1 Daniel	2 Mateo	3 Bea
4 Valeria	5 Farid	6 Manuela

2 Escucha. Copia y completa la tabla. (1–4) (L3)

Listening. Pupils copy out the table. They then listen to four conversations and complete the table – for each conversation, they note what the speaker likes and dislikes doing at Christmas, writing down the appropriate letter from pictures a to f in exercise 1.

Audioscript Track 36

1 – ¿Qué te gusta hacer en Navidad?
 – En Navidad… me gusta ir a la Misa del Gallo y también me gusta mandar postales navideñas, pero no me gusta decorar el árbol de Navidad.

2 – ¿Qué te gusta hacer en Navidad?
 – En Navidad me gusta cantar villancicos y también me gusta hacer una cena especial, pero no me gusta mandar postales navideñas.

3 – ¿Qué te gusta hacer en Navidad?
 – En Navidad me gusta estar de vacaciones y también me gusta decorar el árbol de Navidad, pero no me gusta ir a la Misa del Gallo.

4 – ¿Qué te gusta hacer en Navidad?
 – En Navidad me gusta hacer una cena especial y estar de vacaciones, pero no me gusta cantar villancicos.

Answers

	☺	☹
1	a, e	c
2	b, d	e
3	f, c	a
4	d, f	b

© Pearson Education Ltd 2013. Copying permitted for purchasing institution only. This material is not copyright free.

Mi tiempo libre 2

3 Escribe estas frases en español. (L3)

Writing. Pupils complete the sentences using the picture prompts to fill in the gaps.

Answers

1 *En Navidad me gusta ir a la Misa del Gallo, pero no me gusta mandar postales navideñas.*

2 *En Navidad me gusta mucho decorar el árbol de Navidad, pero no me gusta hacer una cena especial.*

3 *En Navidad me gusta estar de vacaciones y me gusta mucho hacer una cena especial, pero no me gusta decorar el árbol de Navidad y no me gusta nada ir a la Misa del Gallo.*

Starter 2

Aim

To practise the phrase *En Navidad, me gusta… pero no me gusta…*

In pairs, give pupils one minute to tell their partners what they like and dislike about Christmas or another festival that they celebrate, using the sentence structure above. Go round the class and ask a handful of pupils to share their opinions in front of the class.

4 Escucha y lee los textos. Escribe el nombre correcto. (L4)

Listening. Pupils listen to four people talking about how they celebrate Christmas, reading the text at the same time. They then answer the questions in English. Some vocabulary is glossed for support.

Audioscript Track 37

Me llamo Alberto y vivo en Bilbao. En Navidad, me gusta mandar postales navideñas y decorar el árbol, pero no me gusta ir a la Misa del Gallo.

Me llamo Mireia y vivo en Granada. No celebro la Navidad porque no soy cristiana, soy hindú, pero me gusta hacer una cena especial y estar con mi familia el 25 de diciembre.

Me llamo Irene y tengo doce años. En Navidad me gusta cantar villancicos y bailar la jota porque es muy divertido, pero no me gusta mandar postales navideñas porque es aburrido.

Me llamo Mohamed y vivo en Sevilla. Tengo trece años. No celebro la Navidad porque soy musulmán, pero el 25 de diciembre me gusta tocar la zambomba. ¡Es guay!

Answers

1 Alberto	2 Irene	3 Mohamed
4 Mireia	5 Alberto	6 Irene
7 Mohamed	8 Mireia	

5 Trabaja en un grupo de cuatro personas. Habla de la Navidad. (L4)

Speaking. In groups of four, pupils ask and answer the question *¿Qué te gusta hacer en Navidad?* Two sample replies are given as support.

6 Haz una presentación sobre la Navidad u otra celebración. (L4)

Speaking. Pupils prepare a short presentation on celebrating Christmas or another festival. Guidance on what to include and sentence starters are given. Encourage pupils to include intensifiers and connectives to extend their sentences.

7 Escribe un acróstico. Escribe una palabra por cada letra. Decóralo. (L2)

Writing. Pupils write and illustrate an acrostic about Christmas in Spanish. An example one is started.

Plenary

Split the class up into teams. Allow each team three minutes to jot down as many facts about how Christmas is celebrated in Spain as they can remember. Give two points for each completely correct answer, one for an answer with an error. The winning team is the one with the most points.

© Pearson Education Ltd 2013. Copying permitted for purchasing institution only. This material is not copyright free.

¡PROYECTO! Los Reyes Magos

Mi tiempo libre 2

Pupil Book pages
Pages 50–51

Learning objectives
- Learning about the Day of the Three Kings
- Creating a Spanish Christmas calendar

Programme of Study
GV3 Developing vocabulary
LC6 Reading comprehension

FCSE links
Unit 8: Celebrations (Various festivals, Special celebrations)

PLTS
T Team workers

Cross-curricular
Religious Studies: Christian festivals
Computing: internet research

Resources
Audio file:
38_Module2_ZP2_Ex1

Starter 1

Aim

To introduce pupils to the vocabulary of the unit.

Read together through the *Zona Cultura* box text on how the Day of the Three Kings is celebrated in Spain. Write the following English phrases on the board, and ask pupils to skim-read the text in exercise 1 to try to find the Spanish equivalents.

6th January	el seis de enero
on the balcony	en el balcón
I really like Christmas	me gusta mucho la Navidad
it's delicious	¡está delicioso!
my favourite day is	mí día favorito es

1 Escucha y lee. (L3)

Listening. Pupils listen to Jorge talking about how he celebrates *el Día de los Reyes Magos* and follow the text at the same time.

Audioscript Track 38

Me llamo Jorge y vivo en Oviedo. Me gusta mucho la Navidad, pero mi día favorito es el seis de enero, el Día de los Reyes Magos.

El 5 de enero veo la cabalgata de los Reyes Magos. Los Reyes Magos lanzan caramelos a los niños.

Dejo fruta a los Reyes Magos y agua a los camellos. Dejo mis zapatos en el balcón.

El 6 de enero, abro los regalos… y como el roscón de Reyes. ¡Está delicioso!

2 Busca estas palabras en español en el texto del ejercicio 1. (L4)

Reading. Pupils reread the text in exercise 1 in order to find the Spanish sentences or short expressions in the text.

Answers
1 la cabalgata de los Reyes Magos
2 Los Reyes Magos lanzan caramelos
3 a los niños
4 Dejo fruta
5 agua a los camellos
6 mis zapatos
7 abro los regalos
8 como el roscón de Reyes

3 Lee el texto del ejercicio 1 otra vez. ¿Verdadero o falso? Escribe V o F. (L4)

Reading. Pupils read the text in exercise 1 again and decide whether the English statements about it are true (V) or false (F).

Answers
1 F 2 F 3 V 4 V 5 F 6 V

Starter 2

Aim

To review strategies for working out unknown words.

Discuss strategies for working out unknown words that pupils have learned so far. Possible suggestions that are appropriate include using picture clues, finding key words and cognates, using context, using a dictionary or vocabulary list. Encourage pupils to write a checklist and refer to it until the strategies become automatic.

4 Lee el texto. Pon los dibujos en el orden del texto. (L4)

Reading. Pupils read Lucía's text, then put the pictures (a–f) in the order that they appear in the text. Some vocabulary is glossed for support.

© Pearson Education Ltd 2013. Copying permitted for purchasing institution only. This material is not copyright free.

Mi tiempo libre 2

> **Answers**
> f, e, c, b, d, a

5 Trabaja en un grupo de cuatro. Cada persona elige una tradición. Busca información en Internet. Haz una presentación en inglés a tu grupo. (L4)

Reading. In groups of four, pupils carry out some Internet research on a Spanish Christmas tradition of their choice from a list of options provided. Each person chooses a different tradition to research. Pupils answer a list of three questions provided in English.

6 En tu grupo de cuatro, diseña un calendario de Navidad para los turistas de habla inglesa en España. (L2)

Writing. In the same groups of four, pupils design a Christmas calendar with six 'doors', which they label in Spanish, to explain six Christmas traditions. Guidance on what to include behind each of the doors is given.

> **Plenary**
> Split the class up into teams. Allow each team three minutes to jot down as many facts as they can remember about how *el Día de los Reyes Magos* is celebrated in Spain. Give two points for each completely correct answer, one for an answer with an error. The winning team is the one with the most points.

© Pearson Education Ltd 2013. Copying permitted for purchasing institution only. This material is not copyright free.

¡TE TOCA A TI!

Mi tiempo libre 2

Pupil Book pages Self-access reading and writing
Pages 122–123

A Reinforcement

1 Copia y completa las frases. (L2)

Writing. Pupils decipher the picture prompts in order to complete the sentences in Spanish. The gap-fill words are supplied in random order.

Answers
1 Saco **fotos**.
2 Hablo con **mis amigos**.
3 Escucho **música**.
4 Toco la **guitarra**.
5 Mando **SMS**.
6 Canto **karaoke**.

2 Mira el móvil de Gabriel. Escribe los números de las dos frases falsas. (L2)

Reading. Pupils look at the icons on Gabriel's mobile phone screensaver. They then read the nine sentences and identify the two sentences that are false (i.e. those that mention items not shown in the picture).

Answers
3 and 6

3 Eres Solana. Mira el móvil. Escribe seis frases. (L2)

Writing. Pupils write six sentences describing Solana's hobbies, based on the icons supplied of her mobile phone screensaver.

Answers
1 Escucho música.
2 Monto en bici.
3 Hago natación.
4 Juego al voleibol.
5 Hago artes marciales.
6 Juego al tenis.

4 Lee el texto. Copia y completa la tabla (L3)

Reading. Pupils read through the short text then copy and fill in the grid with details in English.

Answers	
weather	activity
nice	cycling
raining	surf the net
cold	listen to music
sunny	take photos
snowing	play the guitar

B Extension

1 Rompecabezas. Lee los textos y mira la gráfica. ¿Cuándo hacen Paco y Julia cada actividad? (L3)

Reading. After reading the texts and looking at the graph, pupils work out which days Paco and Julia do the four activities that they each mention.

Answers	
Julia	
los sábados	hacer artes marciales
los domingos	jugar al fútbol
los lunes	navegar por Internet
los martes	escuchar música
Paco	
los sábados	cantar karaoke
los domingos	jugar al baloncesto
los lunes	hacer equitación
los martes	hablar con mis amigos

2 Empareja a los chicos españoles con un amigo/una amiga posible. Hay dos amigos posibles de sobra. (L4)

Reading. Pupils read about the activities that three Spanish people like doing, then match them to an appropriate English friend who shares similar interests (there are two possible English friends too many). The English speech bubbles contain some words they do not know in Spanish. Encourage pupils who may get confused by this to focus on the words they do know.

Answers
Raúl – Kevin
Juan – Khaled
Denisa – Samantha

© Pearson Education Ltd 2013. Copying permitted for purchasing institution only. This material is not copyright free.

Mi tiempo libre 2

3 Escribe los mensajes de Carlos, Alana y de ti mismo/a a *amigos.es*. (L3)

Writing. Using the picture prompts, pupils write messages on behalf of Carlos and Alana to a penpal site. They then write a message presenting themselves on the site.

> **(Possible) Answers**
>
> **Carlos**: *En mi tiempo libre, me encanta* mandar SMS y ver la televisión, pero no me gusta navegar por Internet.
>
> **Alana**: En mi tiempo libre, me encanta salir con mis amigos y leer, pero no me gusta jugar a los videojuegos.

© Pearson Education Ltd 2013. Copying permitted for purchasing institution only. This material is not copyright free.

MODULE 3 · Mi insti

Unit & Learning objectives	PoS references	Key language	Grammar and other language features
1 ¿Qué estudias? (pp. 54–55) Saying what subjects you study Using -ar verbs to say what 'we' do	**GV3** Developing vocabulary **LC3** Conversation	¿Qué estudias? Estudio… (el) dibujo (el) inglés (la) educación física (la) música (el) francés (el) español (la) religión (la) geografía (la) historia (la) tecnología (la) informática (las) ciencias (las) matemáticas (el) teatro ¿Cuál es tu día favorito? Mi día favorito es el… ¿Por qué? porque (no) estudio/estudiamos… por la mañana por la tarde	**G** 'we' form of -ar verbs – y (meaning 'and') changes to e before words beginning with i- or hi- – pronunciation of c (when hard or soft) – los lunes (on Mondays)
2 ¿Te gustan las ciencias? (pp. 56–57) Giving opinions about school subjects Using me gusta(n) + el/la/los/las	**GV2** Grammatical structures (me gusta(n)) **GV4** Accuracy (grammar) **LC4** Expressing ideas (speaking)	¿Te gusta…? ¿Te gustan…? Me gusta(n)… No me gusta(n)… No me gusta(n) nada… Me encanta(n)… porque… interesante importante aburrido/a divertido/a práctico/a difícil fácil útil el profesor/la profesora es… paciente severo/a raro/a	**G** using the direct article (el/la/los/las) when giving opinions about subjects **G** checking verbs, definite articles and adjectival agreement in sentences giving opinions – pronunciation of g (when hard or soft) – using porque to give reasons for opinions

© Pearson Education Ltd 2013. Copying permitted for purchasing institution only. This material is not copyright free.

Mi insti 3

Unit & Learning objectives	PoS references	Key language	Grammar and other language features
3 ¿Qué hay en tu insti? (pp. 58–59) Describing your school Using the words for 'a', 'some' and 'the'	**GV2** Grammatical structures (articles) **GV4** Accuracy (grammar) **LC8** Writing creatively	En mi instituto hay… no hay… un campo de fútbol un comedor un gimnasio un patio una clase de informática una piscina una biblioteca unos laboratorios unas clases moderno/a bonito/a grande antiguo/a pequeño/a feo/a	**G** plural indefinite articles *unos/unas* (meaning 'some') **G** plural definite articles *los/las* (meaning 'the') – *hay* + indefinite article – *no hay* + no article
4 Durante el recreo (pp. 60–61) Talking about break time Using -*er* and -*ir* verbs	**GV1** Tenses (present) **LC6** Reading comprehension	¿Qué haces durante el recreo? Como… algo unas patatas fritas un bocadillo una chocolatina unos caramelos chicle fruta Bebo… algo agua un zumo un refresco leo mis SMS escribo SMS primero luego normalmente a veces	**G** present tense of regular -*er* and -*ir* verbs (full paradigms) – use of sequencers to extend writing, e.g. *primero*, *luego*, *normalmente*, *a veces*,
5 ¿Te gusta tu instituto? (pp. 62–63) Understanding details about schools Using prediction as a listening strategy	**LC1** Listening and responding **LC5** Speaking coherently and confidently	Review of language from Units 1–4	– developing listening skills – using prediction; questions and pictures as clues – trying to predict while listening

© Pearson Education Ltd 2013. Copying permitted for purchasing institution only. This material is not copyright free.

Mi insti 3

Unit & Learning objectives	PoS references	Key language	Grammar and other language features
6 ¿Cómo es tu insti? (pp. 64–65) Writing a longer text about your school Checking your written work is accurate	**GV4** Accuracy (spelling, grammar) **LC4** Expressing ideas (writing)	Review of language from Units 1–4	– developing writing skills – checking grammar, spelling, accents – using connectives, intensifiers, sequencers and expressions of frequency
Resumen y Prepárate (pp. 66–67) Pupils' checklist and practice exercises			
Gramática (pp. 68–69) Detailed grammar summary and practice exercises			**G** *me gusta/me gustan me encanta/me encantan* **G** adjectives (agreement with sing., plural, masc., fem. nouns) **G** the definite and indefinite articles **G** present tense verbs (regular *-ar*, *-er* and *-ir* verbs)
Zona Proyecto: La educación (pp. 72–73) Reading about the right to education Creating an action plan for a school in Guatemala	**GV3** Opinions and discussions **LC4** Expressing ideas (speaking)		– developing reading strategies: looking for cognates and near-cognates, using context and pictures for clues
Te toca a ti (pp. 124–125) Self-access reading and writing at two levels			

© Pearson Education Ltd 2013. Copying permitted for purchasing institution only. This material is not copyright free.

1. ¿Qué estudias?

Mi insti 3.1

Pupil Book pages
Pages 52–55

Learning objectives
- Saying what subjects you study
- Using -ar verbs to say what 'we' do

Programme of Study
GV3 Developing vocabulary
LC3 Conversation

FCSE links
Unit 2: Education and future plans (School subjects, Timetable)

Grammar
- 'we' form of -ar verbs

Key language
¿Qué estudias?
Estudio…
(el) dibujo
(el) inglés
(la) educación física
(la) música
(el) francés
(el) español
(la) religión
(la) geografía
(la) historia
(la) tecnología
(la) informática
(las) ciencias
(las) matemáticas
(el) teatro
¿Cuál es tu día favorito?
Mi día favorito es…
¿Por qué?
porque
no estudio…/estudiamos…
por la mañana
por la tarde

PLTS
T Team workers

Resources
Audio files:
39_Module3_Unit1_Ex2
40_Module3_Unit1_Ex5
41_Module3_Unit1_Ex8
Workbooks:
Cuaderno 1A & 1B, page 25
ActiveTeach:
p.054 Flashcards
p.055 Grammar presentation
ActiveLearn:
Listening A, Listening B
Reading A, Reading B
Grammar, Vocabulary

Module 3 Quiz (pp. 52–53)

Answers
1 a 2 b 1 c 3   2 b   3 b
4 Answers will vary   5 a
6 Melon with ham   Cauliflower and broccoli
Lasagne   Salmon with salad
Fruit   Yogurt
7 c

Starter 1

Aim

To review -ar verbs escuchar/hablar via a game of noughts and crosses.

Project a 3 x 3 grid on the board and put in nine English forms of the verbs 'to listen' and 'to talk' (e.g. we talk, I listen, you (pl) talk, he listens, etc.). Divide the class into two teams – the noughts and the crosses. Each team takes it in turns to specify which square they will translate, and they gain a nought or cross on that square if they state the Spanish correctly. The object of the game is to be the first team to get three in a row. You can repeat the game with different verbs and do a best of three.

1 Empareja los dibujos con las asignaturas. (L1)

Reading. Pupils match the pictures to the school subjects. This will be the first time that pupils will have encountered the vocabulary, but the vast majority are cognates or near-cognates.

Answers
1 b   2 f   3 k   4 a   5 h   6 i   7 l
8 c   9 e   10 m   11 n   12 d   13 g   14 j

2 Escucha y comprueba tus respuestas. (1–14) (L1)

Listening. Pupils listen and check their answers to exercise 1.

Audioscript Track 39

- ¿Qué estudias?
- Estudio…
1 – inglés
2 – español
3 – informática
4 – dibujo
5 – geografía
6 – historia
7 – ciencias
8 – educación física

© Pearson Education Ltd 2013. Copying permitted for purchasing institution only. This material is not copyright free.

Mi insti 3.1

9 – *francés*
10 – *matemáticas*
11 – *teatro*
12 – *música*
13 – *religión*
14 – *tecnología*

Reinforcement
Working in pairs, pupils take turns to quickly draw a sketch of a school subject for their partner to name.

3 Lee el texto. ¿Qué estudias cada día? Apunta las asignaturas, utilizando los números del ejercicio 1. (L2)

Reading. Pupils read the text and note the numbers of the school subjects (from exercise 1) that are mentioned for each day. Draw pupils' attention to the Tip box, which explains how *y* ('and') changes spelling and pronunciation based on the word that follows.

Answers
Mon, 5, 1
Tues, 3, 11, 10
Wed, 9, 12, 8
Thurs, 2, 14, 6
Fri, 7, 13, 4

4 Habla de tu horario. Con tu compañero/a, pregunta y contesta. (L3)

Speaking. In pairs, pupils ask and answer questions about their school timetable. A sample exchange is given. Point out the *Pronunciación* box, which reminds pupils to revise the rule, if necessary, for when the letter *c* is pronounced with a hard or soft sound (see p. 36, Module 2).

Starter 2
Aim
To review days of the week.

Put anagrams of the days of the week on the board (without accents) and allow pupils one minute to unjumble them and place accents over the correct letters. In pairs, ask pupils to make up sentences using the plural expressions for each day (*los lunes, los martes*, etc.) for each day of the week.

Alternative starter 2:
Use ActiveTeach p.054 Flashcards to review and practice school subjects vocabulary.

5 ¿Cuál es tu día favorito? Copia y completa la tabla en inglés. (1–5) (L4)

Listening. Pupils copy the grid. They then listen and complete it in English, noting the five speakers' favourite school days and the reasons that they give. A list of key language is supplied for support. Point out the *Gramática* box, which highlights the 'we' form endings for *-ar* verbs, including the verb *escuchar*, which they will hear in the audio.

Audioscript Track 40

1 – ¿Cuál es tu día favorito, Laila?
– Mi día favorito es el lunes.
– ¿Por qué?
– Porque estudio inglés por la mañana e historia por la tarde.

2 – ¿Cuál es tu día favorito, Andrés?
– Mi día favorito es el miércoles.
– ¿Por qué?
– Porque estudiamos geografía por la mañana y francés por la tarde.

3 – ¿Cuál es tu día favorito, Almudena?
– Mi día favorito es el martes.
– ¿Por qué?
– Porque estudio ciencias por la mañana y matemáticas y música por la tarde y no estudio tecnología.

4 – ¡Hola Gabriel! ¿Qué tal?
– Bien, gracias.
– ¿Cuál es tu día favorito?
– A ver, mi día favorito es el jueves.
– ¿Por qué, Gabriel?
– Porque estudiamos dibujo y teatro por la mañana y educación física por la tarde.

5 – ¡Hola Sara! ¿Qué tal?
– Bien, gracias.
– ¿Cuál es tu día favorito?
– Bueno… mi día favorito es el viernes.
– ¿Y por qué?
– Porque estudiamos español y tecnología por la mañana e informática por la tarde y no estudiamos matemáticas.

Mi insti 3.1

Answers

	favourite school day	reason
Laila	Monday	has English a.m./history p.m.
Andrés	Wednesday	has geography a.m./French p.m.
Almudena	Tuesday	has science a.m./maths & music p.m., no technology
Gabriel	Thursday	has art & drama a.m./PE p.m.
Sara	Friday	has Spanish & technology a.m./ICT p.m., no maths

6 Con tu compañero/a, pregunta y contesta. (L4)

Speaking. In pairs, pupils ask and answer the question ¿Cuál es tu día favorito? and give reasons for their response using porque. Point out the Tip box, which reminds pupils how to differentiate between *el lunes* and *los lunes*. A sample exchange is given.

7 Lee y completa las frases con los verbos del recuadro. (L4)

Reading. Pupils read the sentences, then fill in the blanks by selecting the correct verbs from the box. Some vocabulary is glossed for support.

Answers

1 *tocamos*   2 calculamos   3 hablamos
4 jugamos   5 navegamos   6 mandamos

8 Escucha y comprueba tus respuestas. Luego canta. (L4)

Listening. Pupils listen and check their answers to exercise 7. Play the song again and encourage pupils to sing along.

Audioscript Track 41

Los lunes en la clase de música, tocamos la guitarra.

Los martes en matemáticas, escuchamos y calculamos.

Los miércoles en la clase de francés, hablamos con los compañeros.

Los jueves en educación física, jugamos al voleibol.

Los viernes estudiamos informática, navegamos por Internet.

Nunca mandamos SMS, tampoco chateamos.

En clase nunca gritamos. ¡Nunca gritamos!

En clase nunca gritamos. ¡Nunca! ¡Ni hablar!

Extension

Pupils draw up their own timetable in Spanish and write five sentences about it. Encourage more able pupils to specify subjects that they study in the morning and afternoon on a given day, as well as what they do not study.

9 ¿Qué estudias? Escribe un párrafo. (L4)

Writing. Pupils write a short paragraph to include details of their school timetable, what their favourite day of the week is and why. A writing frame is supplied for support. Challenge more able pupils to include some other 'we' form verbs in their answer.

Plenary

Ask pupils to prepare a mind map summarising the main points and key vocabulary of the lesson.

Workbook 1A, page 25

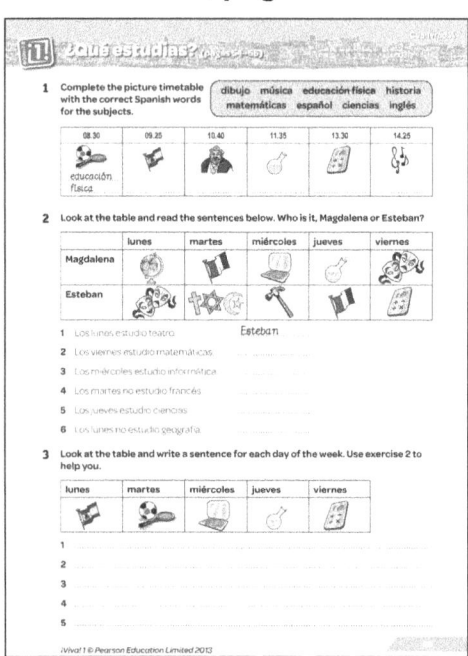

Answers

1 8.30 *educación física*, 9.25 español,
   10.40 historia, 11.35 ciencias,
   13.30 matemáticas, 14.25 música

2 1 *Esteban*   2 Esteban   3 Magdalena
   4 Esteban   5 Magdalena 6 Esteban

3 Own answers.

© Pearson Education Ltd 2013. Copying permitted for purchasing institution only. This material is not copyright free.

Mi insti 3.1

Workbook 1B, page 25

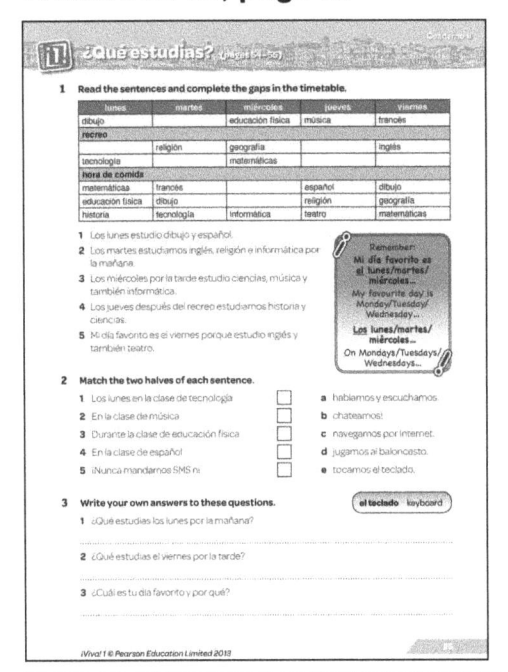

Answers

1

lunes	martes	miércoles
dibujo	inglés	educación física
	recreo	
español	religión	geografía
tecnología	informática	matemáticas
	hora de comer	
matemáticas	francés	ciencias
educación física	dibujo	música
historia	tecnología	informática

jueves	viernes
música	francés
recreo	
historia	inglés
ciencias	teatro
hora de comer	
español	dibujo
religión	geografía
teatro	matemáticas

2 1 c 2 e 3 d 4 a 5 b

3 Own answers

¿Te gustan las ciencias?

Mi insti 3.2

Pupil Book pages
Pages 56–57

Learning objectives
- Giving opinions about school subjects
- Using *me gusta(n)* + *el/la/los/las*

Programme of Study
GV2 Grammatical structures (*me gusta(n)*)
GV4 Accuracy (grammar)
LC4 Expressing ideas (speaking)

FCSE links
Unit 2: Education and future plans (School: teachers, subjects)

Grammar
- using *me gusta(n)* + *el/la/los/las* when giving opinions about subjects
- checking verbs, definite articles and adjectival agreement in sentences giving opinions

Key language
¿Te gusta...?
¿Te gustan...?
Me gusta(n)...
No me gusta(n)...
No me gusta(n) nada...
Me encanta(n)...
porque es...
interesante
importante
aburrido/a
divertido/a
práctico/a
difícil
fácil
útil
el profesor/la profesora es...
paciente
severo/a
raro/a

PLTS
R Reflective learners

Cross-curricular
English: checking grammar

Resources
Audio files:
42_Module3_Unit2_Ex1
43_Module3_Unit2_Ex4
Workbooks:
Cuaderno 1A & 1B, page 26
ActiveTeach:
p.056 Video 5
p.056 Video 5 transcript
p.056 Video worksheet 5
p.056 Grammar presentation
p.057 Extension reading
ActiveLearn:
Listening A, Listening B
Reading A, Reading B
Grammar, Vocabulary

Starter 1

Aim

To review the vocabulary for school subjects.

Ask one pupil to go out of the room. The rest of the class decides on a school subject to mime (separately). The volunteer returns into the room and has to guess the subject that the class is miming. Repeat the exercise several times so that as many of the fifteen school subjects are mimed as possible.

1 Escucha y lee. ¿Quién habla? (1–6) (L3)

Listening. Pupils listen, reading the six speech bubbles at the same time. They identify the correct speaker each time.

Audioscript Track 42

1 – ¿Te gusta la historia?
  – Sí, me gusta la historia.
2 – ¿Te gusta el inglés?
  – No, no me gusta el inglés.
3 – ¿Te gustan las ciencias?
  – Sí, me gustan mucho las ciencias.
4 – ¿Te gustan las matemáticas?
  – ¿Estás loco? No me gustan nada las matemáticas.
5 – ¿Te gusta el español?
  – Sí, me gusta el español.
6 – ¿Te gusta la educación física?
  – ¡Ah, sí! ¡Me encanta la educación física! ¡Es mi asignatura favorita!

Answers		
1 Enrique	2 Marisol	3 Diana
4 Donato	5 Abril	6 Óscar

Gramática

Use the *Gramática* box to remind pupils that they need to include the definite article (*el/la/los/las*) in front of the noun when giving opinions on subjects. A noun in Spanish will virtually always have an article (either definite or indefinite) in front of it, unless a possessive (my, your, etc.) or demonstrative adjective (this, that) is being used. There is more information and further practice on Pupil Book p. 68.

© Pearson Education Ltd 2013. Copying permitted for purchasing institution only. This material is not copyright free.

Mi insti 3.2

2 Con tu compañero/a, haz un diálogo muy positivo y un diálogo muy negativo. (L3/4)

Speaking. In pairs, pupils discuss school subjects, taking it in turns to have a very positive dialogue and a very negative one. Sample exchanges and a Key language box are supplied for support.

Pronunciación

Use the *Pronunciación* box to explain to pupils the rules on how to pronounce the Spanish letter *g*. The *g* is soft and sounds like the Spanish *j* when it comes before *e* or *i* but hard like the English *g* in 'got' in any other case. For a *g* to sound hard before the letters *e/i*, it must be followed by a silent *u* as in *guitarra* (guitar).

Reinforcement

Working in pairs, pupils take turns to prompt with a subject and to respond with an opinion, using an intensifier such as *muy*, *un poco*, or *bastante* (covered in Module 1, Unit 5) + an adjective.

Starter 2

Aim

Revise the key structure *me gusta/me gustan* in the context of sport/activities.

Give pupils three minutes to write sentences using the key structure *me gusta/me gustan* using activities from the following list. Ask pupils to summarise what they have learned.

el críquet	el fútbol	los ordenadores
el ciclismo	el tenis	la Fórmula 1
la música	el voleibol	los deportes

3 Lee las opiniones y completa las frases en inglés. (L3)

Reading. Draw pupils' attention to the Key language box on page 56. Ask them to pick out any words they know already and identify any cognates or near-cognates. Pupils then read the texts and complete the sentences that summarise them in English.

Answers

1 Aitor thinks **art** is interesting and **history** is useful.
2 Gabriela thinks **science** and **maths** are important.
3 Fran thinks **geography** is fun but **English** is boring.
4 Aína thinks **ICT** is practical.
5 She also thinks **PE** is easy but **French** is difficult.
6 Lola thinks the **drama** teacher is patient, but the **RE** teacher is strict.

4 Escucha y escribe la asignatura y la opinión. (1–8) (L4)

Listening. Pupils listen and write the subject and opinion mentioned each time.

Audioscript Track 43

1 – No me gusta nada el dibujo porque es difícil.
2 – Me gusta la informática porque es fácil.
3 – Me encanta la historia porque es interesante.
4 – Me gustan mucho las matemáticas porque son útiles.
5 – Me gustan las ciencias porque son prácticas.
6 – Me encanta el francés porque la profesora es paciente.
7 – No me gusta la educación física porque es el profesor es severo.
8 – Me gusta mucho el inglés porque es importante.

Answers

1 dibujo, difícil
2 informática, fácil
3 historia, interesante
4 matemáticas, útiles
5 ciencias, prácticas
6 francés, la profesora es paciente
7 educación física, el profesor es severo
8 inglés, importante

5 Lee los textos. Escribe los números de las cuatro frases correctas. (L4)

Reading. Pupils read the Spanish texts and the six sentences that follow them in English. They write down the numbers of the four correct sentences.

Answers

The four correct sentences are 1, 4, 5 and 6.

Extension

Pupils translate Paulina, Manuel and Ana's texts without using a dictionary. Remind them to look for key words, and use cognates and context to work out the meaning of words they don't know.

Mi insti 3.2

Gramática

Before asking pupils to attempt exercise 6, read together through the *Gramática* box, which advises on checking for grammatical accuracy in the areas of verb formation, use of the correct definite article and agreement of adjectives.

6 Prepara una presentación. Da tu opinión sobre tres asignaturas y tres profesores. (L4)

Writing. Pupils prepare a detailed presentation, giving their opinion on three school subjects and three teachers, following the framework supplied. Point out the Skills box, which reminds pupils to use *porque* to extend their sentences. Once they have prepared their presentation, pupils could present it to their partner or to the whole class.

Plenary

Play a chain game around the class with the aim of creating the longest sentence possible in the context of school subjects and opinions. Start it off: *Me gusta la educación física.* The next person repeats what you have said and adds an opinion (e.g. ... *porque es divertida*), ensuring the adjective agrees. Continue around the class adding more subjects and opinions. If someone can't remember the chain, makes a mistake, or can't think of anything to add, he or she sits down and the chain starts again.

Workbook 1A, page 26

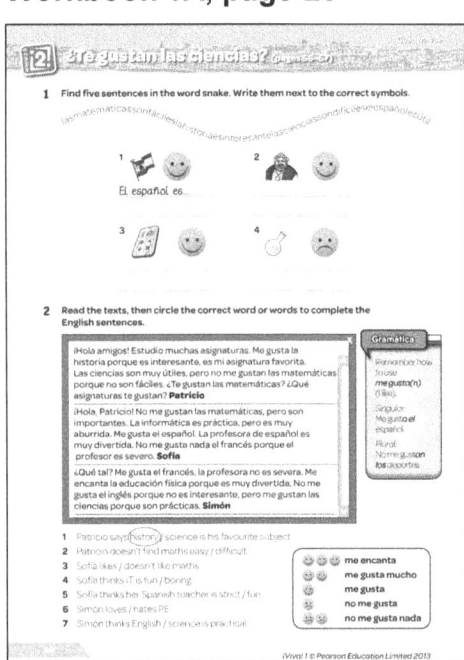

Answers

1 1 *El español es* útil.
 2 La historia es interesante.
 3 Las matemáticas son fáciles.
 4 Las ciencias son difíciles.

2 1 history 2 easy 3 doesn't like
 4 boring 5 fun 6 loves
 7 science

Workbook 1B, page 26

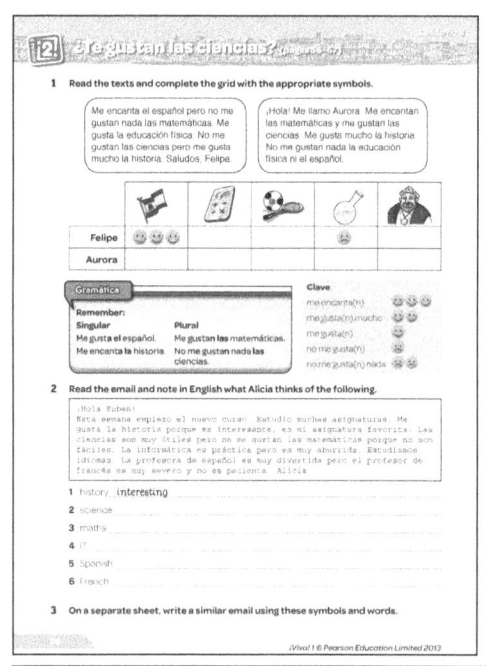

Answers

1

	Spa.	maths	PE	sci.	hist.
Felipe	☺☺☺	☹☹	☺	☹	☺☺
Aurora	☹☹	☺☺☺	☹☹	☺	☺☺

2 1 interesting 2 useful
 3 doesn't like it because not easy
 4 practical but boring
 5 teacher is fun
 6 teacher is strict and not patient

3 Own answers

Mi insti 3.2

ActiveTeach, Extension Reading

Answers (Question 5)

1 Manuel likes **science** because it's useful.
2 Paulina likes maths because the teacher is **patient**.
3 Ana doesn't like **geography** because in her opinion it's not important.
4 Paulina loves art but doesn't like French because it's very **boring**.
5 Manuel doesn't like **Spanish** at all because the teacher is strange.
6 Ana loves **IT** because it's practical.

Video

Episode 5: Las asignaturas

Laura and the team are reporting live from their school, *Colegio Nazaret Oviedo*, to find out which subjects pupils like and why. Video worksheet 5 can be used in conjunction with this episode.

Answers to video worksheet (ActiveTeach)

A

1 Answers will vary and may include the fourteen school subjects introduced in Unit 1 of the Pupil Book.

2 a) útil
  b) divertido/a
  c) paciente
  d) interesante
  e) importante
  f) difícil

B

1 matemáticas, español, inglés, tecnología, religión, historia, geografía

She also mentions *lengua*, which pupils probably haven't seen before.

2 a) technology
  b) art
  c) ICT

3 What is your favourite subject?

C

1 French

2

Name	Subject	Opinion	Correx.
Claudia	maths	~~interesting~~	important
Adrián	science	~~fun~~	boring
Andrés	~~Spanish~~	important	English
Laura	~~geog.~~	useful	ICT

D

1 Which subject is better – drama or PE (Laura prefers drama and José prefers PE).

2 Pupils will probably say 'yes', as she is very dramatic in her role as a presenter!

3 Pupils will probably say 'yes' and make reference to body language clues such as facial expressions (e.g. smiling, frowning etc.), nodding or shaking their head, tone of voice (e.g. speaking with enthusiasm about the subject).

4 It is probably a geography classroom as there are several maps on the wall.

5 Answers will vary.

E

Pupils will produce their own dialogues in small groups.

[3] ¿Qué hay en tu insti?

Mi insti 3.3

Pupil Book pages
Pages 58–59

Learning objectives
- Describing your school
- Using the words for 'a', 'some' and 'the'

Programme of Study
GV2 Grammatical structures (articles)
GV4 Accuracy (grammar)
LC8 Writing creatively

FCSE links
Unit 2: Education and future plans (School facilities, Physical description of school)

Grammar
- plural indefinite articles *unos/unas* (meaning 'some')
- plural definite articles *los/las* (meaning 'the')

Key language
En mi instituto hay…
no hay…
un campo de fútbol
un comedor
un gimnasio
un patio
una clase de informática
una piscina
una biblioteca
unos laboratorios
unas clases
moderno/a
antiguo/a
bonito/a
feo/a
pequeño/a
grande

PLTS
C Creative thinkers

Resources
Audio files:
44_Module3_Unit3_Ex1
45_Module3_Unit3_Ex5
Workbooks:
Cuaderno 1A & 1B, page 27
ActiveTeach:
p.058 Flashcards
p.058 Grammar worksheet
ActiveLearn:
Listening A, Listening B
Reading A, Reading B
Grammar, Vocabulary

Starter 1

Aim

To review definite and indefinite articles.

Write the following list of nouns up on the board for pupils to translate into Spanish from memory.

a dog	a brother
a snake	a sister
a guinea pig	a rabbit

Pupils then change all the indefinite articles to definite articles.

---

1 Escucha y escribe las letras en el orden correcto. (L3)

Listening. Pupils listen to Luis's description of his school and write the letters of the photos in the order that they hear them. Point out the Tip box, which introduces the key phrases *hay* and *no hay*, and highlights that you do not need the definite article after *no hay*.

Audioscript Track 44

– *Hola Luis ¿Qué tal?*
– *Bien gracias. ¿Y tú?*
– *Muy bien, gracias. Dime Luis, ¿qué hay en tu insti?*
– *A ver… en mi instituto hay un patio.*
   También hay una clase de informática.
   Hay un campo de fútbol…
   …y un comedor.
– *¿Qué más?*
– *Bueno… hay unos laboratorios…*
   …y un gimnasio.
   Hay una biblioteca…
   …y unas clases, por supuesto…
– *¿Hay una piscina?*
– *No, no hay piscina.*

Answers
d, e, a, b, h, c, g, i, f

Reinforcement

Ask pupils to translate the following into Spanish:

1 There is a swimming pool.
2 There isn't a football field.
3 There isn't a gymnasium.
4 There is a library.
5 There are some classrooms.
6 There aren't any laboratories.

2 Con tu compañero/a, describe tu instituto. Añade cada vez una cosa más. (L3)

Speaking. In pairs, pupils describe their school. The first person starts the description; the next person repeats what they say and adds on another thing, and so on. The sentence chain becomes progressively more difficult to memorise as more information is added to it.

Gramática

Use the *Gramática* box to draw pupils' attention to the fact that the indefinite articles *un/una* become *unos/unas* in the plural (and the meaning changes to 'some'), while the definite articles *el/la* become *los/las* in the plural (and the meaning stays the same – 'the'). There is more information and further practice on Pupil Book p. 69.

3 Escribe estas frases correctamente. Traduce las frases al inglés. (L2)

Writing. Pupils decipher the mirror-writing sentences and write out the five sentences correctly in Spanish, before translating them into English.

Answers

1 *En mi instituto hay un campo de fútbol.*
   In my school, there is a football field.
2 *En mi instituto hay un comedor y un gimnasio.*
   In my school, there is a dining hall and a gymnasium.
3 *En mi instituto hay un patio pero no hay piscina.*
   In my school, there is a playground, but there isn't a swimming pool.
4 *En mi instituto hay una biblioteca y también hay una piscina pero no hay campo de fútbol.*
   In my school, there is a library and also a swimming pool, but there isn't a football field.

Starter 2

Aim

To review singular and plural adjectives.

Present the following words jumbled up on the board. Pupils sort them into two Venn diagrams: one diagram for singular adjectives and one for plural. Each diagram has overlapping circles for masculine and feminine:

moderno	moderna
paciente	pacientes
difícil	difíciles
fea	feos
pequeños	pequeñas
grande	grandes

Alternative starter 2:

Use ActiveTeach p.058 Flashcards to review and practise school facilities vocabulary.

4 Completa los textos con los adjetivos correctos del recuadro. (L4)

Reading. Pupils read the two texts and complete the gap-fill sentences, choosing the correct adjective from the box each time. Point out the Tip box, which reminds pupils to look at the adjective endings, as these have to agree with the noun. A list of singular and plural adjectives is supplied in the Key language box at the top of the page for further support.

Answers

Ariana
1 grande   2 moderna
3 modernos 4 bonitas

Diego
5 pequeño   6 antigua
7 antiguos 8 feas

5 Escucha y comprueba tus respuestas. (L4)

Listening. Pupils listen and check their answers to exercise 4.

Audioscript Track 45

– ¿Te gusta tu insti, Ariana?
– Sí, me encanta mi instituto porque el patio es grande y la biblioteca es moderna.
  Los laboratorios son modernos y las clases son bonitas.
  Es guay.
– ¿Te gusta tu insti Diego?
– ¡Ni hablar! No me gusta nada mi instituto porque el patio es pequeño y la biblioteca es antigua.
  Los laboratorios son antiguos y las clases son feas.
  Es horrible.

Mi insti 3.3

Extension

Write up sentences on the board, jumbling the order of the words. With books closed, pupils say the sentences in the correct order.

1 *Los laboratorios son antiguos y las clases son feas.*
2 *Me encanta mi instituto porque es bastante moderno.*
3 *No me gusta nada mi instituto porque es muy feo.*
4 *Las clases son modernas y la biblioteca es grande.*
5 *En mi instituto, hay un gimnasio y también un campo de fútbol.*
6 *En mi instituto, hay un comedor, pero no hay piscina.*

6 Vas a un instituto famoso. ¿Qué hay en tu instituto? Escribe una entrada para un blog. (L4)

Writing. Pupils write a blog entry to describe a famous school that they attend, including details on the subjects that they study, the teachers, facilities and their personal opinions. A writing frame is supplied for support.

Plenary

Put one pupil in the 'hot seat' as an expert on the lesson – the other pupils ask them questions on school facilities and adjectival agreement. If they answer them correctly, they get to nominate another pupil to take the hot seat.

Workbook 1A, page 27

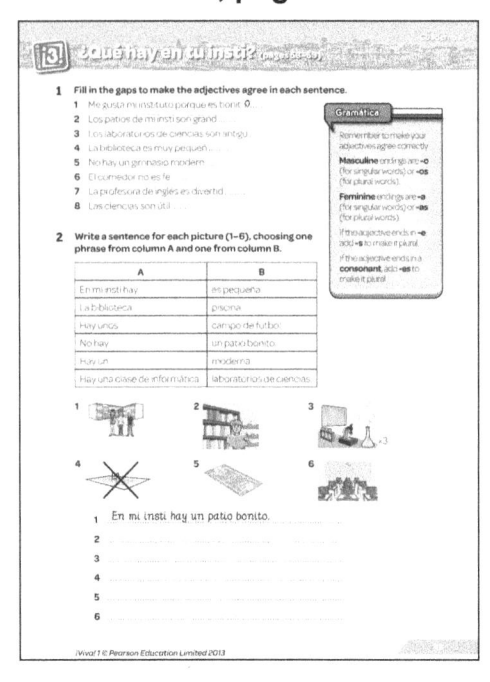

Answers

1 1 *bonito*   2 grandes   3 antiguos
   4 pequeña   5 moderno   6 feo
   7 divertida   8 útiles

2 1 *En mi insti hay un patio bonito.*
   2 La biblioteca es pequeña.
   3 Hay unos laboratorios de ciencias.
   4 No hay piscina.
   5 Hay un campo de fútbol.
   6 Hay una clase de informática moderna.

Workbook 1B, page 27

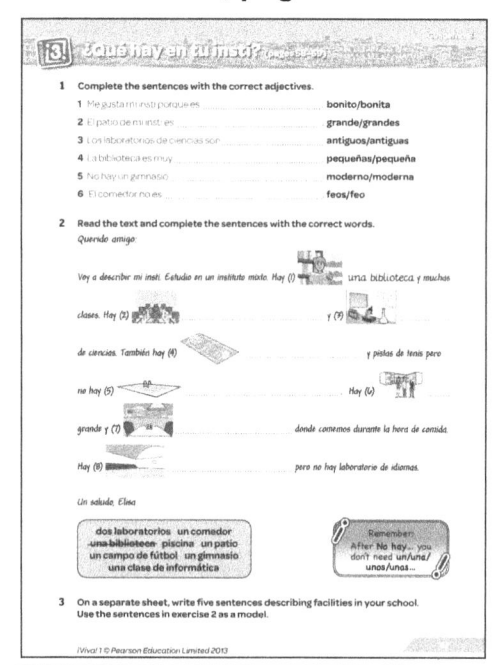

Answers

1 1 *bonito*   2 grande   3 antiguos
   4 pequeña   5 moderno   6 feo

2 1 *una biblioteca*   2 una clase de informática
   3 un laboratorio   4 un campo de fútbol
   5 piscina   6 un patio
   7 un comedor   8 un gimnasio

2 Own answers

Mi insti 3.3

Worksheet 3.3 I think the opposite!

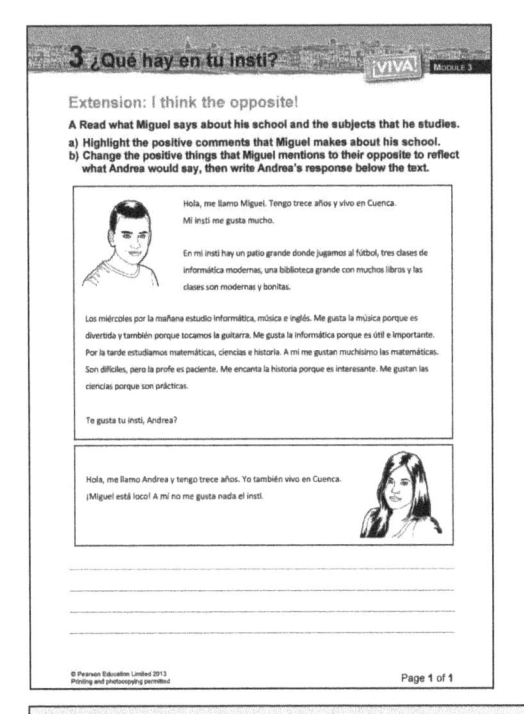

3 ¿Qué hay en tu insti? — VIVA! MODULE 3

Extension: I think the opposite!

A Read what Miguel says about his school and the subjects that he studies.
a) Highlight the positive comments that Miguel makes about his school.
b) Change the positive things that Miguel mentions to their opposite to reflect what Andrea would say, then write Andrea's response below the text.

> Hola, me llamo Miguel. Tengo trece años y vivo en Cuenca.
> Mi insti me gusta mucho.
>
> En mi insti hay un patio grande donde jugamos al fútbol, tres clases de informática modernas, una biblioteca grande con muchos libros y las clases son modernas y bonitas.
>
> Los miércoles por la mañana estudio informática, música e inglés. Me gusta la música porque es divertida y también porque tocamos la guitarra. Me gusta la informática porque es útil e importante. Por la tarde estudiamos matemáticas, ciencias e historia. A mí me gustan muchísimo las matemáticas. Son difíciles, pero la profe es paciente. Me encanta la historia porque es interesante. Me gustan las ciencias porque son prácticas.
>
> Te gusta tu insti, Andrea?

> Hola, me llamo Andrea y tengo trece años. Yo también vivo en Cuenca. ¡Miguel está loco! A mí no me gusta nada el insti.

© Pearson Education Limited 2013
Printing and photocopying permitted
Page 1 of 1

Answers

A

Hola, me llamo Miguel. Tengo doce años y vivo en Cuenca. **Mi insti me gusta mucho**.

En mi insti **hay un patio grande donde jugamos al fútbol, tres clases de informática modernas, una biblioteca grande con muchos libros** y **las clases son modernas y bonitas**.

Los miércoles por la mañana estudio informática, música e inglés. **Me gusta la música porque es divertida y también porque tocamos la guitarra. Me gusta la informática porque es útil e importante**. Por la tarde estudiamos matemáticas, ciencias e historia. **A mí me gustan muchísimo las matemáticas**. Son difíciles, pero **la profe es paciente. Me encanta la historia porque es interesante. Me gustan las ciencias porque son prácticas**.

¿Te gusta tu insti, Andrea?

B (Suggested answer)

Hola, me llamo Andrea y tengo doce años. Yo también vivo en Cuenca. ¡Miguel está loco! **A mí no me gusta nada el insti**.

En mi insti **hay un patio pequeño y no podemos jugar al fútbol, hay tres clases de informática antiguas, una biblioteca pequeña con pocos libros** y **las clases son antiguas y feas**.

Los miércoles por la mañana estudio informática, música e inglés. **No me gusta la música porque es aburrida y porque nunca tocamos la guitarra. No me gusta la informática porque no es útil ni importante**. Por la tarde estudiamos matemáticas, ciencias e historia. **A mí no me gustan nada las matemáticas**. Son difíciles y **la profe es poco paciente. No me gusta la historia porque es aburrida. No me gustan las ciencias porque no son prácticas**.

[4] Durante el recreo

Mi insti 3.4

Pupil Book pages
Pages 60–61

Learning objectives
- Talking about break time
- Using -er and -ir verbs

Programme of Study
GV1 Tenses (present)
LC6 Reading comprehension

FCSE links
Unit 2: Education and future plans (Sequence)
Unit 5: Healthy lifestyle (Food/drink)
Unit 6: Food and drink (Food/drink vocabulary items)

Grammar
- present tense of regular -er and -ir verbs (full paradigms)

Key language
¿Qué haces durante el recreo?
Como…
algo
unas patatas fritas
un bocadillo
una chocolatina
unos caramelos
chicle
fruta
Bebo…
algo
agua
un zumo
un refresco
leo mis SMS
escribo SMS
primero
luego
normalmente
a veces

PLTS
T Team workers

Resources
Audio files:
46_Module3_Unit4_Ex1
47_Module3_Unit4_Ex4
Workbooks:
Cuaderno 1A & 1B, page 28
ActiveTeach:
p.060 Video 6
p.060 Video 6 transcript
p.060 Video worksheet 6
p.060 Flashcards
p.060 Grammar presentation
p.060 Grammar worksheet
Plenary resource
ActiveLearn:
Listening A, Listening B
Reading A, Reading B
Grammar, Vocabulary

Starter 1

Aim

To review the pronunciation of *ca/ce/ci/co/cu* using Spanish towns.

As an incentive, award two points for a completely correct answer and one for a good attempt. Or, set a challenge – bet that no one can read the entire list without making a single mistake, or ask a volunteer to predict how many mistakes he or she will make, then see if he or she can beat that prediction.

Cáceres	Ciudad Real
Córdoba	Cartagena
Cádiz	Albacete
Cuenca	Castellón
Valencia	La Coruña

Alternative starter 1:

Use ActiveTeach p.060 Flashcards to introduce break time vocabulary.

---

1 Escucha y lee. (1–6) (L3)

Listening. Pupils listen, following the text on p. 60 of the Pupil Book.

Audioscript Track 46

- ¡Hola! Hacemos un sondeo en el instituto. ¿Qué haces durante el recreo?

- ¿Qué haces durante el recreo?
- Como algo… unas patatas fritas, por ejemplo.
- ¿Y tú?
- Como un bocadillo o una chocolatina, o a veces unos caramelos.

- ¿Qué haces durante el recreo?
- Como chicle o fruta.

- ¿Y tú? ¿Qué haces durante el recreo?
- Bebo algo. Bebo agua, un zumo o un refresco.

- ¿Y tú? ¿Qué haces durante el recreo?
- Leo mis SMS.
- ¿Y tú?
- Escribo SMS.

2 Busca estas frases en español en el sondeo. (L3)

Reading. Pupils find the Spanish equivalent of the English sentences in the exercise 1 text.

© Pearson Education Ltd 2013. Copying permitted for purchasing institution only. This material is not copyright free.

Mi insti 3.4

Answers
1 ¿Qué haces durante el recreo?
2 Como algo.
3 Bebo algo.
4 Leo mis SMS.
5 Escribo SMS.

Reinforcement
Working in pairs, pupils take turns to draw a sketch of a break-time activity for their partner to name.

Gramática
Use the *Gramática* box to teach the full paradigms of *comer* (regular *-er* verb) and *escribir* (regular *-ir* verb). Once pupils know the patterns, they can apply them to other regular *-er* and *-ir* verbs that they come across. There is more information and further practice of both verbs on Pupil Book p. 69.

3 Con tu compañero/a, haz cinco diálogos. (L3)

Speaking. In pairs, pupils put together five dialogues, using the picture prompts and the sample exchange supplied.

Starter 2
Aim
To review infinitives from the unit.

Ask pupils to make links between the following groups of verbs. They can make any sort of link that they wish, as long as they can justify it. Examples of links might include: verbs that represent things they do in languages or things they can do on a computer, verbs that have the same ending in the infinitive, etc.

comer	escuchar	beber
leer	hablar	mandar
escribir	hacer	jugar

4 Escucha. ¿Qué no se menciona? Escribe las dos letras correctas. (L4)

Listening. Pupils listen to Juana describe what she usually does at break time. They identify the two activities that she does not mention, noting the letters of the two redundant pictures.

Audioscript Track 47
– ¿Qué haces durante el recreo, Juana?
– Durante el recreo... a ver... primero como algo, un bocadillo o a veces una chocolatina.
– Un momentito... primero comes un bocadillo, o a veces una chocolatina... muy bien. ¿Qué más?
– Normalmente bebo agua.
– ...bebes agua... ¿Y luego? ¿Qué haces?
– Luego juego al fútbol o al baloncesto en el patio con mis amigos.
– Juegas al fútbol o al baloncesto... muy bien. ¿Algo más?
– A veces leo mis SMS.

Answers
The two things not mentioned are c and e.

5 Lee los mensajes. ¿Verdadero o falso? Escribe V o F. (L3)

Reading. Pupils read the SMS texts and the six statements that follow them in Spanish, then decide whether each statement is true (V) or false (F). Some key language is glossed for support.

Extension
Ask pupils to rewrite the four false sentences correcting the errors.

Answers
1 V 2 F 3 F 4 F 5 V 6 F

6 Escribe una tira cómica. Con tu compañero/a, lee la tira cómica en voz alta. (L4)

Writing. Pupils write a short comic strip about on their school break-time activities, making full use of the sequencers they have met in the unit (e.g. *primero, luego, normalmente, a veces*), to add variety to their sentences. Pupils read their comic strips to their partners once finished.

Plenary
Allow pupils three minutes to work in pairs to find the five errors (which are highlighted) in this passage (Plenary resource):

*Primero como algo, un**a** bocadillo y a veces una chocolatina. Normalmente bebo agua. L**eu**go juego al fútbol o **a la** baloncesto en el patio con mis amigos. A veces **leer** mis SMS**S**.*

© Pearson Education Ltd 2013. Copying permitted for purchasing institution only. This material is not copyright free.

Mi insti 3.4

Workbook 1A, page 28

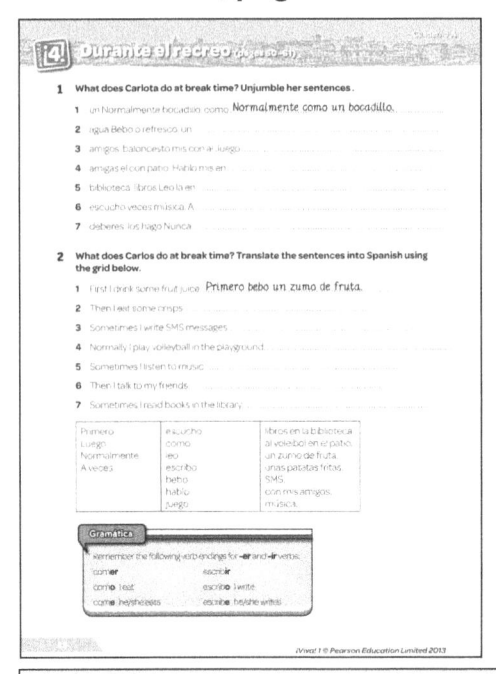

Answers

1
1 *Normalmente como un bocadillo.*
2 Bebo agua o un refresco.
3 Juego al baloncesto con mis amigos.
4 Hablo con mis amigas en el patio.
5 Leo libros en la biblioteca.
6 A veces escucho música.
7 Nunca hago los deberes.

2
1 Primero bebo un zumo de fruta.
2 Luego como unas patatas fritas.
3 A veces escribo SMS.
4 Normalmente juego al voleibol en el patio.
5 A veces escucho música.
6 Luego hablo con mis amigos.
7 A veces leo libros en la biblioteca.

Workbook 1B, page 28

Answers

1 Marisa, Juan
2 Own answers
3 Own answers

Worksheet 3.4 Adapting a verb pattern

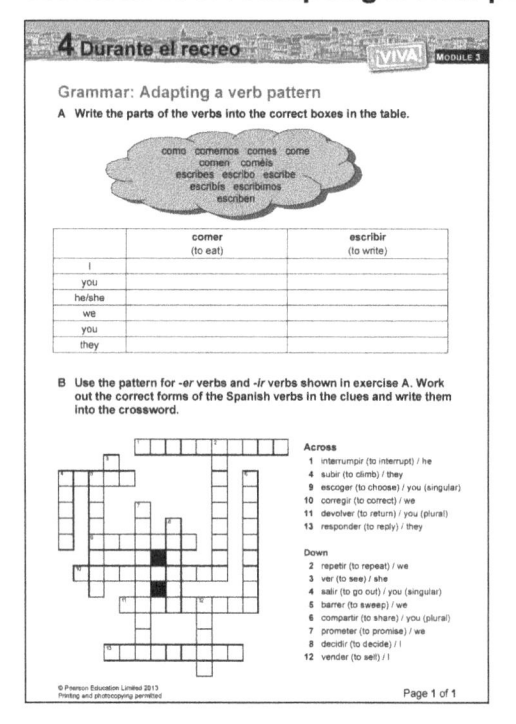

Mi insti 3.4

Answers

A

	comer	**escribir**
(I)	como	escribo
(you)	comes	escribes
(he/she)	come	escribe
(we)	comemos	escribimos
(you)	coméis	escribís
(they)	comen	escriben

B

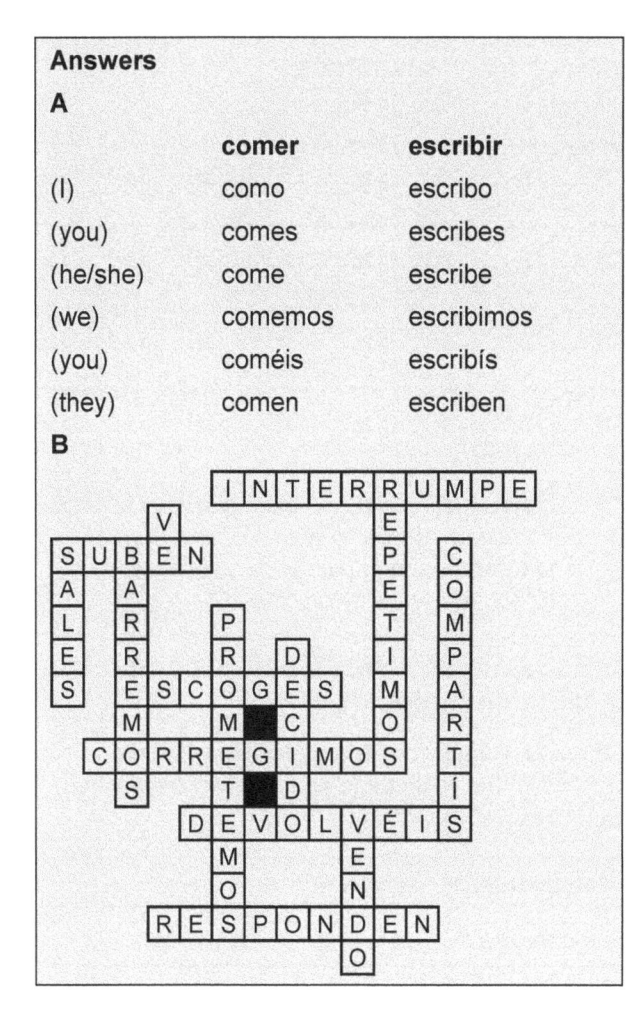

Crossword answers: INTERRUMPE, SUBEN, ESCOGES, CORREGIMOS, DEVOLVÉIS, RESPONDEN, COMPARTÍS, COMPROMETIDO, ALES, ARRRES, APRENDEMOS, VEPETI, CSMOS, etc.

Video

Episode 6: En el instituto

Marco goes on a secret mission to show us around his school. Video worksheet 6 can be used in conjunction with this episode.

Answers to video worksheet (ActiveTeach)

A

1 Answers will vary and may include the nine rooms and facilities introduced in Unit 3 of the Pupil Book.

2 a antiguo – moderno
  b grande – pequeño
  c bonito – feo

B

1 clases, laboratorios, biblioteca, clase de informática, clase de matemáticas, clase de historia, gimnasio, campo de fútbol, piscina, comedor, patio

2 football field, swimming pool, dining hall

3 He eats crisps in the playground.

C

1 ICT, maths, history

2 b big, modern
  c small
  d big, a little bit old
  e small

D

1 Pupils will probably say 'yes' as he really gets into the role of being on a secret mission (e.g. creeping around)/he likes the idea of being like James Bond/he says it's really cool ('*superguay*').

2 Many Spanish schools do not have a lunch hour as pupils go home for lunch when school finishes at around two/three o'clock (because lunchtime is much later in Spain).

3 Answers will vary. Most state schools in Spain do not have a school uniform, though many private schools do.

4 Pupils will say probably 'no'. Reasons given may include:

   He taps the microphone.

   He eats crisps whilst the microphone is on.

   Ramona and Estela describe his wobbly camerawork as '*fatal*'.

   They sigh at the end of his report.

5 Literally 'Until the next one'. It is the equivalent of 'Until next time' or 'See you next time'.

E

Pupils will prepare their own video tour of their school.

5. Listening Skills: ¿Te gusta tu instituto? Mi insti 3.5

Pupil Book pages
Pages 62–63

Learning objectives
- Understanding details about schools
- Using prediction as a listening strategy

Programme of Study
LC1 Listening and responding
LC5 Speaking coherently and confidently

Key language
Review of language from Units 1–4

PLTS
S Self-managers

Resources
Audio files:
48_Module3_Unit5_Ex2
49_Module3_Unit5_Ex3
50_Module3_Unit5_Ex5
51_Module3_Unit5_Ex7
ActiveTeach:
Starter 1 resource
Starter 2 resource

Starter 1

Aim

To review language from the module.

Allow pupils one minute to make as many words as possible from the following sentence (Starter 1 resource), by taking away any letters from any word to make new words (e.g. *es, come, el, las, toca...*). The words that they make must not already be in the sentence. You could repeat the exercise, this time adding up to two letters to a word in order to create new words.

A la hora de comer, primero como y bebo algo y luego leo libros en la biblioteca o a veces escribo SMS en la clase de informática.

1 Con tu compañero/a, mira las fotos y haz una lista de palabras posibles para cada una. (L1/2)

Writing. Draw pupils' attention to the Skills box, which advises using prediction as a listening strategy. Pupils predict what the three speakers will talk about in exercise 2 based on their photos and captions. Working in pairs, they make a list of possible words for each one.

2 Escucha. ¿Cuántas palabras adivinaste? (L4)

Listening. Pupils listen and count how many words they guessed correctly for each person.

Audioscript Track 48

– ¿Te gusta el dibujo, Hugo?
– Sí, me gusta mucho el dibujo porque es divertido e interesante. La profesora es paciente y también muy simpática.

– Durante el recreo.
  Primero como algo... unas patatas fritas, por ejemplo. Normalmente bebo agua, un zumo o un refresco. Luego leo mis SMS.

– Mi insti.
  En mi instituto hay un gimnasio muy grande y muchas clases. Hay un comedor, unos laboratorios, una biblioteca y un campo de fútbol, pero no hay piscina.

3 Escucha otra vez. Copia y completa la tabla en inglés. (L4)

Listening. Pupils copy the table. They listen and note down the main topic and any two details that each speaker mentions.

Audioscript Track 49

See exercise 2

Answers		
	main topic	two details
Hugo	Art	(any 2 of:) likes it, fun, interesting, teacher is nice and patient
Nuria	Break	(any 2 of:) eats something (e.g. chips), drinks water, juice or fizzy drink, reads texts
Marcos	School/What school is like	(any 2 of:) has very big gym, lots of classrooms, canteen, labs, library, football pitch, but no swimming pool

4 Con tu compañero/a, lee las frases en inglés. Tradúcelas al español e inventa algo para completar cada frase. (L3)

Writing. In pairs, pupils translate five sentences into Spanish, filling the gaps with possible answers of their own. Point out the Skills box, which advises pupils to look closely at the exercise questions first in order to try to predict what the task will be about.

Answers (will vary)

Mi insti 3.5

5 Escucha y comprueba tus respuestas. (L4)

Listening. Pupils listen and check their answers to exercise 4.

Audioscript Track 50

Hola, me llamo Alberto. Tengo trece años y vivo en Oviedo, en España. Me gustan mucho las ciencias porque son útiles e interesantes. También me gusta la historia porque es fácil y bastante divertida, pero no me gusta nada el español porque es difícil y el profesor es raro y muy severo.

Answers

1 Me llamo Alberto. Tengo trece años y vivo en **Oviedo, en España**.
2 Me gustan mucho las ciencias porque son útiles e **interesantes**.
3 También me gusta **la historia** porque es fácil y bastante divertida.
4 No me gusta nada el español porque es **difícil**.
5 Mi profesor de español es raro y muy **severo**.

Reinforcement

Pupils write five things they like and five things they dislike about school (e.g. the subjects, teachers, building) using *me encanta(n)/me gusta(n) (mucho)* and *no me gusta(n) (nada)*.

Starter 2

Aim

To review language of the module.

Present the following twenty vocabulary items on the board in a random order (Starter 2 resource). Allow pupils three minutes to group the words into the four categories (school facilities, school subjects, break-time activities, time expressions).

un campo de fútbol	como un bocadillo
unas clases	bebo un zumo
un comedor	escribo SMS
un patio	juego al baloncesto
una biblioteca	hablo con mis amigos
el dibujo	por la tarde
las matemáticas	por la mañana
la historia	los viernes
las ciencias	normalmente
la educación física	a veces

6 Con tu compañero/a, juega al 'bip'. Di seis frases de este módulo. En cada frase, haz 'bip' en vez de una palabra. Tu compañero/a adivina la palabra. (L2)

Speaking. In pairs, and using any six sentences from Module 3, pupils play 'beep', a game of prediction, whereby one person beeps out a word in a sentence and the other tries to guess what it would have been. Point out the Skills box, which offers further advice to pupils on how to predict while listening.

7 Escucha y completa las frases. (L4)

Listening. Pupils try to predict which words are missing from the Spanish gap-fill sentences. They then listen to Silvia talk about her school to check their answers.

Audioscript Track 51

¡Hola! Me llamo Silvia, tengo catorce años y vivo en Alicante, en España.

Mi instituto es muy moderno y me gusta. Hay un patio bastante grande donde hablo con mis amigas y como mi bocadillo en el recreo.

Hay un campo de fútbol y también un campo de baloncesto.

Hay clases para todo, hay laboratorios, clases de informática y de tecnología. También hay un gimnasio y una biblioteca.

El gimnasio es un poco feo, pero la biblioteca es muy grande y me gusta mucho.

Answers

1 años	2 instituto
3 patio	4 campo de fútbol
5 gimnasio	6 muy grande

8 Elige A, B o C y prepara una presentación en secreto. Tu compañero/a escucha y apunta cinco datos importantes. (L3/4)

Speaking. In pairs, pupils take it in turns to prepare a short presentation on one of three possible topics: school facilities, break-time activities or school subjects (some sentence starters are provided for support). Their partner listens and notes down five important details.

Extension

Pupils choose a topic from two of those in exercise 8 (school facilities or school subjects) and carry out a survey to find other pupils' opinions of them. Pupils could use a computer to design a word-processed document showing the results of their survey, with a graph and written sentences on their findings.

Plenary

Ask pupils to summarise what they have learned about listening skills. They need to say:

(a) what they find difficult about listening

(b) what strategies they will use from now on to help them when tackling listening exercises.

Writing Skills: ¿Cómo es tu insti?

Mi insti 3.6

Pupil Book pages	Programme of Study	Cross-curricular
Pages 64–65	**GV4** Accuracy (spelling, grammar)	**English:** checking spelling and grammar
Learning objectives	**LC4** Expressing ideas (writing)	**Resources**
• Writing a longer text about your school	**Key language**	Workbooks:
• Checking your written work is accurate	Review of language from Units 1–4	Cuaderno 1A & 1B, page 29
	PLTS	ActiveTeach:
	R Reflective learners	p.065 Grammar worksheet

Starter 1

Aim

To review common mistakes.

In pairs, pupils brainstorm the types of mistakes that they tend to make, including words that they often misspell, and also discuss how they check their work. Pupils feedback their thoughts and findings as a class.

1 Haz una lista de palabras que no escribes correctamente, e inventa una forma de recordarlas. (L1)

Writing. Pupils make a list of the words that they tend to have difficulty spelling, whether simply due to their length, or the number of vowels or accents they contain. Their task is to try to find an inventive way to remember them, such as visualisation, mnemonics, spider diagrams or learning games.

2 Busca los dos errores en cada frase. (L4)

Reading. Pupils look for the two errors in each sentence.

Answers

1 Estud**i**o español, ma**t**emáticas y francés.
2 En mi institu**t**o hay una cla**s**e de informática muy grande.
3 Dur**a**nte el recreo bebo un zumo y como un bocadi**ll**o.
4 Me gustan las ci**e**ncias porque son intere**s**antes.
5 El profesor de histori**a** es bastan**t**e severo y no es divertido.
6 Primero leo mis SMS y **lu**ego nav**e**go por Internet.

3 Con tu compañero/a, busca tres ejemplos de cada letra en este libro. (L1)

Reading. In pairs, pupils find three examples of words containing one of the accented vowels in the book or module.

Answers (will vary, examples below)

á: fácil, informática, matemáticas
é: francés, inglés, qué
í: tecnología, escribís, física
ó: religión, educación, jamón
ú: música, fútbol, útil
ñ: español, mañana, pequeño

4 Busca los siete acentos y la ñ que faltan en este mensaje. (L4)

Reading. Pupils read Cristina's message and find the seven words that are missing accents and the word missing a tilde. First, read through the Skills box together, which stresses the importance of accents and the Spanish tilde.

Answers

Perú, matemáticas, geografía, inglés, informática, música, español, simpático.

5 Busca los seis errores gramaticales en este SMS. (L4)

Reading. Read through the Skills box together, which highlights the importance of checking for grammatical accuracy in written work. Areas of concern for pupils to be particularly aware of are: verb endings; definite and indefinite articles; adjectival agreement and the structures *me gusta(n)/me encanta(n)*. Pupils find the six grammatical mistakes in the message.

Mi insti 3.6

Answers
Mi día favorito es el jueves porque <u>estudio</u> dibujo y teatro por la mañana y educación física por la tarde. Me encanta <u>el</u> dibujo y me <u>gustan</u> <u>las</u> ciencias porque son <u>divertidas</u> y la profesora es muy <u>simpática</u>.

Reinforcement
Pupils write their own text message about school containing six deliberate grammatical mistakes, using exercise 5 as a model. Each pupil then swaps work with a partner, who attempts to make the necessary corrections.

Starter 2
Aim

To review high-frequency words.

In pairs, allow pupils four minutes to brainstorm as many high-frequency verbs, connectives and intensifiers as they can remember, including what they mean in English. Pupils feedback their findings as a class.

6 Lee el texto de Guillermo y haz un mapa mental en inglés. (L4)

Reading. Pupils read Guillermo's text about his school and make a spider diagram in English to show how the report has a solid structure with clearly defined topics. A sample diagram is started off for pupils as support.

Extension
Pupils read aloud Guillermo's text in Spanish round the class, a sentence at a time, translating it into English.

7 Haz un mapa mental para tu instituto y luego escribe un reportaje. Utiliza el reportaje de Guillermo como modelo. (L4)

Writing. Pupils draw their own spider diagram. This will form the basis of a structured school report, which they are to write, using Guillermo's report as a model. Make sure that pupils have read and understood the advice in the Skills box, which suggests using connectives, intensifiers, sequencers and expressions of frequency to make their writing more interesting.

8 Comprueba el trabajo de tu compañero/a y da tu opinión. (L4)

Reading. Pupils swap their reports from exercise 7 with a partner, then read through and assess each other's work. Before asking pupils to comment on their partner's work, check that they understand the meanings of the three Spanish feedback comments.

Plenary
Ask pupils to compile a list of five accented words that they find difficult to spell, which they can resolve to learn by heart.

Workbook 1A, page 29

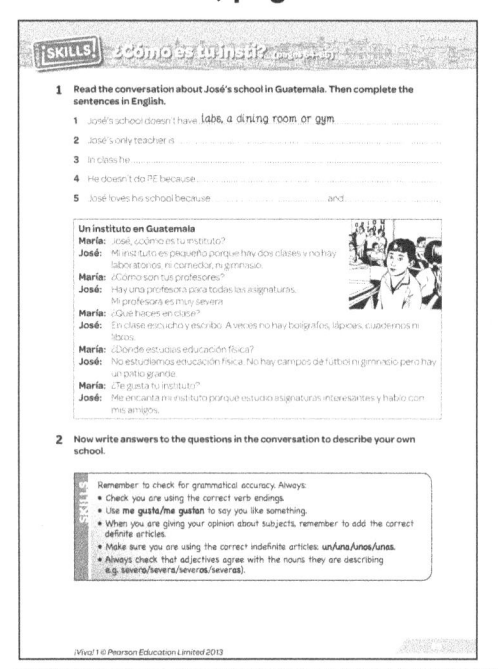

Answers
1
1 *labs, a dining room or gym.*
2 very strict
3 listens and writes
4 there are no football pitches or gym
5 he studies interesting subjects/ alks to his friends

2 Own answers.

Mi insti 3.6

Workbook 1B, page 29

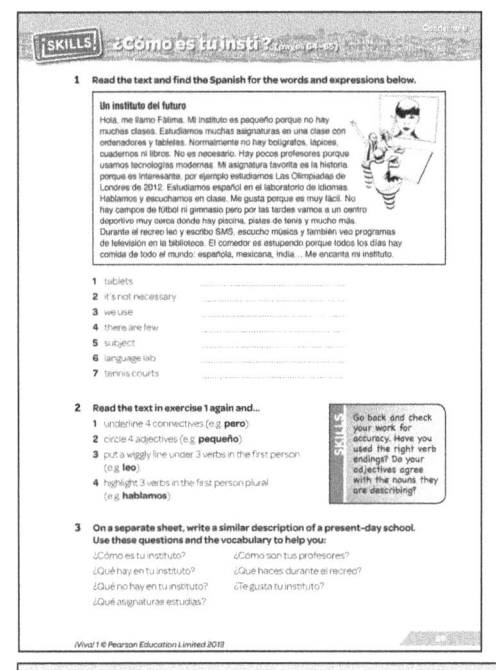

Worksheet 3.6 High-frequency words

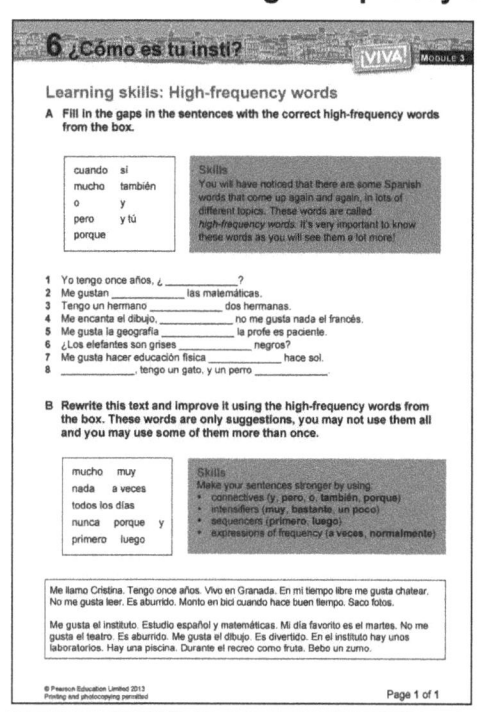

Answers

1
1 tabletas
2 no es necesario
3 usamos
4 hay pocos
5 asignatura
6 laboratorio de idiomas
7 pistas de tenis

2 Answers might include the following:

1 connective: porque, y, ni, también

2 adjectives: muchas, pocos, moderna, favorita, interesante, fácil, mucho, estupendo

3 verbs in first person: escribo, escucho, veo

4 verbs in first person plural: estudiamos, usamos, escuchamos, vamos

3 Own answers

Answers

A
1 y tú   2 mucho   3 y
4 pero   5 porque   6 o
7 cuando   8 Sí, también

B (Suggested answer)

Me llamo Cristina **y** tengo once años. Vivo en Granada. En mi tiempo libre me gusta **mucho** chatear. No me gusta leer **porque** es aburrido. Monto en bici cuando hace buen tiempo. **A veces** saco fotos.

Me gusta el instituto. Estudio español y matemáticas **todos los días.** Mi día favorito es el martes. No me gusta **nada** el teatro **porque** es **muy** aburrido. Me gusta el dibujo **porque** es divertido. En el instituto hay unos laboratorios **y** una piscina. Durante el recreo **primero** como fruta, **luego** bebo un zumo.

© Pearson Education Ltd 2013. Copying permitted for purchasing institution only. This material is not copyright free.

Mi insti 3

Pupil Book pages
Pages 66–67

Resumen
Pupils use the checklist to review language covered in the module, working on it in pairs in class or on their own at home. Encourage them to follow up any areas of weakness they identify. There are Target Setting Sheets included in the Assessment Pack and an opportunity for pupils to record their own levels and targets on the Self-assessment pages in the Workbooks, p. 33. You can also use the *Resumen* checklist (available in the ActiveTeach) as an end-of-module plenary option.

Prepárate
These revision exercises can be used for assessment purposes or for pupils to practise before tackling the assessment tasks in the Assessment Pack.

Resources
Audio files:
52_Module3_Prep_Ex1
53_Module3_Prep_Ex2
Workbooks:
Cuaderno 1A & 1B, pages 30 & 31
ActiveTeach:
p.030 *Resumen* checklist

1 Escucha. Escribe la letra correcta y apunta si la opinión es positiva (P) o negativa (N). (1–6) (L3)

Listening. Pupils listen to the six statements. For each one, they note the letter of the subject mentioned and whether the opinion of the speaker is positive (P) or negative (N).

Audioscript Track 52

1 – No me gusta el inglés porque es aburrido.
2 – Me gusta mucho la informática porque es útil.
3 – Me gustan las ciencias porque son prácticas.
4 – Me gusta la historia porque es fácil.
5 – No me gustan las matemáticas porque la profesora es severa.
6 – No me gusta nada la geografía porque es difícil.

Answers
1 c, N   2 a, P   3 e, P   4 d, P   5 f, N   6 b, N

2 Escucha otra vez. Apunta la razón en inglés. (1–6) (L4)

Listening. Pupils listen to the statements again and make a note of the reason the speaker gives for liking or disliking the school subject.

Audioscript Track 53

See exercise 1

Answers
1 boring	2 useful
3 practical	4 easy
5 teacher is strict	6 difficult

3 Con tu compañero/a, haz cuatro diálogos. (L3)

Speaking. In pairs, pupils take turns to ask and answer questions about school facilities. A sample dialogue and picture prompts for pupils' answers are supplied.

4 Lee el texto y completa las frases en inglés. (L4)

Reading. Pupil's read Cristina's letter, in which she describes her school experience. They then complete the gap-fill sentences that summarise the letter in English.

Answers
1 seven	2 French
3 Thursday	4 morning
5 football pitch	6 small
7 talks to her friends	

5 Describe tu insti. Utiliza el texto del ejercicio 4 como modelo. (L4)

Writing. Pupils write a description of their own school experience, using Cristina's letter in exercise 4 as a model. A writing frame is supplied.

© Pearson Education Ltd 2013. Copying permitted for purchasing institution only. This material is not copyright free.

Workbook 1A, page 30

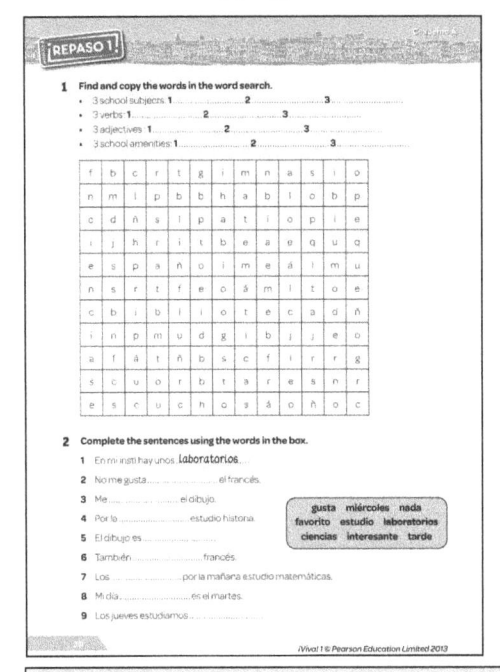

Workbook 1A, page 31

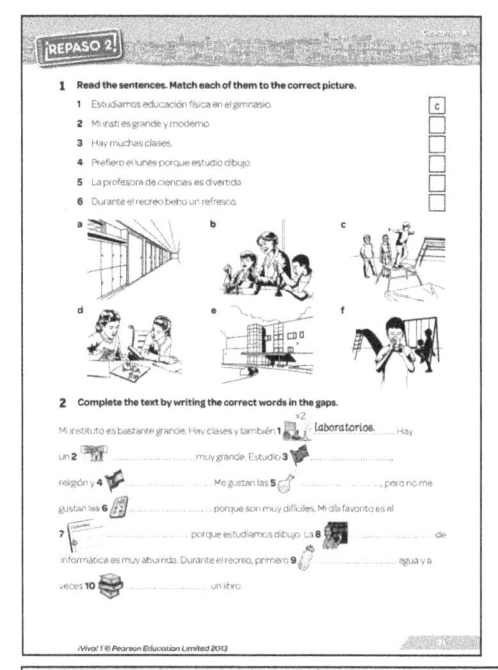

Answers

1. **3 school subjects:** matemáticas, ciencias, español

   3 verbs: hablo, escucho, leo

   3 adjectives: pequeño, moderno, feo

   3 amenities: patio, biblioteca, gimnasio

f	b	c	r	t	g	i	m	n	a	s	i	o
n	m	l	p	b	b	h	a	b	f	h	b	p
c	d	ñ	s	l	p	a	t	i	o	p	l	e
i	j	h	r	i	t	b	e	a	e	q	u	q
e	s	p	a	ñ	o	l	m	e	á	l	m	u
n	s	r	t	f	e	o	á	m	l	t	o	e
c	b	i	b	l	i	o	t	e	c	a	d	ñ
i	n	p	m	u	d	g	i	b	j	j	e	o
a	f	á	t	ñ	b	s	c	f	l	r	r	g
s	c	u	o	r	b	t	a	r	e	s	n	r
e	s	c	u	c	h	o	s	á	o	ñ	o	c

2.
   1 *laboratorios* 2 nada
   3 gusta 4 tarde
   5 interesante 6 estudio
   7 miércoles 8 favorito
   9 ciencias

Answers

1. 1 c 2 e 3 a 4 d 5 b 6 f

2. 1 *laboratorios* 2 patio
   3 inglés 4 español
   5 ciencias 6 matemáticas
   7 martes 8 profesora
   9 bebo 10 leo

Mi insti 3

Workbook 1B, page 30

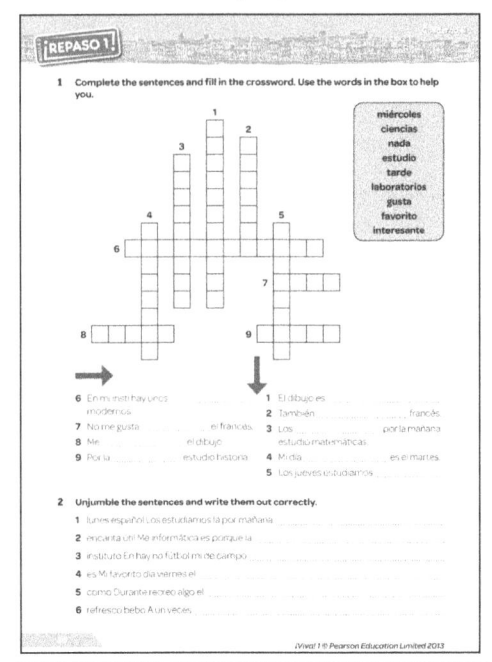

Workbook 1B, page 31

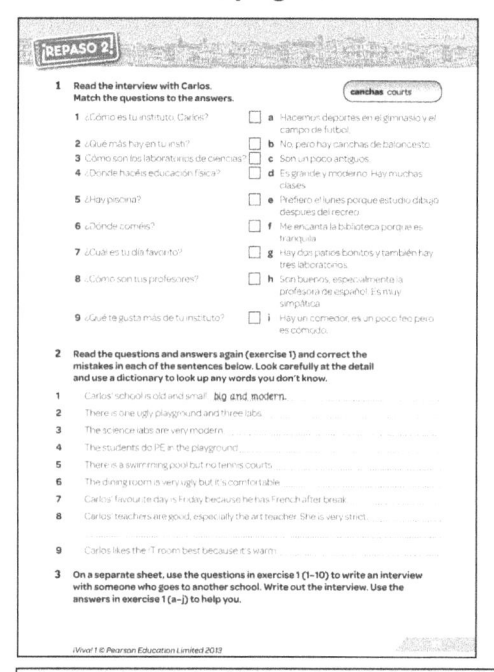

Answers

1 horizontales   verticales

6 laboratorios   1 interesante

7 nada   2 estudio

8 gusta   3 miércoles

9 tarde   4 favorito

            5 ciencias

2 1 Los lunes por la mañana estudiamos español.

     2 Me encanta la informática porque es útil.

     3 En mi instituto no hay campo de fútbol.

     4 Mi día favorito es el viernes.

     5 Durante el recreo como algo.

     6 A veces bebo un refresco.

Answers

1 1 d   2 g   3 c   4 a   5 b   6 i   7 e   8 h   9 f

2 1 *big and modern*

     2 two pretty playgrounds

     3 The science labs are a bit old.

     4 PE in the gym and on the football ground

     5 basketball courts but no swimming pool

     6 a bit ugly

     7 Monday, because he has art

     8 Spanish teacher, she is very friendly

     9 library because it's quiet

3 Own answers

© Pearson Education Ltd 2013. Copying permitted for purchasing institution only. This material is not copyright free.

¡GRAMÁTICA!

Mi insti 3

Pupil Book pages
Pages 68–69

The *Gramática* section provides a more detailed summary of the key grammar covered in the module, along with further exercises to practise these points.

Grammar topics
- *me gusta/me gustan*
  me encanta/me encantan
- adjectives (agreement with sing., plural, masc., fem. nouns)
- the definite and indefinite articles
- present tense verbs (regular *-ar*, *-er* and *-ir* verbs)

Resources
Workbooks:
Cuaderno 1A & 1B, page 32
ActiveTeach:
p.068 Grammar presentation
p.068 Grammar presentation
p.069 Grammar presentation

Me gusta/Me gustan

1 Choose the correct words and complete the sentences.

Pupils write out the completed sentences using the picture prompts, choosing the correct form of the verbs from the two options given each time.

Answers
1 *Me gusta la historia.*
2 Me gustan mucho las matemáticas.
3 Me encantan las ciencias.
4 No me gusta el francés.
5 No me gusta nada la educación física.
6 ¿Te gusta la informática?

Adjectives

2 Choose an adjective from the box to complete each sentence. There may be more than one answer, but the adjective must agree with the noun. The sentence must be logical!

Pupils complete the gap-fill sentences with an appropriate word from the box.

Answers
1 No me gusta nada el inglés porque es **aburrido**.
2 Me encantan las matemáticas porque son **interesantes**.
3 Me gusta mucho la informática porque es **fácil**.
4 Me gusta el español porque la profesora es **simpática**.
5 El profesor de religión es **severo**.
6 En mi instituto, la piscina es **pequeña**.
7 El comedor es **antiguo**.
8 Los laboratorios son **modernos**.

The definite and indefinite articles

3 Complete these sentences.

Pupils fill in the progressively more challenging gap-fill sentences using the picture prompts.

Answers
1 En mi insti hay un patio. **El** patio es grande.
2 En mi insti hay una piscina. **La** piscina es pequeña.
3 En mi insti hay **una biblioteca**. **La biblioteca** es antigua.
4 En **mi insti hay unos laboratorios**. **Los laboratorios** son modernos.

Present tense verbs

4 Choose the correct answer.

Pupils choose the correct verb form from the three options given each time.

Answers
1 b 2 c 3 a 4 a

5 Translate these sentences into Spanish.

Pupils translate the English sentences into Spanish, paying particular attention to verb conjugation.

Answers
1 (Él) Bebe agua.   2 Leo mis SMS.
3 Estudias inglés.   4 Comen bocadillos.
5 Bailáis.   6 Tocamos la guitarra.
7 (Ella) Vive en Madrid.   8 Escriben.

© Pearson Education Ltd 2013. Copying permitted for purchasing institution only. This material is not copyright free.

Mi insti 3

Workbook 1A, page 32

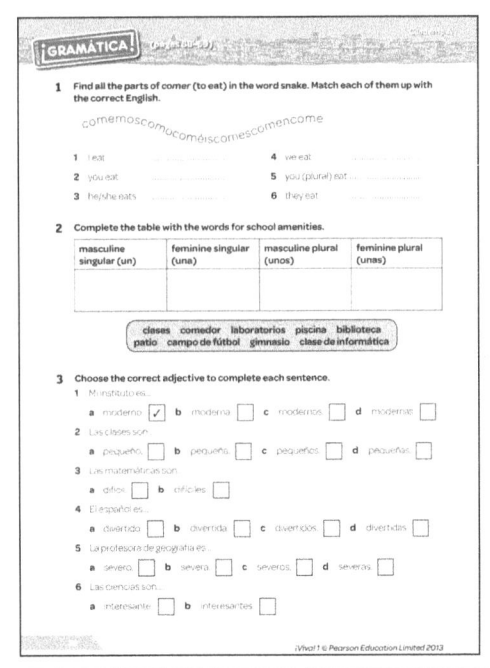

Answers

1. 1 como 2 comes 3 come 4 comemos 5 coméis 6 comen

2.

masc. sing.	fem. sing.	masc. pl.	fem. pl.
comedor patio campo de fútbol gimnasio	piscina biblioteca clase de informática	laboratorios	clases

3. 1 a 2 d 3 b 4 a 5 b 6 b

Workbook 1B, page 32

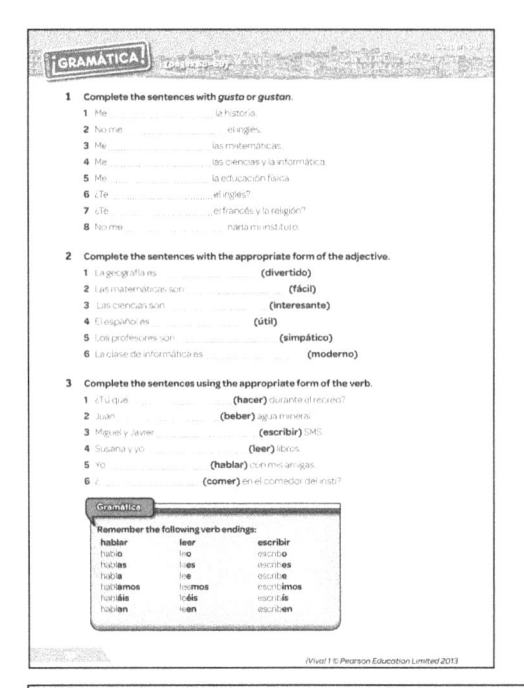

Answers

1. 1 gusta 2 gusta 3 gustan 4 gustan 5 gusta 6 gusta 7 gustan 8 gusta

2. 1 divertida 2 fáciles 3 interesantes 4 útil 5 simpáticos 6 moderna

3. 1 haces 2 bebe 3 escriben 4 leemos 5 hablo 6 coméis

¡PROYECTO! La educación

Mi insti 3

Pupil Book pages
Pages 72–73

Learning objectives
- Reading about the right to education
- Creating a plan for a school in Guatemala

Programme of Study
GV3 Opinions and discussions
LC4 Expressing ideas (speaking)

FCSE links
Unit 2: Education and future plans (School facilities)

PLTS
T Team workers

Cross-curricular
Citizenship: charity work
Mathematics: model realistic situations mathematically

Resources
Audio files:
54_Module3_ZP_Ex1
55_Module3_ZP_Ex3

Starter 1

Aim

To introduce the countries of Latin America.

With books closed, pupils work in pairs to brainstorm all the countries that they know in Central America and the rest of Latin America. Ask pupils to feed back their answers and discuss how each of the countries is pronounced in Spanish.

1 Escucha. Copia y completa la tabla. (1–4) (L3)

Listening. Before starting this exercise, read through the *Zona Cultura* box together. Pupils copy the table. They listen to four young people introduce themselves and complete the table. For each person, they note which country they live in and whether they go to school. Some vocabulary is glossed for support.

Audioscript Track 54

1 – *Me llamo Enrique y vivo en Costa Rica. Mi colegio es muy grande y muy moderno. Me gusta mucho porque los profesores son simpáticos.*

2 – *Me llamo María. Vivo en Honduras, en Centroamérica. No voy al colegio porque no hay colegio en mi pueblo.*

3 – *¡Hola! ¿Qué tal? Me llamo César y vivo en la Ciudad de Panamá. Mi día favorito en el colegio es el jueves porque estudiamos educación física.*

4 – *Me llamo Alejandra y vivo en El Salvador. Tengo una hermana. No voy al colegio porque está demasiado lejos.*

Answers

	vive en	va al colegio	no va al colegio
Enrique	Costa Rica	✓	✗
María	Honduras	✗	✓
César	Panamá	✓	✗
Alejandra	El Salvador	✗	✓

2 Lee los textos. Apunta los detalles en inglés. (L4)

Reading. Pupils read the texts and make notes, in English, of the details mentioned in the bullet points. *Nuevo/a* is glossed for support. Draw pupils' attention to the Skills box, which lists the reading strategies pupils can adopt to help them tackle longer texts.

Answers

Name: Virginia **Age:** 13
How ActionAid helped the school: gave 4 computers
Other details: she likes using them

Name: Marta **Age:** 9
How ActionAid helped the school: built 8 new classrooms
Other details: it's easy to study

Name: Edgar **Age:** 8
How ActionAid helped the school: they built it
Other details: they sing and study numbers and letters, he likes playing football in the playground

Starter 2

Aim

To introduce vocabulary for school equipment.

Working in pairs and referring to the pictures on p. 73 of the Pupil Book, pupils take turns to mime the materials or equipment from exercise 3 for their partners to name. Their partner guesses the noun and reads out the Spanish.

© Pearson Education Ltd 2013. Copying permitted for purchasing institution only. This material is not copyright free.

3 ¿Qué necesitan los niños en el colegio? Escucha y escribe la letra correcta. (1–8) (L3)

Listening. Pupils listen to eight brief conversations and identify what it is that the children need in school, noting the letter of the correct item (a–h) on p. 73 of the Pupil Book. *Cada niño* is glossed for support.

Audioscript Track 55

1 – ¿Qué necesitas en tu colegio?
 – Necesitamos una pizarra.
2 – ¿Y tú, José? ¿Qué necesitas en tu colegio?
 – Necesitamos materiales para deportes.
3 – ¿Qué necesitas en tu colegio?
 – Necesitamos un servicio de agua potable.
4 – ¿Qué necesitas en tu colegio?
 – Necesitamos una clase nueva.
5 – ¿Qué necesitas en tu colegio, Alejandra?
 – Necesitamos una mesa y una silla para cada niño.
6 – ¿Qué necesitas en tu colegio, Darwin?
 – Necesitamos una tablet para estudiar. Una tablet para cada niño.
7 – ¿Qué necesitas en tu colegio, Rodrigo?
 – Necesitamos un lápiz y un cuaderno para cada niño.
8 – ¿Qué necesitas en tu colegio?
 – Necesitamos un bloc de dibujo y lápices de colores para cada niño.

Answers
1 c 2 e 3 g 4 h 5 d 6 f 7 a 8 b

4 Escribe tu opinión sobre los objetos del ejercicio 3. (L3)

Writing. Pupils write their opinion on the importance of the items mentioned in exercise 3. An example and some phrases are given for support.

5 Trabaja en un grupo de cuatro personas. Cada persona da tres opiniones. Las otras personas hacen comentarios. (L4)

Speaking. In groups of four, pupils practise exchanging opinions on the importance of having certain items in school. Each person gives three opinions, which the other three comment upon. Sample replies are given for support.

6 Vas a equipar un colegio en Guatemala. ¿Qué material se necesita? En tu grupo de cuatro, haz un plan. (L3)

Writing. In groups of four, pupils create an action plan for a school in Guatemala. An imaginary budget is allocated and the group needs to decide what to spend the money on. A comprehensive list of tasks to be undertaken is supplied.

Plenary

Play a chain game around the class. Start it off: *Los niños necesitan una pizarra.* The next person repeats what you have said and adds another item (e.g. *...y materiales para deportes*). Continue around the class. If someone can't remember the chain, makes a mistake, or can't think of anything to add, he or she sits down and the chain starts again with another topic, i.e. *En mi opinión, tener una mesa es muy importante.*

¡TE TOCA A TI!

Mi insti 3

Pupil Book pages Self-access reading and writing
Pages 124–125

A Reinforcement

1 ¿Qué día es? ¿Qué estudia? (L2)

Reading. Pupils read the sentences and decide which school subjects are studied on which day.

Answers
1 Monday, f
2 Tuesday, d
3 Thursday, c
4 Wednesday, b
5 Thursday, a
6 Friday, e

2 Escribe cinco frases sobre tu semana en el insti. (L3)

Writing. Pupils write five sentences to describe what they study each day at school, using the sentences in exercise 1 as a framework.

3 Lee los textos y mira los dibujos. Para cada dibujo escribe Sofía o David. (L3)

Reading. Pupils read the texts describing Sofía and David's experiences of school. They then look at the pictures and decide whether they refer to Sofía or David.

Answers		
1 David	2 Sofía	3 David
4 David	5 Sofía	6 Sofía

B Extension

1 ¿Lógico o absurdo? Escribe L o A. (L3)

Reading. Pupils read the sentences and decide whether each one is logical (L) or absurd (A).

Answers
1 A 2 A 3 L 4 L 5 A 6 L 7 L 8 A

2 Cambia las frases absurdas del ejercicio 1 para hacer frases lógicas. (L3)

Writing. Pupils write out corrected versions of the four absurd sentences in exercise 1, using their own ideas.

Answers (may vary)
1 No me gustan las matemáticas porque son aburridas.
2 Me gusta la historia porque es interesante.
5 Me gustan las ciencias porque son interesantes.
8 No me gusta nada la tecnología porque es muy difícil y el profesor es severo.

3 Lee el texto y completa las frases en inglés. (L4)

Reading. Pupils read Juan Pedro's text describing his experiences at school, then complete the gap-fill sentences about it in English.

1 Juan Pedro lives in **Burgos**.
2 He studies English, Spanish, **maths**, **science**, **history**, **geography**, **ICT and also PE**.
3 He doesn't study **RE**.
4 His favourite day is **Thursday** because **in the morning he studies science and maths and in the afternoon he studies PE**.
5 At break **he plays football or basketball in the playground or chats with his friends**.
6 Normally he eats **a sandwich or sometimes a chocolate bar**.

4 Escribe un blog. Utiliza el texto de Juan Pedro como modelo. (L4)

Writing. Pupils write a blog about their own school experience, adapting Juan Pedro's text in exercise 3. A list of topics to include is given. Encourage pupils to include connectives and intensifiers in their writing.

© Pearson Education Ltd 2013. Copying permitted for purchasing institution only. This material is not copyright free.

MODULE 4: Mi familia y mis amigos

Unit & Learning objectives	PoS references	Key language	Grammar and other language features
1 ¿Cuántas personas hay en tu familia? (pp. 76–77) Describing your family Using possessive adjectives	**GV2** Grammatical structures (possessive adjectives) **GV3** Developing vocabulary **LC1** Listening and responding	*mi madre* *mi padre* *mis padres* *mi hermano/a* *mi hermanastro/a* *mi abuelo/a* *mis abuelos* *mi bisabuelo/a* *mi tío/a* *mis tíos* *mi primo/a* *mis primos* *tiene/tienen… años* *se llama/se llaman* *veinte* *treinta* *cuarenta* *cincuenta* *sesenta* *setenta* *ochenta* *noventa* *cien* *cuarenta y tres*, etc.	**G** possessive adjectives: *mi/tu/su* and *mis/tus/sus*
2 ¿De qué color tienes los ojos? (pp. 78–79) Describing your hair and eye colour Using the verbs *ser* and *tener*	**GV2** Grammatical structures (irregular verbs, adjectival word order) **LC6** Reading comprehension **LC8** Writing creatively	*¿De qué color tienes los ojos?* *Tengo los ojos…* *azules* *grises* *marrones* *verdes* *Llevo gafas.* *¿Cómo tienes el pelo?* *Tengo el pelo…* *negro* *rubio* *castaño* *azul* *liso* *rizado* *largo* *corto* *Soy pelirrojo/a.* *Soy calvo.*	**G** irregular verbs *tener* and *ser* **G** position of adjectives (after the noun) – pronunciation of *l* and *ll*

© Pearson Education Ltd 2013. Copying permitted for purchasing institution only. This material is not copyright free.

Mi familia y mis amigos 4

Unit & Learning objectives	PoS references	Key language	Grammar and other language features
3 ¿Cómo es? (pp. 80–81) Saying what other people look like Using verbs in the third person	**LC6** Reading comprehension **LC8** Writing creatively	*(No) Es…* *alto/a* *bajo/a* *pequeño/a* *joven* *viejo/a* *guapo/a* *gordo/a* *delgado/a* *feo/a* *simpático/a* *inteligente* *Tiene pecas.* *Tiene barba.*	**G** agreement of adjectives with nouns – pronunciation of diphthongs – using intensifiers – using the correct part of the verb
4 ¿Cómo es tu casa o tu piso? (pp. 82–83) Describing where you live Using the verb *estar* (to be)	**GV2** Grammatical structures (the verb *estar*) **LC5** Speaking coherently and confidently	*Vivo en…* *una casa* *un piso* *bonito/a* *antiguo/a* *cómodo/a* *pequeño/a* *grande* *moderno/a* *Está en…* *la montaña* *un pueblo* *una ciudad* *la costa* *el campo* *el desierto* *el norte* *el este* *el sur* *el oeste* *el centro*	**G** the verb *estar*
5 El carnaval en familia (pp. 84–85) Reading about the carnival in Cadiz Looking up new Spanish words in a dictionary	**GV3** Developing vocabulary **LC6** Reading comprehension	Review of language from Units 1–4	– developing dictionary skills – looking up nouns, adjectives and verbs

© Pearson Education Ltd 2013. Copying permitted for purchasing institution only. This material is not copyright free.

Mi familia y mis amigos 4

Unit & Learning objectives	PoS references	Key language	Grammar and other language features
6 Autorretrato (pp. 86–87) Creating a video about yourself Planning and giving a presentation	**LC4** Expressing ideas (speaking) **LC5** Speaking coherently and confidently	Review of language from Units 1–4	– developing speaking skills – using connectives, intensifiers, adjectives and giving opinions – developing presentation skills: speaking from notes and practising
Resumen y Prepárate (pp. 88–89) Pupils' checklist and practice exercises			
Gramática (pp. 90–91) Detailed grammar summary and practice exercises			**G** possessive adjectives: *mi/tu/su* and *mis/tus/sus* **G** adjectives (agreement with nouns) **G** irregular verbs (*tener, ser*) **G** *ser* and *estar*
Zona Proyecto: Las Meninas (pp. 94–95) Describing a painting Recording an audio or video guide to a painting	**GV3** Developing vocabulary to give opinions and take part in discussions **LC5** Speaking coherently and confidently		
Te toca a ti (pp. 126–127) Self-access reading and writing at two levels			

© Pearson Education Ltd 2013. Copying permitted for purchasing institution only. This material is not copyright free.

¿Cuántas personas hay en tu familia?

Mi familia y mis amigos 4.1

Pupil Book pages
Pages 74–77

Learning objectives
- Describing your family
- Using possessive adjectives

Programme of Study
GV2 Grammatical structures (possessive adjectives)
GV3 Developing vocabulary
LC1 Listening and responding

FCSE links
Unit 1: Relationships, family and friends (Family and step family, Personal details, Numbers, Family/friends)

Grammar
- Possessive adjectives *mi/tu/su* and *mis/tus/sus*

Key language
mi madre
mi padre
mis padres
mi hermano/a
mi hermanastro/a
mi abuelo/a
mis abuelos
mi bisabuelo/a
mi tío/a
mis tíos
mi primo/a
mis primos
tiene/tienen… años
se llama/se llaman
veinte
treinta
cuarenta
cincuenta
sesenta
setenta
ochenta
noventa
cien
cuarenta y tres, etc.

PLTS
I Independent enquirers

Resources
Audio files:
56_Module4_Unit1_Ex1
57_Module4_Unit1_Ex5
58_Module4_Unit1_Ex7
Workbooks:
Cuaderno 1A & 1B, page 36
ActiveTeach:
p.076 Flashcards
p.076 Grammar presentation
ActiveLearn:
Listening A, Listening B
Reading A, Reading B
Grammar, Vocabulary

Module 4 Quiz (pp. 74–75)

Answers

1 c 2 a 3 b 4 c 5 Answers will vary 6 c

Starter 1

Aim

To review vocabulary for family members.

Ask pupils to create anagrams of vocabulary for family members in Spanish (e.g. *hermano, hermana, hermanastro, hermanastra, hijo único, hija única, bisabuela*, etc.) for their partners to decipher. Allow each pair three minutes to make up the anagrams and to work through each other's lists.

1 Escucha y lee. (L3)

Listening. Pupils listen and follow the text on p. 76 of the Pupil Book at the same time.

Audioscript Track 56

¡Hola! Me llamo Tray. Tengo doce años y vivo en Malibú.

Mis padres son muy famosos. Mi madre se llama Carolina. Tiene treinta y ocho años. Mi padre se llama Spencer y tiene cincuenta años.

Tengo una hermana y un hermanastro. Se llaman Violeta y Knox.

Mi abuelo tiene setenta y un años y mi abuela tiene setenta y dos. ¡Mi bisabuela tiene noventa años!

Mi tío Jaime tiene cuarenta años y mi tía Jennifer tiene cuarenta y tres años. Mis primos se llaman Madison y Tyler. Mi prima Kiki tiene catorce años.

2 Busca estas palabras en español en el ejercicio 1. (L3)

Reading. Pupils find in the exercise 1 text the Spanish for the English words given.

Answers

1 mi madre	2 mi padre
3 mi tío	4 mis primos
5 mi abuelo	6 mi abuela
7 mi tía	8 mi bisabuela
9 mi prima	10 mis padres

© Pearson Education Ltd 2013. Copying permitted for purchasing institution only. This material is not copyright free.

Mi familia y mis amigos 4.1

Gramática

Use the *Gramática* box to teach the possessive articles *mi*, *tu* and *su* (my, your, his and her), which only have two forms: singular and plural. With no masculine and feminine forms, they stay the same regardless of the gender of the nouns they modify, e.g. *mi amigo/mi amiga* and *tus hermanos/tus hermanas*. There is more information and practice on Pupil Book p. 90.

3 Juego de memoria. Con tu compañero/a, contesta en lugar de Tray. (L3)

Speaking. In pairs, pupils play a memory game with the information given in exercise 1. They take it in turns to ask each other the names of the members of Tray's family, while the other person (whose book is closed), tries to remember them all. Two sample questions are supplied. Draw pupils' attention to *se llama* (he/she is called) changing to *se llaman* (they are called) when the noun being described is plural (i.e. parents, cousins).

Reinforcement

Write the following sentences on the board, jumbling the word order. With books closed, pupils say the sentences in the correct order.

1 *Mis tíos se llaman Tom y James.*
2 *Mi hermanastro Ben tiene catorce años.*
3 *Mi abuelo se llama George.*
4 *Mi prima es hija única.*
5 *Mi bisabuela tiene noventa y dos años.*
6 *Mi tía se llama Jane y tiene cincuenta años.*

Starter 2

Aim

To review numbers 1–30.

Do a few drills around the class to practise numbers up to 30 in Spanish: count through the times tables forwards and backwards; you say a sequence and stop (or insert 'beep') for pupils to complete it; you make a deliberate mistake in a sequence, and pupils put up their hands as soon as they spot it.

4 Copia y completa la tabla. (L3)

Reading. Pupils copy and fill in the blanks in the table. The missing words can all be found in the text in exercise 1. Draw their attention to the Tip box, which offers a strategy for working out higher numbers and remind them, if necessary, to look for cognates and patterns.

Answers	
veinte	**twenty**
treinta	thirty
cuarenta	forty
cincuenta	fifty
sesenta	**sixty**
setenta	seventy
ochenta	eighty
noventa	ninety
cien	**a hundred**

5 Escucha. Copia y completa la tabla. (1–6) (L3)

Listening. Pupils copy and complete the table in Spanish with the correct family relationship and age of the person being described each time.

Audioscript Track 57

1 – ¿Cuántas personas hay en tu familia?
   En mi familia hay siete personas. Mi padre se llama Santiago y tiene cincuenta años.
2 – Mi madre se llama Karina. Tiene cuarenta y tres años.
3 – Mi hermanastro se llama Roberto. Tiene quince años.
4 – Mi bisabuela tiene noventa años. Se llama María.
5 – Mi abuela se llama Ana. Tiene sesenta y ocho años.
6 – Mi hermana se llama Alba. Tiene nueve años.

Answers		
	persona	**edad**
1	*padre*	50
2	madre	43
3	hermanastro	15
4	bisabuela	90
5	abuela	68
6	hermana	9

6 Con tu compañero/a, describe a estas dos familias. (L3)

Speaking. In pairs, pupils take it in turns to describe a figurative family including their names and ages, using the picture prompts provided. A framework is provided for support.

Mi familia y mis amigos 4.1

7 Escucha y canta. Pon los dibujos en el orden de la canción. (L4)

Listening. Pupils listen to the song, following the text at the same time. Play the song again and encourage pupils to sing along. Pupils then place the pictures in the order that they are mentioned.

Audioscript Track 58

En mi familia hay seis personas,
Mi tía, mis abuelas, yo y mis padres.

Mi abuela Valeria toca la batería.
Los jueves baila tango en la cafetería.

Mi tía favorita es tía Trini.
Monta en bici y juega a la Wii.

Mi padre tiene sesenta años.
Baila flamenco y habla con sus amigos.

Mi madre, Sara, saca fotos con su cámara.
Tiene cuarenta años y canta ópera.

Mi bisabuela Mía escucha música
Los lunes hace yoga ¡Es fanática!

Mi familia es rara, pero a mí me gusta.
¿Cuántas personas hay en tu familia?

Answers
c, d, a, e, b

8 Eres miembro de una familia famosa. Describe a tu familia. (L3/4)

Writing. Pupils choose a child of a celebrity and write a description of his/her family. A writing frame is supplied for support, along with a Tip box reminding pupils to pay attention to possessive adjectives and verb forms in their writing.

Extension

Ask pupils to draw their own family tree and describe it orally to their partner. Without taking notes, their partner has to remember as many details as possible about the names and ages of the family members and recite them back, e.g. *Tu abuelo se llama... y tiene... años.*

Plenary

Ask pupils to brainstorm their 'progress pyramid': three things that they already knew but now understand more clearly; two things that they have recently learned and one thing that they need to work on. They then feedback their thoughts to the class.

Workbook 1A, page 36

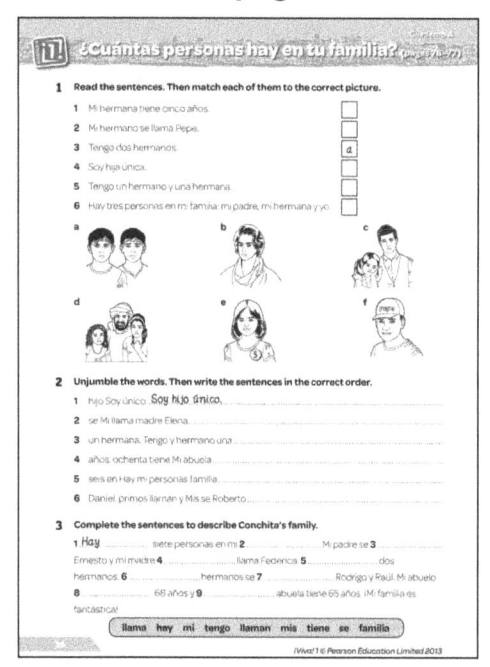

Answers

1 1 e   2 f   3 a   4 b   5 c   6 d

2 1 Soy hijo único.
   2 Mi madre se llama Elena.
   3 Tengo un hermano y una hermana.
   4 Mi abuela tiene ochenta años.
   5 Hay seis personas en mi familia.
   6 Mis primos se llaman Roberto y Daniel.

3 1 hay   2 familia   3 llama
   4 se   5 tengo   6 mis
   7 llaman 8 tiene   9 mi

Workbook 1B, page 36

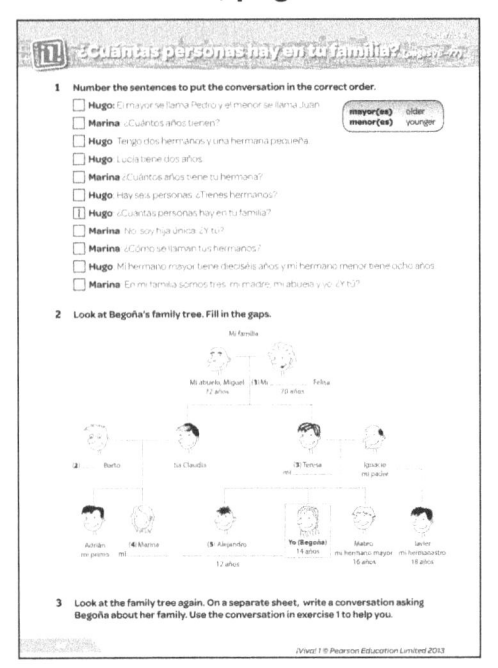

Answers

1 11, 6, 5, 9, 8, 3, *1*, 4, 10, 7, 2

2 **1** abuela **2** tío **3** madre **4** prima
  5 mi hermano menor

3 Own answers

2 ¿De qué color tienes los ojos?

Mi familia y mis amigos 4.2

Pupil Book pages
Pages 78–79

Learning objectives
- Describing your hair and eye colour
- Using verbs *ser* and *tener*

Programme of Study
GV2 Grammatical structures (irregular verbs, adjectival word order)
LC6 Reading comprehension
LC8 Writing creatively

FCSE links
Unit 1: Relationships, family and friends (Personal details, Descriptions)

Grammar
- irregular verbs *tener* and *ser*
- position of adjectives (after the noun)

Key language
¿De qué color tienes los ojos?
Tengo los ojos…
azules
grises
marrones
verdes
Llevo gafas.
¿Cómo tienes el pelo?
Tengo el pelo…
negro
rubio
castaño
azul
liso
rizado
largo
corto
Soy pelirrojo/a.
Soy calvo.

PLTS
T Team workers

Resources
Audio files:
59_Module4_Unit2_Ex1
60_Module4_Unit2_Ex3
61_Module4_Unit2_Ex5
Workbooks:
Cuaderno 1A & 1B, page 37
ActiveTeach:
p.078 Video 7
p.078 Video 7 transcript
p.078 Video worksheet 7
p.078 Flashcards
p.078 Grammar presentation
p.078 Grammar worksheet
ActiveLearn:
Listening A, Listening B
Reading A, Reading B
Grammar, Vocabulary

Starter 1

Aim

To review family members and ages.

Prepare eight jumbled up sentences that recap on all family members from Unit 1 and read them out slowly to the class. Ask pupils to write out the sentences, putting the words back in the correct order. For example:

llaman James Mis y tíos Tom se.

bisabuela años Mi tiene noventa.

1 Escucha y escribe la letra o letras correcta(s). (1–4) (L2)

Listening. Pupils listen to the exchanges and look at the pictures. They note the correct letter of the picture(s) for each person mentioned.

Audioscript Track 59

1 – ¿De qué color tienes los ojos?
Tengo los ojos verdes.

2 – ¿De qué color tienes los ojos?
Tengo los ojos grises.

3 – ¿De qué color tienes los ojos?
Tengo los ojos marrones.

4 – ¿De qué color tienes los ojos?
Tengo los ojos azules y llevo gafas.

Answers
1 d 2 b 3 c 4 a, e

Reinforcement

Write up the following on the board. Ask pupils to find someone in the class who fits each description. You could also use the opportunity to clarify the meanings of the subject pronouns *él* and *ella*.

1. *Él tiene el pelo rubio. Tiene los ojos marrones.*
2. *Ella tiene el pelo negro. Tiene los ojos verdes.*
3. *Él es pelirrojo. Tiene los ojos azules.*
4. *Ella tiene el pelo castaño. Tiene los ojos grises.*
5. *Él tiene el pelo corto y rizado. Tiene los ojos azules.*
6. *Ella tiene el pelo largo y castaño. Tiene los ojos marrones.*

2 Con tu compañero/a, pregunta y contesta. (L3)

Speaking. In pairs, pupils take it in turns to choose to be one of the celebrities pictured. One pupil describes their eye colour while the other guesses his or her identity. A sample exchange is given. Use the *Pronunciación* box to review pronunciation of the letters *ll* and *l*.

© Pearson Education Ltd 2013. Copying permitted for purchasing institution only. This material is not copyright free.

Mi familia y mis amigos 4.2

3 Escucha y escribe la letra correcta. (1–10) (L2)

Listening. Pupils listen to the ten descriptions of hair types and look at the pictures. They note the letter of the correct picture for each person.

Audioscript Track 60

1 – *Tengo el pelo rubio.*
2 – *Tengo el pelo azul.*
3 – *Tengo el pelo castaño.*
4 – *Tengo el pelo negro.*
5 – *Tengo el pelo liso.*
6 – *Tengo el pelo largo.*
7 – *Tengo el pelo corto.*
8 – *Tengo el pelo rizado.*
9 – *Soy calvo.*
10 – *Soy pelirrojo.*

Answers
1 b 2 d 3 c 4 a 5 f 6 h 7 i 8 g 9 j 10 e

Gramática
Use the *Gramática* box to teach the full paradigms of *tener* and *ser*, two extremely important irregular verbs that pupils will need to learn by heart. There is more information and further practice on Pupil Book p. 91.

Starter 2
Aim
To review language for describing hair and eyes.

Dictate the following short description to the class. Ask pupils to transcribe it and then draw it. To differentiate, more able pupils can write out the complete sentence, while others can write down any 3–10 words that they recognise.

Me llamo Diego. Tengo once años. Tengo el pelo negro y tengo los ojos marrones.

Alternative starter 2:
Use ActiveTeach p.078 Flashcards to review and practise hair and eyes vocabulary.

4 Con tu compañero/a, elige a uno de los personajes. Describe las dos fotos. (L3)

Speaking. In pairs, pupils take it in turns to compare the appearance of a famous celebrity in two separate photos. Sample sentence openers are given. Draw pupils' attention to the *Gramática* box, which highlights how most adjectives come <u>after</u> the noun they are describing in Spanish.

5 ¿Cómo es la familia de Alma? Copia y completa la tabla. (1–3) (L4)

Listening. Pupils copy the table. They listen and note down the hair, eye colour and other details mentioned about Alma's family members. Point out the Glossary box accompanying exercise 6, which includes *además*, a new connective that they will hear several times.

Audioscript Track 61

1 – *Mi hermana se llama Carlota. Tiene el pelo castaño y largo y tiene los ojos marrones. Es simpática y además, muy, muy lista.*
2 – *Mi padre se llama José. Tiene el pelo negro y corto y tiene los ojos azules. Es divertido y además muy generoso.*
3 – *Mi hermano se llama Ricardo. Tiene los ojos marrones y el pelo castaño. Navega por Internet todo el tiempo. Es aburrido y además muy tonto.*

Answers

	name	hair	eye colour	other details
1	Carlota	brown, long	brown	nice, very clever
2	José	short, black	blue	funny, very generous
3	Ricardo	brown	brown	surfs the net, boring, very silly

6 Lee las descripciones. Escribe el nombre correcto para cada dibujo. (L4)

Reading. Pupils read the descriptions and write the name of the person being described in each picture (a–c). *Además* and *guapo/a* are glossed for support.

Answers
a Emiliano b Angelina c Rafael

Extension
Pupils rework the three texts in exercise 6 using the first person singular. This can be done orally or in writing.

Mi familia y mis amigos 4.2

7 Rellena una ficha en inglés para cada miembro del grupo. (L4)

Reading. Pupils fill in an identity card in English for each of the three members of the band described in exercise 6.

Answers	
Name	Rafael
Age	19
Appearance	blond straight hair, green eyes
Personality	intelligent, nice
Role in group	singer

Name	Emiliano
Age	20
Appearance	black hair, wears glasses
Personality	funny
Role in group	plays guitar

Name	Angelina
Age	21
Appearance	blond hair, grey eyes
Personality	interesting
Role in group	plays drums

8 Inventa otro miembro del grupo 'Supergenial'. Escribe su descripción. (L4)

Writing. Pupils invent a fourth member of the band described in exercise 6 and write a description of him or her in Spanish, using the text in exercise 6 as a model. A writing frame is provided.

Plenary

Allow pupils a few minutes to write a short description of someone in the class, describing their hair and eyes. You could suggest that they use the subject pronouns *él* (he) and *ella* (she) in front of the verbs in order to emphasise the person's gender. Pupils exchange their descriptions with their partner and try to work out who is being described in the fewest number of guesses.

Workbook 1A, page 37

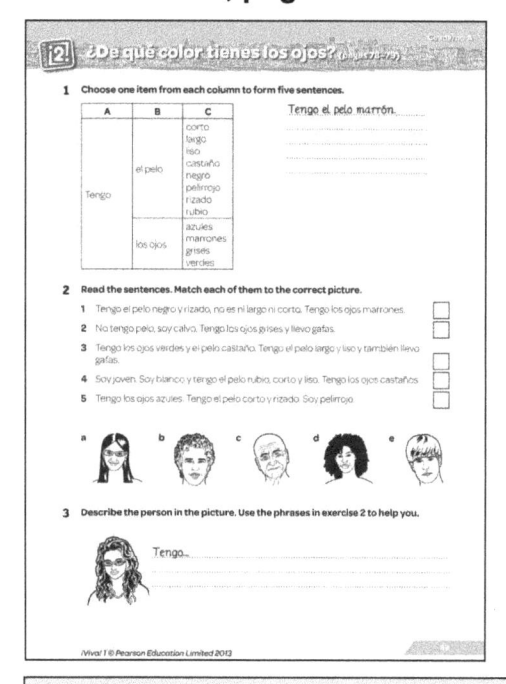

Answers

1 Own answers.

2 1 d 2 c 3 a 4 e 5 b

3 Own answers.

Workbook 1B, page 37

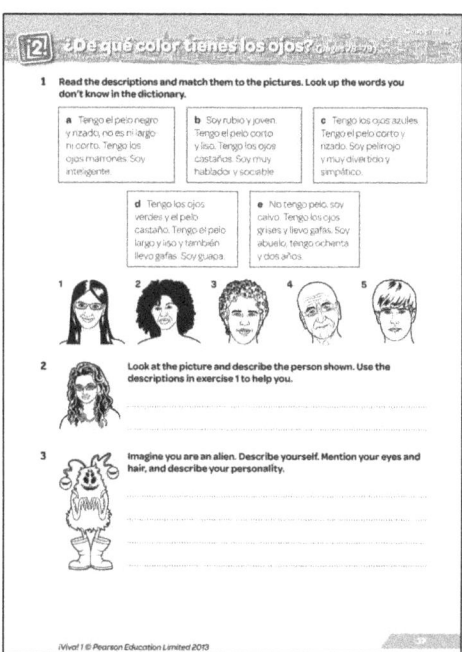

Answers

1 1 d 2 a 3 c 4 e 5 b

2 Own answers

3 Own answers

© Pearson Education Ltd 2013. Copying permitted for purchasing institution only. This material is not copyright free.

Worksheet 4.2 What a picture!

Answers

A

1 lentillas	2 ondulado
3 reflejos rojos	4 un tatuaje de una flor
5 en el cuello	6 un *piercing* en el labio
7 pendientes	8 multicolores
9 con forma de animales	10 pecas
11 en la nariz	12 un poco rara

B (Suggested answer)

Te presento a Sergio. Es mi novio y tiene veintidós años. Primero, tiene los ojos verdes y lleva unas gafas pequeñas. Tiene el pelo corto, liso y negro. Mi novio es interesante porque tiene un *piercing* en la nariz y lleva dos pendientes pequeños. Sergio es el hermano de una amiga. Es un poco raro, como yo, y ¡creo que es muy guapo!

Video

Episode 7: La familia

Laura presents a report on her family in Spain and Bolivia. Video worksheet 7 can be used in conjunction with this episode.

Answers to video worksheet (ActiveTeach)

A

1 Answers will vary and may include the ten words introduced in Unit 1 of the Pupil Book, as well as words such as '*hermano*' introduced on page 13.

2 a) Tengo los ojos azules y (tengo) el pelo castaño y rizado.

  b) Tengo los ojos verdes y (tengo) el pelo rubio y largo.

  c) Tengo los ojos marrones y (tengo) el pelo negro y corto.

B

1 familia, padres, hermano, prima, hermana, madre, padre, abuela, hermanos, hijo único, primos, tía, primo, hermanastro, hijo, tío, primas

The word '*marido*' is also mentioned, which pupils have not seen before.

2 a) true

  b) false (He is called Jaime, not José.)

  c) false (He is ten years old, not twelve.)

3 in Bolivia

C

Name: *Flora*

Age: *15*

Eyes: *brown*

Hair: *curly*, *blond*

Interests: *sport*, *piano*

2 b) Flora — sister
  c) Isabel — mother
  d) Luca — father
  e) Soby — grandmother
  f) Mateo and Andrés — brothers

3 *Rodri* is <u>25</u> years old. He has short <u>black</u> hair and <u>brown</u> eyes. He likes <u>music</u> and has a <u>stepbrother</u>.

D

1 He interrupts her / looks fed up / rolls his eyes / says that her family is strange / says that her report is boring.

2 Because they keep on arguing and interrupting filming.

3 Answers will vary.

4 Answers will vary.

5 I have coffee-coloured eyes (literally 'I have coffee eyes').

6 Pupils will probably say 'yes', because he says he has fifty people in his family / he appears to be getting back at Laura.

E

Pupils will produce their own video report.

3 ¿Cómo es?

Mi familia y mis amigos 4.3

Pupil Book pages
Pages 80–81

Learning objectives
- Saying what other people look like
- Using verbs in the third person

Programme of Study
LC6 Reading comprehension
LC8 Writing creatively

FCSE links
Unit 1: Relationships, family and friends (Personal details, Family/friends, Descriptions)

Grammar
- Agreement of adjectives with nouns

Key language
(No) Es…
alto/a
bajo/a
pequeño/a
joven
viejo/a
guapo/a
gordo/a
delgado/a
feo/a
simpático/a
inteligente
Tiene pecas.
Tiene barba.

PLTS
C Creative thinkers

Resources
Audio files:
62_Module4_Unit3_Ex2
63_Module4_Unit3_Ex5
Workbooks:
Cuaderno 1A & 1B, page 38
ActiveTeach:
p.080 Flashcards
p.080 Grammar presentation
p.081 Extension reading
Starter 2 resource
ActiveLearn:
Listening A, Listening B
Reading A, Reading B
Grammar, Vocabulary

Starter 1

Aim

To review singular forms of *ser* and *tener*.

As a class, allow pupils a few minutes to revise the singular forms of *ser* and *tener* via a game of 'sentence tennis'. To 'bat', one pupil says the form of the verb plus another pupil's name. That pupil translates the verb, then chooses another pupil to whom he or she will bat a new verb.

1 Empareja los nombres con las descripciones. (L3)

Reading. Pupils read the six descriptions and identify the person being described in each one. Some vocabulary is glossed for support.

Answers
1 Manuel el Cruel
2 Paquito el Pequeño
3 Fernando el Feo
4 Daniela la Delgada
5 Guillermo el Gordo
6 Diego el Diabólico

2 Escucha y comprueba tus respuestas. (L3)

Listening. Pupils listen and check their answers to exercise 1.

Audioscript Track 62

1 – Es muy alto. Tiene los ojos azules y tiene el pelo largo y liso. No es muy simpático. Se llama Manuel el Cruel.

2 – Es bastante joven y es pelirrojo. Tiene el pelo corto. Lleva gafas y también tiene pecas. Se llama Paquito el Pequeño.

3 – Es bajo y no es muy guapo. Tiene el pelo corto y negro, los ojos marrones y una barba roja. Se llama Fernando el Feo.

4 – Es delgada y muy guapa. Tiene el pelo largo, rubio y rizado. Tiene los ojos grises. Es la capitana. Se llama Daniela la Delgada.

5 – Es negro, tiene los ojos verdes, es viejo y también muy gordo. Se llama Guillermo el Gordo.

6 – Es calvo, tiene una barba negra enorme y un ojo verde. Es terrible. Es muy feo. Se llama Diego el Diabólico.

Reinforcement

Working in pairs, pupils take turns to describe a person in the class and to identify him or her.

Gramática

Use the *Gramática* box to review adjectival agreement with nouns. There is more information and practice on Pupil Book p. 90.

Mi familia y mis amigos 4.3

3 Busca estas frases en el ejercicio 1. (L3)

Reading. Pupils find in the exercise 1 text the Spanish equivalents of the English sentences.

Answers
1 Es muy alto.
2 Es bastante joven.
3 Es bajo y no es muy guapo.
4 Es delgada y muy guapa.
5 Es viejo y también muy gordo.
6 Es muy feo.

4 Con tu compañero/a, describe a estos piratas. (L3)

Speaking. In pairs, pupils take it in turns to describe two of the pirates pictured. Draw their attention to the *Pronunciación* box on diphthongs. In Spanish, there are 'strong' vowels (the letters *a*, *e* and *o*), which normally carry the stress in a word, and 'weak' vowels (the letters *i* and *u*), which are usually not stressed. Also point out to pupils that while Spanish words that end in -*o* are nearly always masculine, and words that end in -*a* are nearly always feminine, there are exceptions, such as *el pirata*.

Extension
Pupils choose two of the cartoon characters pictured in exercise 4 and write a sentence describing each one (hair and eyes).

Starter 2

Aim
To review language for describing people.
Play 'Odd-one-out' using the following lists (Starter 2 resource). Ask pupils to explain the reason for their choices.
For example: **1** *alto* (all the others begin with 'g').

1	*guapo*	*gordo*	*gigante*	*alto*
2	*soy*	*son*	*tengo*	*eres*
3	*delgado*	*fea*	*inteligente*	*bajo*
4	*altos*	*guapos*	*bajas*	*feos*
5	*somos*	*sois*	*es*	*son*

Ask pupils to create a couple of their own odd-one-out lists on the same theme.

Alternative starter 2:
Use ActiveTeach p.080 Flashcards to review and practice descriptions vocabulary.

5 Escucha. ¿Verdadero o falso? Escribe V o F. (1–5) (L4)

Listening. Pupils listen to the exchanges and read the sentences. They decide whether the sentences are true (V) or false (F). Some vocabulary is glossed for support. Point out the Skills box to remind pupils of the intensifiers *muy*, *bastante* and *un poco*, which they will hear in this exercise.

Audioscript Track 63

1 – ¿Cómo es tu mejor amigo?
 – Eh, a ver… es bastante delgado y bastante simpático.
2 – ¿Cómo es tu mejor amiga?
 – Es muy guapa pero muy baja.
3 – ¿Cómo es tu mejor amigo?
 – Eh…es un poco gordo.
4 – ¿Cómo es tu mejor amiga?
 – Es muy alta y también muy delgada.
5 – ¿Cómo es tu mejor amigo?
 – Es muy feo, muy gordo y muy bajo y también muy estúpido.

Answers
1 V 2 F 3 V 4 F 5 F

6 Lee el texto. Escribe el nombre correcto. (L4)

Reading. Pupils read the text, then answer the questions that follow, identifying who is being described each time. *Como yo* is glossed for support.

Answers
1 Ray   2 Elizabeth Vélez
3 Roberto   4 Rudy
5 Rony   6 Reyna

7 Describe a una de estas familias. Utiliza el texto del ejercicio 6 como modelo. (L4)

Writing. Pupils write a description of one of the families pictured, using the text in exercise 6 as a model. Point out the Skills box, which advises pupils to think carefully about verb formation. *El vampiro/la vampira* and *el payaso/la payasa* are glossed for support.

© Pearson Education Ltd 2013. Copying permitted for purchasing institution only. This material is not copyright free.

Mi familia y mis amigos 4.3

Plenary

In pairs, ask pupils to play the 'beep game' to test each other on what they have learned about adjectival endings during the lesson. For example, one pupil prompts with:

Mi madre tiene el pelo (beep) *y los ojos* (beep).

Their partner supplies the complete sentence.

Workbook 1A, page 38

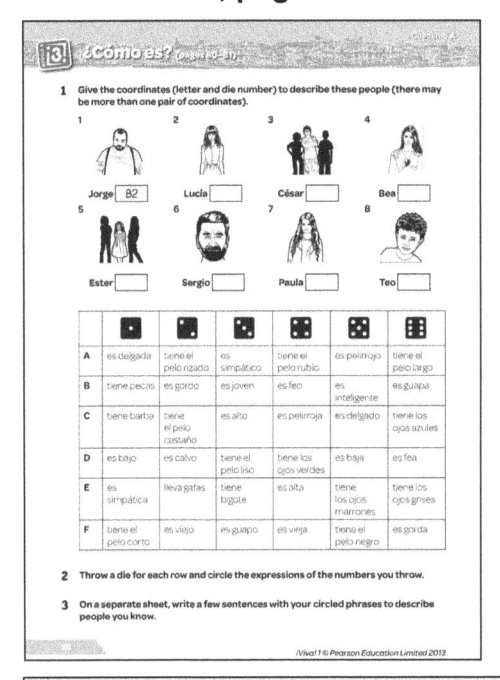

Answers

1 (Answers may vary) **1** (Jorge) B2
  2 (Lucía) A1   **3** (César) C3
  4 (Bea) B6   **5** (Ester) D5
  6 (Sergio) C1   **7** (Paula) A6
  8 (Teo) A2
2 Own answers.   3 Own answers.

Workbook 1B, page 38

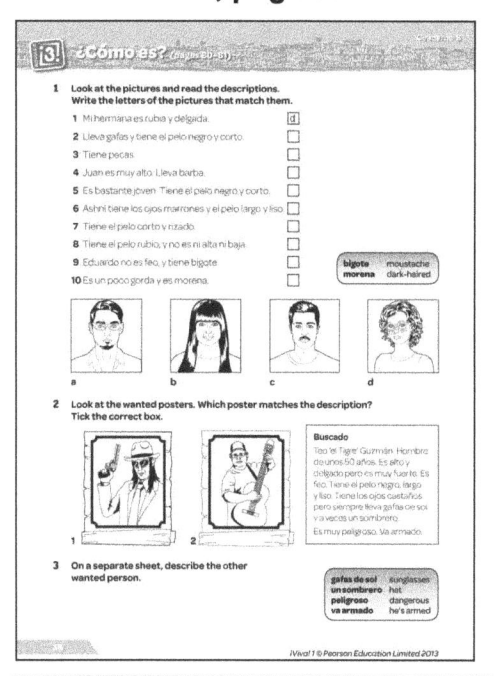

Answers

1 **1** 1d   **2** a   **3** d   **4** a   **5** c   **6** b   **7** d
  8 d   **9** c   **10** b
2 1   3 Own answers.

ActiveTeach, Extension Reading

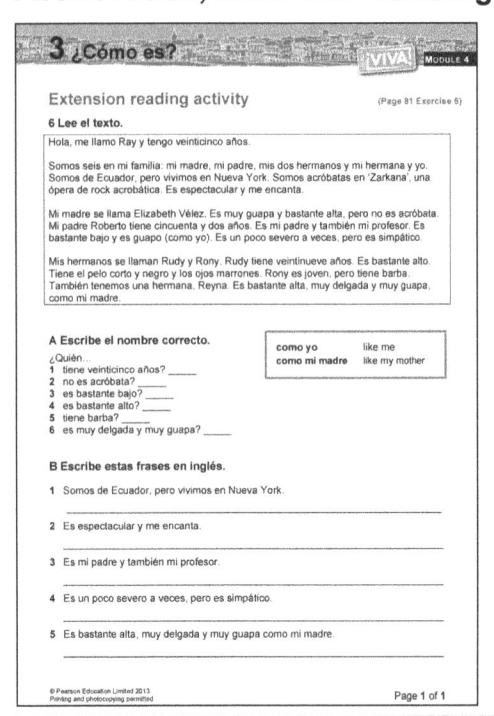

3 ¿Cómo es?

Extension reading activity (Page 81 Exercise 5)

6 Lee el texto.

Hola, me llamo Ray y tengo veinticinco años.

Somos seis en mi familia: mi madre, mi padre, mis dos hermanos y mi hermana y yo. Somos de Ecuador, pero vivimos en Nueva York. Somos acróbatas en 'Zarkana', una ópera de rock acrobática. Es espectacular y me encanta.

Mi madre se llama Elizabeth Vélez. Es muy guapa y bastante alta, pero no es acróbata. Mi padre Roberto tiene cincuenta y dos años. Es mi padre y también mi profesor. Es bastante bajo y es guapo (como yo). Es un poco severo a veces, pero es simpático.

Mis hermanos se llaman Rudy y Rony. Rudy tiene veintinueve años. Es bastante alto. Tiene el pelo corto y negro y los ojos marrones. Rony es joven, pero tiene barba. También tenemos una hermana, Reyna. Es bastante alta, muy delgada y muy guapa, como mi madre.

A Escribe el nombre correcto.

¿Quién...
1 tiene veinticinco años? _____
2 no es acróbata? _____
3 es bastante bajo? _____
4 es bastante alto? _____
5 tiene barba? _____
6 es muy delgada y muy guapa? _____

| como yo | like me |
| como mi madre | like my mother |

B Escribe estas frases en inglés.

1 Somos de Ecuador, pero vivimos en Nueva York.

2 Es espectacular y me encanta.

3 Es mi padre y también mi profesor.

4 Es un poco severo a veces, pero es simpático.

5 Es bastante alta, muy delgada y muy guapa como mi madre.

Answers (Question 6)

A

1 Ray   2 Elizabeth Vélez
3 Roberto   4 Rudy
5 Rony   6 Reyna

B

1 We are from Ecuador but we live in New York.
2 It is spectacular and I love it.
3 He is my father and also my teacher.
4 He is strict from time to time, but nice.
5 She is quite tall, very slim and very pretty like my mother.

¿Cómo es tu casa o tu piso?

Mi familia y mis amigos 4.4

Pupil Book pages
Pages 82–83

Learning objectives
- Describing where you live
- Using the verb *estar* (to be)

Programme of Study
GV2 Grammatical strcutures (the verb *estar*)
LC5 Speaking coherently and confidently

FCSE links
Unit 7: Local area and environment (Locations)

Grammar
- the verb *estar*

Key language
Vivo en…
una casa
un piso
bonito/a
antiguo/a
cómodo/a
pequeño/a
grande
moderno/a
Está en…
la montaña
un pueblo
una ciudad
la costa
el campo
el desierto
el norte
el este
el sur
el oeste
el centro

PLTS
C Creative thinkers

Resources
Audio files:
64_Module4_Unit4_Ex1
65_Module4_Unit4_Ex3
Workbooks:
Cuaderno 1A & 1B, page 39
ActiveTeach:
p.082 Video 8
p.082 Video 8 transcript
p.082 Video worksheet 8
p.082 Flashcards
p.082 Grammar presentation
p.083 Flashcards
p.083 Grammar worksheet
ActiveLearn:
Listening A, Listening B
Reading A, Reading B
Grammar, Vocabulary

Starter 1

Aim

To review pronunciation rules met so far.

Ask pupils to predict the pronunciation of the following words, which they will meet in Unit 4:

montaña, pequeño/a
está, cómodo/a
vivo, bonito/a
campo, casa, ciudad
pueblo, desierto

1 Escucha y escribe la letra correcta para cada persona. (1–6) (L3)

Listening. Read through the *Zona Cultura* box together before starting the exercise. Pupils listen to the six exchanges and look at the photos. They note the letter of the correct photo for each person.

Audioscript Track 64

1 – ¿Cómo es tu casa o tu piso?
– Vivo en una casa antigua.
– ¿Dónde está?
– Está en un pueblo.

2 – ¿Cómo es tu casa o tu piso?
– Vivo en un piso cómodo.
– ¿Dónde está?
– Está en una ciudad.

3 – ¿Cómo es tu casa o tu piso?
– Vivo en un piso pequeño.
– ¿Dónde está?
– Está en la costa.

4 – ¿Cómo es tu casa o tu piso?
– Vivo en una casa bonita.
– ¿Dónde está?
– Está en la montaña.

5 – ¿Cómo es tu casa o tu piso?
– Vivo en una casa moderna.
– ¿Dónde está?
– Está en el desierto.

6 – ¿Cómo es tu casa o tu piso?
– Vivo en una casa grande.
– ¿Dónde está?
– Está en el campo.

Answers
1 b 2 c 3 d 4 a 5 f 6 e

© Pearson Education Ltd 2013. Copying permitted for purchasing institution only. This material is not copyright free.

Mi familia y mis amigos 4.4

> **Gramática**
>
> Use the *Gramática* box to teach the full paradigm of the verb *estar* (to be), used to describe location and temporary conditions, unlike *ser* (also to be), which is used for permanent states. There is more information and practice in choosing when to use *estar* or *ser* on Pupil Book p. 91.

2 Con tu compañero/a, tira un dado tres veces y haz diálogos. (L3)

Speaking. In pairs, pupils play a dice game. One pupil asks two fixed questions; the other throws the dice three times to find the answers using the key provided (the first two throws determine whether they live in a house or flat and what sort of building it is, and the third throw determines where it is).

> **Starter 2**
>
> **Aim**
>
> To review adjectives for describing the home.
>
> Give pupils three minutes to copy and complete this table, placing the eight adjectives and their English meanings in the correct columns below.
>
> | adjetivo | opuesto | inglés |
> | --- | --- | --- |
> | moderno | antiguo | modern/old |
> | bonito | feo | pretty/ugly |
> | grande | pequeño | big/small |
> | cómodo | incómodo | comfortable/uncomfortable |

3 Escucha y apunta los datos. (1–5) (L4)

Listening. Pupils listen to the five people talking about their homes and make notes in Spanish.

> **Audioscript Track 65**
>
> 1 – *Vivo en un piso en una ciudad en el oeste de España. Me gusta mucho porque es muy, muy grande.*
>
> 2 – *Vivo en una casa en el campo. Está en el este de España. Me gusta mucho porque hace buen tiempo y mi casa es muy bonita.*
>
> 3 – *Vivo en un piso en la costa. Está en el sur de España. No me gusta nada porque es muy pequeño y además hay muchos turistas.*
>
> 4 – *Vivo en una casa bastante grande y muy antigua. Está en el norte de España, en la montaña. Me encanta porque es muy tranquilo.*
>
> 5 – *Vivo en un piso moderno. Está en el centro de España. Me gusta mucho porque la ciudad es interesante.*

> **Extension**
>
> To differentiate this exercise according to ability, increase the number of details pupils have to listen out for.

> **Answers**
>
> 1 piso – ciudad – oeste – me gusta mucho – muy grande
>
> 2 casa – campo – este – me gusta mucho – hace buen tiempo – casa es muy bonita
>
> 3 piso – costa – sur – no me gusta nada – muy pequeño – hay muchos turistas
>
> 4 casa bastante grande – muy antigua – norte – montaña – me encanta – muy tranquilo
>
> 5 piso moderno – centro – me gusta mucho – ciudad es interesante

4 Lee los textos y completa las frases. (L4)

Reading. Pupils read the texts, then complete the gap-fill sentences that follow in Spanish. *Madrastra* is glossed for support.

> **Answers**
>
> 1 Arturo vive en una **casa** en el campo.
>
> 2 Le gusta su casa porque es muy **cómoda**.
>
> 3 Rosa vive en un piso moderno con su **familia**.
>
> 4 Le gusta porque está **en la costa**.
>
> 5 Irene vive en una casa **antigua**.
>
> 6 Para Irene, vivir en la montaña es **aburrido**.
>
> 7 Jesús **vive** con su padre, su madrastra y su hermanastra.
>
> 8 En el pueblo donde vive hay una **piscina**.

> **Reinforcement**
>
> Pupils read aloud the four texts in Spanish round the class, a sentence at a time, translating it into English.

Mi familia y mis amigos 4.4

5 Elige una foto y haz una presentación. (L4)

Speaking. Pupils prepare a presentation on living in a choice of three cities, to include details of the type of building they live in, its geographical location, the people they live with and whether they like it or not. A framework is supplied for support. Once complete, pupils could present it to their partner (who could note down five important details), or to the whole class, as preferred.

6 Eres muy famoso y tienes mucho dinero. Escribe un tuit describiendo donde vives. (L3/4)

Writing. Imagining they are a wealthy celebrity, pupils write a creative tweet of no more than 140 characters to describe their palatial home.

Plenary

Put one pupil in the 'hot seat' as an expert on topics covered in Unit 4 – the other pupils ask him or her questions on what they have learned. If the pupil answers them correctly, he or she gets to nominate another pupil to take the hot seat.

Workbook 1A, page 39

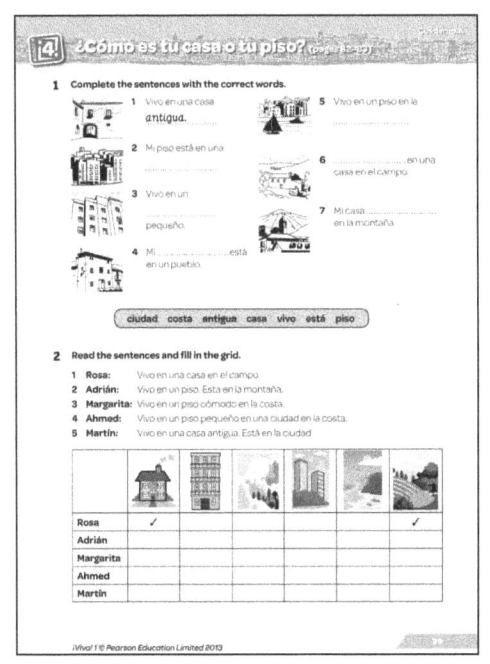

Answers

1 **1** *antigua* **2** ciudad **3** piso **4** casa **5** costa **6** vivo **7** está

2

	house	flat	mt.	city	coa.	coun.
Rosa	✓					✓
Adri.		✓	✓			
Marg.		✓			✓	
Ahm.		✓	✓	✓		
Mart	✓			✓		

Workbook 1B, page 39

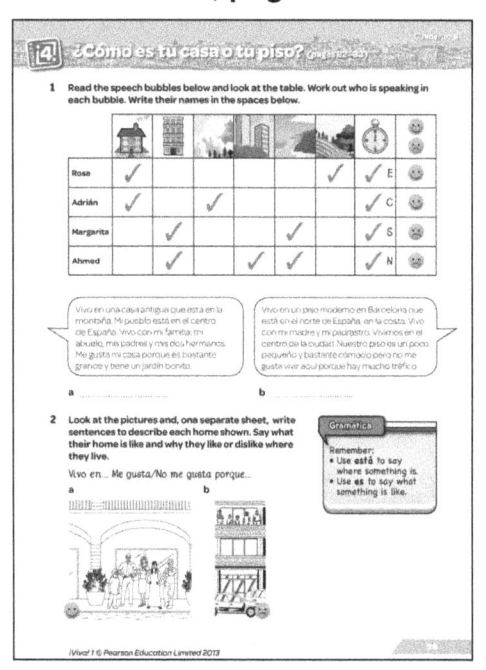

Answers

1 **a** Adrián **b** Ahmed

2 Own answers

Mi familia y mis amigos 4.4

Worksheet 4.4 Where do they live?

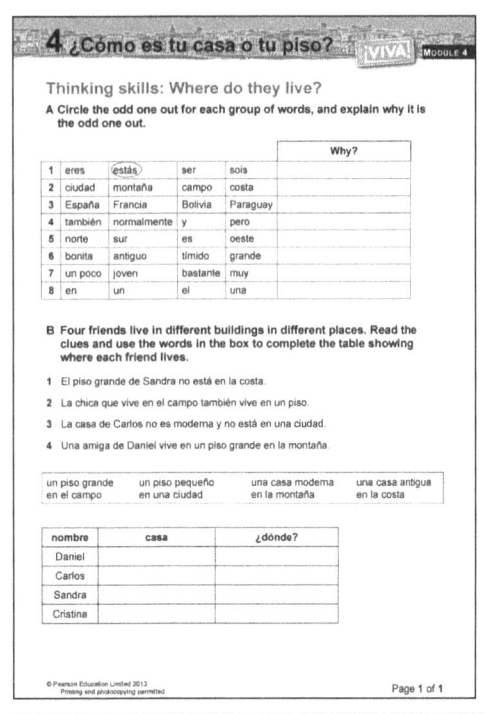

4 ¿Cómo es tu casa o tu piso? MODULE 4

Thinking skills: Where do they live?

A Circle the odd one out for each group of words, and explain why it is the odd one out.

					Why?
1	eres	estás	ser	sois	
2	ciudad	montaña	campo	costa	
3	España	Francia	Bolivia	Paraguay	
4	también	normalmente	y	pero	
5	norte	sur	es	oeste	
6	bonita	antiguo	tímido	grande	
7	un poco	joven	bastante	muy	
8	en	un	el	una	

B Four friends live in different buildings in different places. Read the clues and use the words in the box to complete the table showing where each friend lives.

1 El piso grande de Sandra no está en la costa.
2 La chica que vive en el campo también vive en un piso.
3 La casa de Carlos no es moderna y no está en una ciudad.
4 Una amiga de Daniel vive en un piso grande en la montaña.

| un piso grande en el campo | un piso pequeño en una ciudad | una casa moderna en la montaña | una casa antigua en la costa |

nombre	casa	¿dónde?
Daniel		
Carlos		
Sandra		
Cristina		

Answers

A

1 *estás* – This is the 2nd person singular of the verb '*estar*'. The other three verb forms correspond to the verb '*ser*'.

2 *ciudad* – This means 'town' or 'city'. The other three are rural settings.

3 *Francia* – French is spoken in this country. In the other three countries, they speak Spanish.

4 *normalmente* – This word is an expression of frequency. The other three words are connectives/adverbs.

5 *es* – This is the 2nd person singular of the verb '*ser*'. The other three words are nouns and the names of the cardinal points.

6 *tímido* – This adjective is used to describe personality. The other three words are adjectives that can be used to describe what a house/flat is like.

7 *joven* – This adjective is used to describe physical appearance. The other three words are intensifiers/adverbs.

8 *en* – This is a preposition. The other three words are articles: definite and indefinite.

B

nombre	casa	¿dónde?
Daniel	una casa moderna	en una ciudad
Carlos	una casa antigua	en la costa
Sandra	un piso grande	en la montaña
Cristina	un piso pequeño	en el campo

Video

Episode 8: ¿Cómo es tu casa o tu piso?

From the studio, the ¡TeleViva! team describe and show us where they live. Video worksheet 8 can be used in conjunction with this episode.

Answers to video worksheet (ActiveTeach)

A

1 Answers will vary and may include the six locations introduced in Unit 4 of the Pupil Book.

2 a) Vivo en una casa moderna.
   b) Vivo en un piso cómodo.
   c) Vivo en una casa antigua.

B

1 el campo, el centro, la ciudad, la montaña

2 a) Estela likes her house because it is very <u>pretty</u>.
   b) Marco likes his flat because he lives near his <u>cousins</u>.
   c) Aroa's grandparents live in a house in the <u>countryside</u>.
   d) Aroa's grandparents have a <u>dog</u> called Tino.

C

1 a) true
   b) false (He has a big family, not a small one.)
   c) true
   d) false (She has a cat called Mickey.)

2 antigua

3 Because her house is small.

Mi familia y mis amigos 4.4

D

1. Because she interrupts when he is interviewing Aroa (pupils may also say that she appears to be showing off).
2. Answers will vary.
3. Significantly more people have cats and dogs in the UK. Pupils may suggest that this is because many more people live in flats in Spain than in the UK.
4. Answers will vary.

E

Pupils will produce their own survey.

5. Reading Skills: El carnaval en familia

Mi familia y mis amigos 4.4

Pupil Book pages
Pages 84–85

Learning objectives
- Reading about the carnival in Cadiz
- Looking up new Spanish words in a dictionary

Programme of Study
GV3 Developing vocabulary
LC6 Reading comprehension

FCSE links
Unit 8: Celebrations (Carnival)

Key language
Review of language from Units 1–4

PLTS
R Reflective learners

Resources
Audio file:
66_Module4_Unit5_Ex4
Workbooks:
Cuaderno 1A & 1B, page 40
ActiveTeach:
p.084 Grammar worksheet

Starter 1

Aim

To practise reading for gist.

Provide a series of words from the spread on the board words (some cognates, near-cognates and non-cognates). Ask pupils to work in groups to decide how many words they would need to look up in the dictionary.

1 Empareja estas palabras con los dibujos. Utiliza el minidiccionario. Añade el/la/los/las. (L1)

Reading. Pupils match up the six words with the pictures, noting the correct definite article *el* or *la*. Before pupils start, read together through the Skills box on looking up nouns in the dictionary. Point out how to find or check the gender of nouns (most dictionaries use the notations *f* or *m*). Then ask pupils to find the gender and meaning of the following words in the mini-dictionary: (*el*) *castillo*, (*la*) *flor*, (*el*) *regalo*.

Answers

1 la mariposa	2 el desfile
3 los fuegos artificiales	4 los mariscos
5 el coro	6 la calle

2 Busca seis adjetivos. Escríbelos en inglés. Utiliza el minidiccionario si es necesario. (L1)

Reading. Read together through the Skills box on looking up adjectives in the dictionary. Ask pupils to find the meaning of the following words: *fuerte, real, largo* (strong, royal/real, long). Pupils unravel the wordsnake to find six adjectives, then translate them using the mini-dictionary if necessary.

Answers

loca/crazy, impresionante/impressive, estupendo/brilliant, ruidoso/noisy, disfrazados/in fancy dress, emocionante/exciting

3 Escribe los infinitivos de estos verbos y búscalos en el minidiccionario. (L1)

Reading. Read together through the Skills box on the listing of infinitives in the dictionary before asking pupils to find the meanings of the following in the mini-dictionary: *correr, abrir, gritar.*

Answers

andar (to walk)	durar (to last)
participar (to participate)	correr (to run)
salir (to go out)	llegar (to arrive)

Extension

Pupils list six of the nine new words they looked up and learn them at home. They can test each other in pairs on this vocabulary.

Starter 2

Aim

To review finding words in a Spanish dictionary.

Working in pairs, pupils make a list of what they already know about bilingual dictionaries. They define infinitives, nouns, adjectives and verbs and give three examples of each in Spanish.

4 Escucha y lee. (L4)

Listening. Pupils listen, following the texts on p. 85 of the Pupil Book at the same time.

Audioscript Track 66

– A mi abuela le gusta el Carnaval de Cádiz porque es emocionante y le gusta hacer disfraces para sus nietos.

– Me gusta porque el Carnaval dura diez días. Hay coros y grupos de personas que tocan instrumentos. Mi madrastra toca la guitarra y canta canciones.

© Pearson Education Ltd 2013. Copying permitted for purchasing institution only. This material is not copyright free.

Mi familia y mis amigos 4.5

– *Me gusta muchísimo el Carnaval de Cádiz porque me encanta el desfile y me gusta comer mariscos, sobre todo erizos.*

– *A mi padrastro no le gusta nada el Carnaval de Cádiz porque es ruidoso y caótico y no le gustan nada los fuegos artificiales.*

Reinforcement

Write the following phrases from the exercise 4 texts on the board, jumbling the order of the phrases in the right-hand column. With books closed, pupils match the Spanish to the English meanings.

me gusta comer mariscos	I like eating seafood
es ruidoso y caótico	it's noisy and chaotic
dura diez días	it lasts ten days
toca la guitarra	she plays the guitar
le gusta hacer disfraces	she likes making costumes
me encanta el desfile	I love the procession
los fuegos artificiales	the fireworks
hay coros	there are choirs

5 Lee los textos otra vez y, con tu compañero/a, busca las palabras en naranja en el minidiccionario. (L4)

Reading. Pupils read the exercise 4 texts again and, working in pairs, use the mini-dictionary to find the meanings of the words in orange.

Answers
nietos/grandchildren	madrastra/stepmother
erizos/sea urchins	caótico/chaotic

6 Lee los textos otra vez. Contesta a las preguntas. (L4)

Reading. Pupils read the exercise 4 text a third and final time and answer the questions that follow in English.

Answers
1 Ignacio's stepfather 2 Ana's grandmother
3 Sonia 4 Ignacio's stepfather
5 Mateo's stepmother

7 Lee el texto. Busca las palabras. (L4)

Reading. Pupils read the text about carnivals in Spain. They then list four words that they already knew, four new words that they worked out without a dictionary, and four words that they needed to look up in the mini-dictionary.

8 Escribe en inglés una descripción del Carnaval de Cádiz para un sitio web turístico. (L4)

Writing. Pupils write a description of the Cadiz carnival in English for a tourist website. They can use the text in exercise 7 as a basis for their information, and/or carry out further research of their own, if preferred.

Plenary

Allow pupils a few minutes to come up with five key points that summarise what they have learned about dictionary skills.

Workbook 1A, page 40

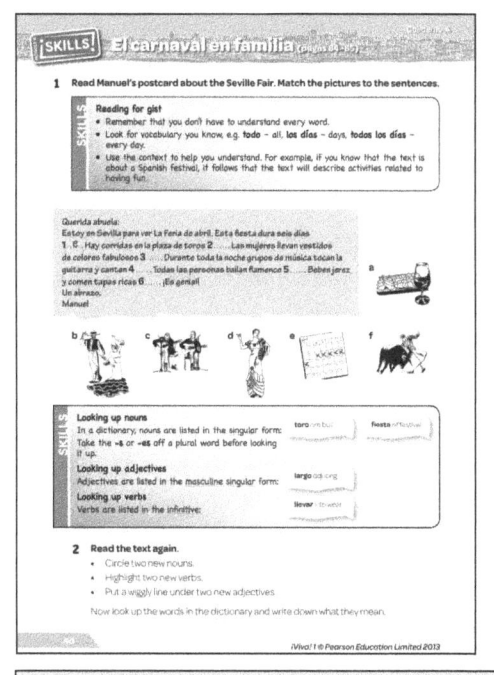

Answers
1 1 e 2 f 3 d 4 c 5 b 6 a
2 Answers might include the following:
   Nouns: feria, corridas, vestidos, jerez, tapas
   Verbs: durar, llevar, tocar, cantar
   Adjectives: fabulosos, ricas, genial

Mi familia y mis amigos 4.5

Workbook 1B, page 40

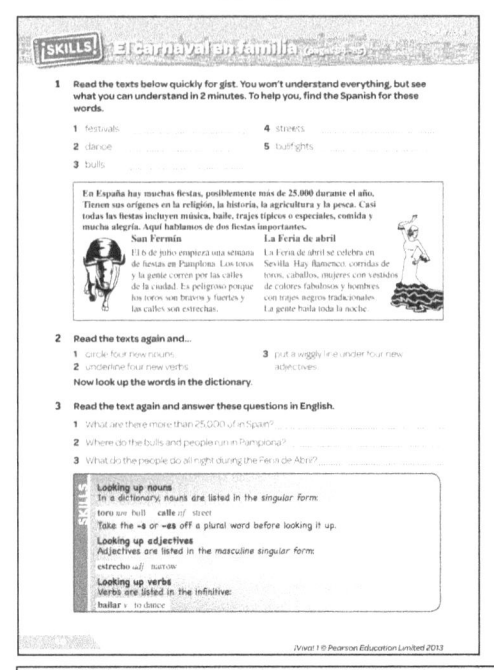

Answers

1 1 fiestas   2 baile   3 toros
   4 calles   5 corridas de toros

2 Answers might include the following:

   1 fiestas, orígenes, religión, agricultura, pesca, baile, trajes, comida, alegría, toros, calles, feria, flamenco, corridas, vestidos, gente

   2 incluyen, empieza, corren, baila

   3 típicos, peligroso, bravos, fuertes, estrechas, tradicionales

3 1 festivals   2 through the streets
   3 they dance

Worksheet 4.5 To be or not to be?

Answers

A

ser	estar
azul	en el norte
bastante pequeño	en la calle
caótico	en la costa oeste
de Perú	en mi pueblo
el dos de marzo	en Santiago de Chile
español	en una ciudad
grande y delgado	
muy interesante	
tranquilo y listo	
un poco calvo	

B

1 somos   2 están   3 son
4 está   5 soy   6 Estoy
7 es   8 Sois   9 estás
10 estamos

© Pearson Education Ltd 2013. Copying permitted for purchasing institution only. This material is not copyright free.

Writing Skills: Autorretrato

Mi familia y mis amigos 4.6

Pupil Book pages
Pages 86–87

Learning objectives
- Creating a video about yourself
- Planning and giving a presentation

Programme of Study
LC4 Expressing ideas (speaking)
LC5 Speaking coherently and confidently

Key language
Review of language from Units 1–4

PLTS
S Self-managers

Cross-curricular
English: Presentation skills

Resources
Audio files:
67_Module4_Unit6_Ex1
68_Module4_Unit6_Ex5
ActiveTeach:
Starter 2 Resource

Starter 1

Aim

To review phrases that pupils are likely to see in the unit.

Play a chain game around the class with the aim of creating the longest sentence possible in the context of describing yourself (appearance and personality; where you live; your family). The teacher starts the ball rolling: *¡Hola! Tengo trece años.* A pupil repeats what the teacher has said and adds another statement (e.g. *Tengo el pelo castaño y los ojos verdes*). Continue round the class adding more personal description statements. If someone can't remember the chain, makes a mistake, or can't add anything, he or she sits down and the chain starts again.

1 Escucha y lee. (L4)

Listening. Pupils listen and follow the text on p. 86 of the Pupil Book at the same time.

Audioscript Track 67

¡Hola! Me llamo Marcos y tengo doce años. Soy bastante alto. Tengo el pelo castaño y los ojos marrones. Soy simpático, bastante inteligente y además, muy guapo.

Vivo en La Paz, en un piso moderno. Me gusta mucho porque es muy grande. La Paz está en la montaña, en el oeste de Bolivia, y me encanta porque es una ciudad bonita. Me gusta mucho vivir aquí. Es genial.

En mi familia hay cuatro personas. Vivo con mi padre, mi madre y mi hermana Daniela. Mi madre se llama Laura. Es guapa y muy inteligente. Tiene cuarenta y tres años. Mi padre se llama Antonio. Tiene cincuenta y dos años. Es inteligente y también muy simpático.

Mi hermana tiene catorce años. Tiene los ojos marrones y el pelo largo. Es delgada, pero no es muy alta.

Mi perro se llama Ricky. Es negro y muy gordo, y come mucho. Es muy divertido.

¿Y tú? ¿Cómo eres?
Hasta luego.

2 Lee el texto del ejercicio 1 otra vez y pon estas fotos en el orden correcto. (L4)

Reading. Pupils reread the text and put the photos into the order they are mentioned in the text.

Answers
c, b, f, g, d, e, a

Extension

Pupils read aloud Marcos's letter round the class, a sentence at a time in Spanish, translating it into English.

3 Escribe tu descripción. Utiliza el texto del ejercicio 1 como modelo. (L4)

Writing. Pupils write an extended description of themselves using the text in exercise 1 as a model and covering the list of topics provided. Read together through the Skills box on including connectives, intensifiers, range of adjectives and opinions. Encourage pupils to work these features into their writing.

Starter 2

Aim

To practise writing notes on a cue card.

Ask pupils to reduce the following sentences (Starter 2 resource) to prompts that they could use on a cue card.

* *Soy bajo y delgado y tengo los ojos verdes y el pelo rubio.*
* *Vivo en Madrid en una casa moderna.*
* *Madrid está en el centro de España.*

Mi familia y mis amigos 4.6

> * Me gusta mucho vivir aquí porque es una ciudad bonita.
> * En mi familia hay cinco personas.
> * Vivo con mi madre, mi padre y mis dos hermanas.

4 Con tu compañero/a, mira esta tarjeta. ¿Qué va a decir esta persona? (L4)

Speaking. Before attempting this exercise, ask pupils to read through the Skills box on giving a presentation. In pairs, pupils read Lara's cue card, then decide what she wants to say. They take it in turns to create a sentence from Lara's speech notes and say it out loud.

5 Escucha y comprueba tus respuestas. (L4)

Listening. Pupils listen and check their answers to exercise 4.

Audioscript Track 68

¡Hola! Me llamo Lara y tengo trece años. Soy baja y delgada y tengo los ojos verdes y el pelo rubio. Soy simpática, bastante lista y soy muy generosa.

Vivo en Alicante en una casa moderna. Me gusta mucho porque es muy cómoda. Alicante está en la costa, en el sureste de España. Me gusta mucho vivir aquí porque es una ciudad bonita.

En mi familia hay tres personas. Vivo con mi madre y mi hermano. Mi madre se llama María. Es baja y muy delgada. No es muy severa. Tiene treinta y ocho años. Mi hermano se llama Tadeo. Tiene los ojos azules y el pelo rubio. Tiene quince años. Es inteligente y bastante simpático.

Mi gato se llama Ulises. Es blanco y muy pequeño. Tiene cinco años de edad.

6 Utiliza tu descripción del ejercicio 3 y haz tu tarjeta para una presentación. (L2)

Writing. Using their written description from exercise 3, pupils make a cue card to use for delivering a presentation. They can refer to the card in exercise 4 as a model.

7 Cuidado con la pronunciación. Con tu compañero/a, repite estas palabras. (L2)

Speaking. In pairs, pupils practise reading the words aloud, taking care to pronounce correctly the letters that are highlighted in red.

8 Haz tu presentación con tu compañero/a. Tu compañero/a escucha y comprueba: (L4)

Speaking. Ask pupils to read through the Skills box on how to rehearse for a presentation. Check that they understand the Spanish feedback comments. In pairs, one pupil reads his or her presentation, while the other fills in the feedback table, which rates pronunciation, volume, fluency and confidence.

9 Comenta el trabajo de tu compañero/a. (L2)

Writing. Pupils comment on their partner's work, awarding them a mark out of three for their efforts. *Más alto* is glossed for support.

Plenary

Pupils list three words that they have had difficulty pronouncing, and decide what their strategy will be to improve their pronunciation.

RESUMEN Y PREPÁRATE

Mi familia y mis amigos 4

Pupil Book pages
Pages 88–89

Resumen
Pupils use the checklist to review language covered in the module, working on it in pairs in class or on their own at home. Encourage them to follow up any areas of weakness they identify. There are Target Setting Sheets included in the Assessment Pack and an opportunity for pupils to record their own levels and targets on the Self-assessment pages in the Workbooks, p. 44. You can also use the *Resumen* checklist (available in the ActiveTeach) as an end-of-module plenary option.

Prepárate
These revision exercises can be used for assessment purposes or for pupils to practise before tackling the assessment tasks in the Assessment Pack.

Resources
Audio file:
69_Module4_Prep_Ex1
Workbooks:
Cuaderno 1A & 1B, pages 41 & 42
ActiveTeach:
p.088 *Resumen* checklist

1 Escucha y completa las frases. (L3)

Listening. Pupils listen to Laura talking about her family and complete the gap-fill sentences that follow in English.

Audioscript Track 69

Me llamo Laura. Vivo en una casa, en la costa.

En mi familia hay cinco personas: mi madre, mi padre, mi hermano, mi hermana y yo.

Mi padre tiene treinta y cinco años y mi madre tiene cuarenta años.

Mi hermano se llama Gabriel. Es muy alto y bastante inteligente. Mi hermana se llama Ana. Tiene los ojos azules… y el pelo largo y rubio.

Answers

1 Laura lives in a **house** by the seaside.
2 In her family, there are **five** people.
3 Her **mother** is 40 years old.
4 Her brother Gabriel is very **tall** and quite intelligent.
5 Her sister Ana has **blue** eyes.
6 Ana also has long, **blond** hair.

2 Con tu compañero/a, pregunta y contesta. (L3)

Speaking. In pairs, pupils ask and answer questions about their personal appearance, family and where they live. A sample exchange is given.

3 Mira los dibujos. ¿Quién es? ¿Nuria o Jorge? Escribe N o J. (L4)

Reading. Pupils read Nuria and Jorge's descriptions of themselves. They then look at the pictures and choose whether each one best describes Nuria or Jorge.

Answers
a N b J c J d N e N f J g J h N

4 ¿Qué dice Miranda? Escribe su descripción. (L3/4)

Writing. Pupils write a detailed description of Miranda, using the picture and vocabulary prompts in the cue card and the texts in exercise 3 as a model. A sample starter sentence is provided.

Mi familia y mis amigos 4

Workbook 1A, page 41

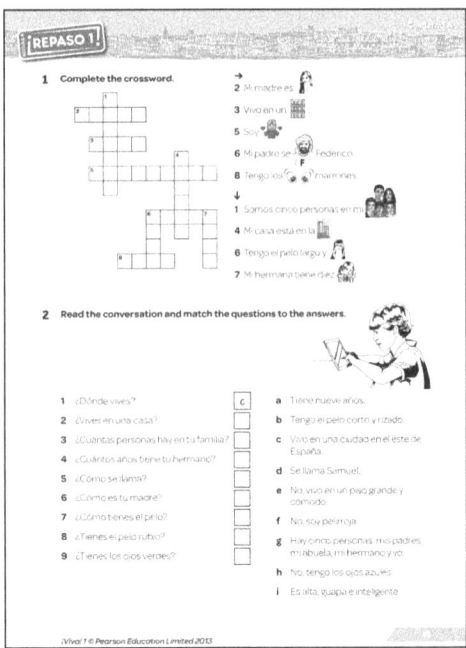

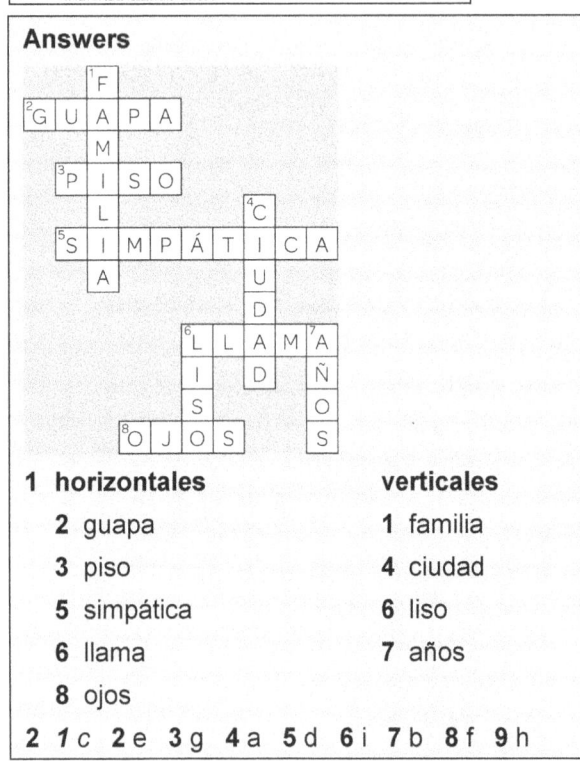

Answers

1 horizontales
- 2 guapa
- 3 piso
- 5 simpática
- 6 llama
- 8 ojos

verticales
- 1 familia
- 4 ciudad
- 6 liso
- 7 años

2 1 c 2 e 3 g 4 a 5 d 6 i 7 b 8 f 9 h

Workbook 1A, page 42

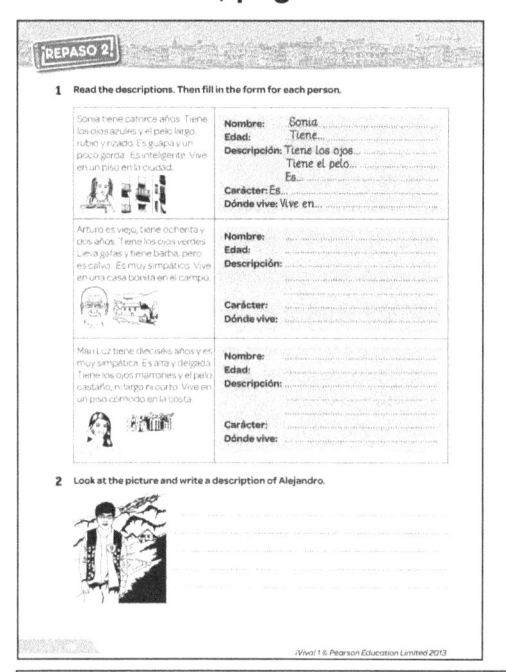

Answers

1

Nombre:	Sonia
Edad:	Tiene 14 años.
Descripción:	Tiene los ojos azules. Tiene el pelo largo, rubio y rizado. Es guapa y un poco gorda.
Carácter:	Es inteligente.
Dónde vive:	Vive en un piso en la ciudad.
Nombre:	Arturo
Edad:	Tiene 82 años.
Descripción:	Tiene los ojos verdes. Lleva gafas. Tiene barba. Es calvo.
Carácter:	Es (muy) simpático.
Dónde vive:	Vive en una casa (bonita) en el campo.
Nombre:	Mari Luz
Edad:	Tiene 16 años.
Descripción:	Es alta y delgada. Tiene los ojos marrones. Tiene el pelo castaño, ni largo ni corto.
Carácter:	Es (muy) simpática.
Dónde vive:	Vive en un piso (cómodo) en la costa.

2 Example answer: Alejandro tiene 9 años. Es bajo y delgado. Tiene los ojos marrones y lleva gafas. Tiene el pelo negro, liso y corto. Es simpático. Vive en una casa pequeña en las montañas.

Mi familia y mis amigos 4

Workbook 1B, page 41

Answers

1.
   1. Mi abuela tiene setenta años.
   2. Hay cuatro personas en mi familia.
   3. Mi hermano se llama Roberto.
   4. Vivo en una casa.
   5. Tengo los ojos azules.
   6. Mi padre es bastante alto.
   7. Mi madre tiene el pelo largo y liso.
   8. Mi casa está en la ciudad.

2. Own answers

Workbook 1B, page 42

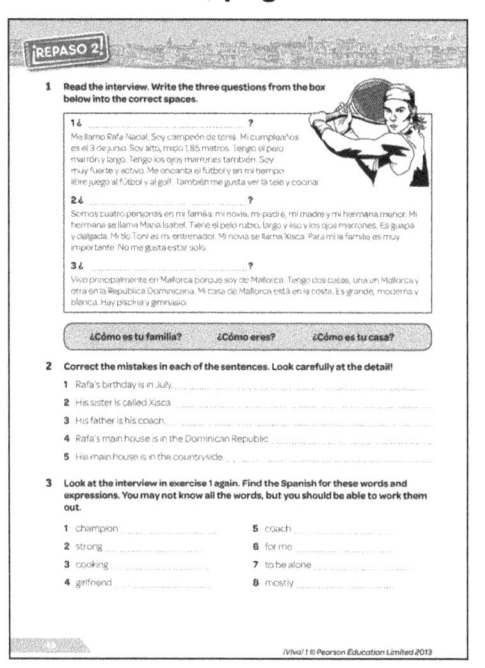

Answers

1.
   1. ¿Cómo eres?
   2. ¿Cómo es tu familia?
   3. ¿Cómo es tu casa?

2.
   1. Rafa's birthday is in June.
   2. His sister is called María Isabel./His girlfriend is called Xisca.
   3. His uncle is his coach.
   4. Rafa's main house is in Mallorca./ Rafa's other house is in the Dominican Republic.
   5. His main house is on the coast.

3.
   1. campeón 2. fuerte 3. cocinar
   4. novia 5. entrenador 6. para mí
   7. estar solo 8. principalmente

¡GRAMÁTICA!

Mi familia y mis amigos 4

Pupil Book pages	Grammar topics	Resources
Pages 90–91	• possessive adjectives (*mi/tu/su* and *mis/tus/sus*)	Workbooks: Cuaderno 1A & 1B, page 43
The *Gramática* section provides a more detailed summary of the key grammar covered in the module, along with further exercises to practise these points.	• adjectives (agreement with nouns)	ActiveTeach:
	• irregular verbs (*tener, ser*)	p.090 Grammar presentation
	• *ser* and *estar*	p.090 Grammar presentation
		p.091 Grammar presentation
		p.091 Grammar presentation
		p.091 Grammar presentation

Possessive adjectives

1 Choose the correct possessive adjective.

Pupils complete the sentences by choosing from the two possessive adjective options each time.

Answers		
1 Mis	2 Mi	3 Mi
4 Mi	5 mis	

2 Rewrite the text in exercise 1 in the he/she form.

Pupils rewrite the sentences in exercise 1, replacing the *mi, mis* possessive adjectives with *su* or *sus*.

Answers
1 *Sus padres son* muy famosos.
2 *Su* madre se llama Valeria. Tiene cuarenta y ocho años.
3 *Su* padre se llama Toni y tiene cincuenta años.
4 *Su* hermana se llama Vera y (5) **sus** hermanastros se llaman Kevin y Kelly.

Adjectives

3 Describe this family of criminals. Make sure your adjectives match the person you are talking about.

Pupils use the picture prompts to write sentences about the criminal family members, paying attention to the agreement of adjectives.

Answers (may vary)
– *Víctor el Violento tiene el pelo rubio y* los ojos azules. Es feo y muy viejo.
– *Fabiana la Fea es bastante fea y vieja. Es pelirroja y tiene los ojos verdes.*
– *Miguel el Malo y Tadeo el Terrible son jóvenes. Tienen el pelo rubio y los ojos marrones.*

Irregular verbs

4 Unjumble these sentences. Then translate them into English.

Pupils write out the jumbled sentences in the correct order, paying attention to the form of *tener* they need to use each time. They then translate the sentences into English.

Answers
1 **Tengo los ojos azules.** I have blue eyes.
2 **¿Tienes hermanos?** Do you have any brothers (and sisters)?
3 **Tiene tres hermanas.** He/She has three sisters.
4 **¿Tenéis un perro?** Do you have a dog?/Have you got a dog?
5 **Mis hermanas tienen los ojos marrones.** My sisters have brown eyes.
6 **Mi hermano y yo tenemos el pelo rubio.** My brother and I have blond hair.

5 Write these sentences in Spanish.

Using the word and picture prompts, pupils write out the sentences in Spanish, paying particular attention to using the correct form of *tener*.

Answers
1 (Ella) Tiene el pelo rubio.
2 Tenemos los ojos azules.
3 Tengo el pelo largo.
4 (Él) Tiene una hermanastra.
5 Mis hermanos tienen los ojos grises.
6 Tienes tres hermanos.

Mi familia y mis amigos 4

6 Unjumble the forms of *ser* and write a sentence using each one. Then translate the sentences into English.

Pupils work out the verb anagrams and write sentences using all the forms of *ser* in Spanish. They then translate the sentences into English.

Answers		
1 eres	2 sois	3 soy
4 son	5 es	6 somos

Ser and estar

7 Choose the correct verb and copy out the sentences.

Pupils complete the sentences by choosing from the forms of *ser* and *estar* options each time.

Answers
1 ¿Cómo **es** tu casa o tu piso?
2 **Es** muy cómodo.
3 ¿Dónde **está**?
4 **Está** en el norte de España, en la montaña.

Workbook 1A, page 43

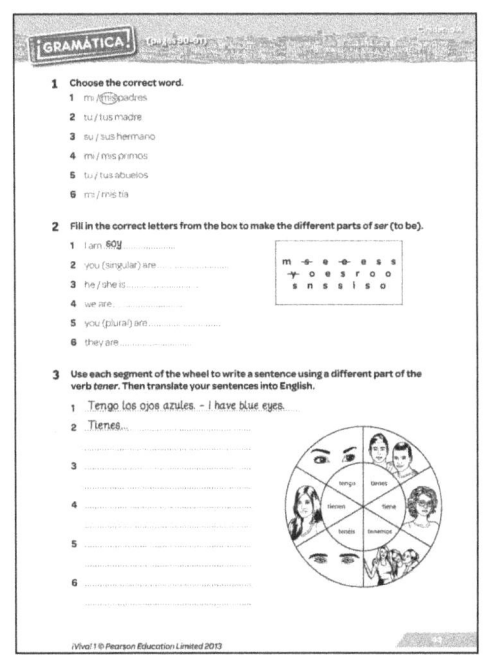

Answers
1 1 mis   2 tu   3 su   4 mis
   5 tus   6 mi
2 1 soy   2 eres   3 es   4 somos
   5 sois   6 son

3 Example answers:
1 *Tengo* los ojos azules. I have blue eyes
2 *Tienes* los ojos marrones. You have brown eyes.
3 Tiene el pelo largo y liso. He/She has long, straight hair,
4 Tenemos el pelo corto y rizado. We have short, curly hair.
5 Tenéis dos hermanos. You have two brothers.
6 Tienen tres hermanas. They have three sisters.

Workbook 1B, page 43

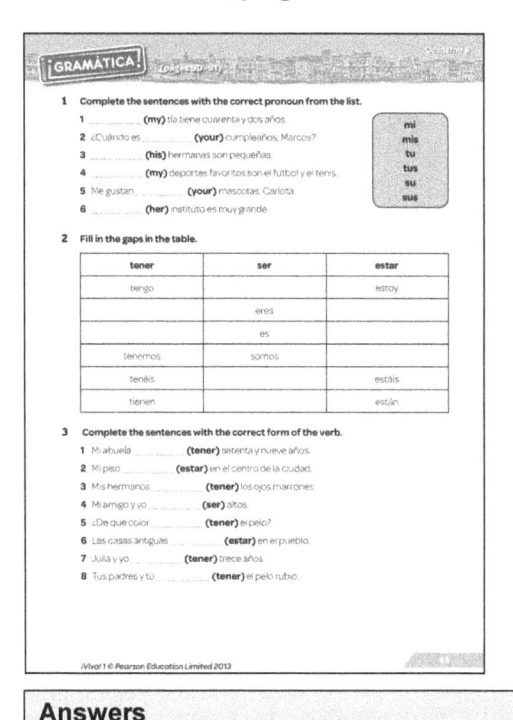

Answers
1 1 Mi   2 tu   3 Sus
   4 Mis   5 tus   6 Su
2 tienes, tiene, soy, sois, son, estás, está, estamos
3 1 tiene   2 está   3 tienen   4 somos
   5 tienes 6 están 7 tenemos 8 tienen

© Pearson Education Ltd 2013. Copying permitted for purchasing institution only. This material is not copyright free.

¡PROYECTO! Las Meninas — Mi familia y mis amigos 4

Pupil Book pages
Pages 94–95

Learning objectives
- Describing a painting
- Recording an audio or video guide to a painting

Programme of Study
GV3 Developing vocabulary to give opinions and take part in discussions
LC5 Speaking coherently and confidently

PLTS
E Effective participators

Cross-curricular
Art and Design: history of art

Resources
Audio file:
70_Module4_ZP_Ex1
ActiveTeach:
Starter 2 resource

Starter 1

Aim

To review adjectives.

Give pupils three minutes to list as many Spanish adjectives as they can remember. Check the answers, asking for the English translations.

On the board, write up *rojo, un cuaderno, una mesa, unos lápices, unas gafas*. Ask the class the Spanish for 'a red exercise book', 'a red table', 'red pencils' and 'red glasses' to review agreement and position of adjectives.

1 Mira el cuadro. Escucha y lee el texto. (L4)

Listening. Read together through the *Zona Cultura* box before starting this exercise. Pupils then study the painting of *Las Meninas* by Diego Velázquez and listen, following the text on p. 94 of the Pupil Book at the same time. *El chico/la chica* are glossed for support.

Audioscript Track 70

Este cuadro se llama 'Las Meninas' y el pintor se llama Diego Velázquez.

En el cuadro hay once personas. En el centro está la Infanta Margarita. Es bastante pequeña. Tiene el pelo largo y rubio.

Al lado de la Infanta Margarita están 'las Meninas'. Se llaman María e Isabel.

A la izquierda está el pintor, Diego Velázquez. Es bastante alto y tiene el pelo castaño. A la derecha hay un chico y un perro.

Los colores principales en el cuadro son el negro, el beige, el gris y el marrón.

2 Lee el texto otra vez. Busca el equivalente de estas palabras en español. (L4)

Reading. Pupils find in the exercise 1 text the Spanish for the English phrases given.

Answers
1 Este cuadro se llama
2 el pintor se llama
3 En el centro
4 A la izquierda
5 A la derecha
6 Los colores principales en el cuadro son

Starter 2

Aim

To review language for expressing opinions.

Write the following on the board, jumbling up the order of the right-hand column (Starter 2 resource). Allow three minutes for pupils to match the sentence halves.

1	Me gusta	a	el cuadro.
2	No me gusta el cuadro	b	porque es feo.
3	Me encantan	c	los colores.
4	Prefiero el cuadro	d	de Eleazar.
5	En mi	e	opinión, es muy bonito.
6	Para mí,	f	no es interesante.
7	Mi cuadro favorito es	g	Las Meninas.

Check pupils' answers, asking them to explain their rationale, then translate the sentences into English.

3 Mira este cuadro de 'Las Meninas' de Eleazar. Con tu compañero/a, pregunta y contesta. (L4)

Speaking. Pupils look at Spanish painter Eleazar's version of *Las Meninas* and ask each other to identify the location of the people or animals listed (a–e). A sample exchange is supplied and *aquí* is glossed for support. Draw pupils' attention to the fact that *está* (it is) changes to *están* (they are) when the noun being described is plural.

© Pearson Education Ltd 2013. Copying permitted for purchasing institution only. This material is not copyright free.

Mi familia y mis amigos 4

4 Lee los textos. Completa las frases en inglés. (L4)

Reading. Pupils read the opinions of Tomás and Emanuela on the paintings of Velázquez and Eleazar, then complete the gap-fill sentences that summarise them in English.

Answers
1 Velázquez
2 Eleazar
3 old, interesting
4 colours, dog
5 Princess, the painter on the left
6 ugly, old, boring

5 Haz un sondeo en tu clase. Pregunta a seis personas. (L4)

Speaking. Pupils do a mini class survey to find out six pupils' opinions of the paintings of Velázquez and Eleazar. Sample questions and answers are given for support. Encourage pupils to use negatives to make their answers more interesting.

6 Elige un cuadro (o pinta una obra maestra tú mismo). Escribe una audioguía o una videoguía y luego grábala. (L4)

Writing. Pupils research a painting of their own choice (or you could suggest *Las Meninas* by Antonio Mingote, *La familia de Juan Bautista* by Juan Bautista Martínez del Mazo or *Las Meninas* by Salvador Dalí). They then write a description of the painting, which they can later record in the form of an audio guide. A list of features to be included and sentence starters are supplied.

Plenary
Ask pupils to tell the class which picture they chose to research in exercise 6 and to say one thing about it in Spanish using an opinion phrase.

¡TE TOCA A TI!

Mi familia y mis amigos 4

Pupil Book pages
Pages 126–127

Self-access reading and writing

A Reinforcement

1 Lee las frases. Escribe las dos letras correctas para cada frase. (L2)

Reading. Pupils read the sentences and choose two letters to describe each one using the visual prompts provided.

Answers
1 a, e **2** b, d **3** a, f **4** b, h **5** b, c **6** a, g

2 Escribe estas frases. Utiliza las frases del ejercicio 1 como modelo. (L3)

Writing. Pupils write out six sentences, supplying the Spanish for the picture prompts and using the sentences in exercise 1 as a framework. The Tip box reminds pupils to check adjectival agreement.

Answers
1 *Vivo en una casa antigua. Está en el campo.*
2 Vivo en un piso bonito. Está en el desierto.
3 Vivo en una casa cómoda. Está en un pueblo.
4 Vivo en un piso grande. Está en la ciudad.
5 Vivo en una casa pequeña. Está en la costa.
6 Vivo en un piso moderno. Está en la montaña.

3 Lee el blog y contesta a las preguntas en inglés. (L3)

Reading. Pupils read Rafa's blog about his family and answer the questions in English.

Answers
1 5
2 5 years old
3 Gabriel
4 Tall and funny and quite intelligent.
5 She has blue eyes and is very pretty.

B Extension

1 Rompecabezas. Lee las frases. Copia y completa la tabla con la información del recuadro. (L3)

Reading. Pupils read the sentences and, using logic, fill in the grid using information from the blue box provided.

Answers

nombre	edad	madre	padre
Mateo	11	Dolores	Carlos
Antonio	12	Carmen	*Pepe*
Carolina	14	María	Jorge
Enrique	13	Laura	Juan

2 Lee el mensaje de Miguel. Escribe el nombre correcto para cada dibujo. (L4)

Reading. Pupils read Miguel's message, then identify which members of his family are being depicted in the pictures that follow.

Answers		
1 *David*	**2** Miguel	**3** Lara
4 Javi	**5** Adela	

3 Describe a tu familia. Utiliza el texto del ejercicio 2 como modelo. (L4)

Writing. Pupils write a few short paragraphs about their own family, adapting Miguel's text in exercise 2. A list of details to include is given. Encourage pupils to include connectives and intensifiers in their writing.

© Pearson Education Ltd 2013. Copying permitted for purchasing institution only. This material is not copyright free.

MODULE 5: Mi ciudad

Unit & Learning objectives	PoS references	Key language	Grammar and other language features
1 ¿Qué hay en tu ciudad? (pp. 98–99) Describing your town or village Using 'a', 'some' and 'many' in Spanish	**GV2** Grammatical structures (*un/una*, *unos/unas* and *muchos/muchas*) **LC1** Listening and responding **LC4** Expressing ideas (writing)	¿Qué hay en tu pueblo o tu ciudad? Hay… un castillo un mercado un estadio un centro comercial un polideportivo una piscina una universidad unos museos unas plazas muchos parques muchos restaurantes muchas tiendas No hay museo. No hay nada.	**G** *un/una*, *unos/unas* and *muchos/muchas*
2 ¿Qué haces en la ciudad? (pp. 100–101) Telling the time Using the verb *ir* (to go)	**GV2** Grammatical structures (the verb *ir*, *a + el*) **LC1** Listening and responding **LC5** Speaking coherently and confidently	¿Qué hora es? Es la una. Son… las dos, las tres las cuatro, las cinco las seis, las siete las ocho, las nueve las diez, las once las doce y cinco, y diez, y cuarto, y veinte, y veinticinco, y media menos veinticinco, menos veinte, menos cuarto, menos diez, menos cinco ¿Qué haces en la ciudad? Salgo con mis amigos. Voy… al cine al parque a la cafetería a la bolera a la playa de paseo con mi familia de compras No hago nada.	**G** *ir* – to go (present tense) – pronunciation of *z* – contraction of *a* and *el* to form *al*

© Pearson Education Ltd 2013. Copying permitted for purchasing institution only. This material is not copyright free.

Mi ciudad 5

3 En la cafetería (pp. 102–103) Ordering in a café Using the verb *querer* (to want)	**GV2** Grammatical structures (the verb *querer*) **LC3** Conversation	*una bebida* *un café* *un té* *una Fanta limón* *un batido de chocolate* *un batido de fresa* *una Coca-Cola* *una granizada de limón* *una ración (de)…* *gambas* *jamón* *calamares* *croquetas* *patatas bravas* *tortilla* *pan con tomate* *¿Qué quieren?* *Yo quiero…* *¿Algo más?* *No, nada más.* *¿Y de beber?* *¿Cuánto es por favor?* *Son… euros …*	**G** stem-changing verb *querer*
4 ¿Qué vas a hacer? (pp. 104–105) Saying what you are going to do at the weekend Using the near future tense	**GV1** Tenses (the near future tense) **LC3** Conversation **LC6** Translation into English	*¿Qué vas a hacer este fin de semana?* *el sábado por la mañana* *el viernes por la tarde* *(No) Voy a…* *jugar a los videojuegos* *ir de compras* *ir de paseo* *ir al parque* *bailar* *salir con mis amigos* *navegar por Internet* *ver la televisión* *hacer los deberes* *montar en bici* *jugar al fútbol* *chatear*	**G** the near future tense (*voy, vas, va*, etc. + infinitive) – pronunciation of *b* and *v* – using sequencers *primero, luego, finalmente*
5 ¿Te gusta tu ciudad? (pp. 106–107) Understanding people describing their town Listening for detail	**GV3** Opinions and discussions **LC1** Listening and responding	Review of language in Units 1–4	– developing listening skills – listening for small words, positive and negative opinions using adjectives, distractors, distinguishing between two different voices

© Pearson Education Ltd 2013. Copying permitted for purchasing institution only. This material is not copyright free.

Mi ciudad 5

6 Mi vida en La Habana (pp. 108–109) Writing a blog about your town and activities Using two tenses together	**GV4** Accuracy (spelling, grammar) **LC4** Expressing ideas (writing) **LC8** Writing creatively	Review of language from Units 1–4	– developing writing skills – using two tenses, connectives, intensifiers, and time expressions – checking written work
Resumen y Prepárate (pp. 110–111) Pupils' checklist and practice exercises			
Gramática (pp. 112–113) Detailed grammar summary and practice exercises			**G** 'a' (*un/una*), 'some' (*unos/unas*) and 'many' (*muchos/muchas*) **G** the verb *ir* (to go) **G** the near future tense **G** using two tenses together
Zona Proyecto I: ¡Pasaporte fiesta! (pp. 116–117) Learning about Spanish festivals Creating a brochure about a fiesta	**LC6** Reading comprehension **LC7** Literary texts		
Zona Proyecto II: El Día de los Muertos (pp. 118–119) Learning about *el Día de los Muertos* Making a skull mask or paper flowers	**LC1** Listening and responding **LC6** Reading comprehension		
Te toca a ti (pp. 128–129) Self-access reading and writing at two levels			

1 ¿Qué hay en tu ciudad?

Mi ciudad 5.1

Pupil Book pages
Pages 96–99

Learning objectives
- Describing your town or village
- Using 'a', 'some' and 'many' in Spanish

Programme of Study
GV2 Grammatical structures (*un/una, unos/unas* and *muchos/muchas*)
LC1 Listening and responding
LC4 Expressing ideas (writing)

FCSE links
Unit 7: Local area and environment (Facilities, Local area)

Grammar
- *un/una, unos/unas* and *muchos/muchas*

Key language
¿Qué hay en tu pueblo o tu ciudad?
Hay…
un castillo
un mercado
un estadio
un centro comercial
un polideportivo
una piscina
una universidad
unos museos
unas plazas
muchos parques
muchos restaurantes
muchas tiendas
No hay museo.
No hay nada.

PLTS
T Team workers

Cross-curricular
Geography: physical characteristics of Spanish-speaking countries

Resources
Audio files:
71_Module5_Unit1_Ex1
72_Module5_Unit1_Ex3
73_Module5_Unit1_Ex6
Workbooks:
Cuaderno 1A & 1B, page 47
ActiveTeach:
p.098 Flashcards
p.098 Grammar presentation
ActiveLearn:
Listening A, Listening B
Reading A, Reading B
Grammar, Vocabulary

Module 5 Quiz (pp. 96–97)

Answers
1 a, c, d **2** a, d, e **3** c **4** b **5** d
6 a Bolivia **b** Venezuela **c** Uruguay
   d Argentina **e** Perú

Starter 1

Aim
To review singular and plural indefinite articles for places in town.

Ask pupils to use the correct indefinite articles for the following list of words:

estadio, parques, centro comercial, restaurantes, castillo, museos, tiendas, universidad, mercado, polideportivo, piscina, plazas

Prompt with *En mi pueblo hay* (beep) *estadio*. Ask pupils to supply the complete sentence. Once you have exhausted the entire list using positive prompts, repeat the exercise, asking pupils to supply the complete negative sentence, e.g. *En mi pueblo no hay estadio*.

1 Escucha y escribe la letra correcta. (1–12) (L2)

Listening. Pupils listen to the statements and look at the pictures. They note the correct letter of the picture for each statement.

Audioscript Track 71

– *¿Qué hay en tu pueblo o tu ciudad? ¿Qué hay en Oviedo?*
1 – *Hay un estadio.*
2 – *Hay muchos parques.*
3 – *Hay un centro comercial.*
4 – *Hay muchos restaurantes.*
5 – *Hay un castillo.*
6 – *Hay unos museos.*
7 – *Hay muchas tiendas.*
8 – *Hay una universidad.*
9 – *Hay un mercado.*
10 – *Hay un polideportivo.*
11 – *Hay una piscina.*
12 – *Hay unas plazas.*

Answers
1 c **2** j **3** d **4** k **5** a **6** h **7** l **8** g **9** b
10 e **11** f **12** i

Reinforcement
Working in pairs, pupils take turns to draw a sketch of a building or place in town for their partner to name.

© Pearson Education Ltd 2013. Copying permitted for purchasing institution only. This material is not copyright free.

Mi ciudad 5.1

Gramática

Use the *Gramática* box to teach the Spanish words for 'a/an' (*un/una*), 'some' (*unos/unas*) and 'many' (*muchos/muchas*), which all change according to the gender of the noun and whether it is singular or plural. There is more information and further practice on Pupil Book p. 112.

2 Juego de memoria. Con tu compañero/a, cierra el libro. ¿Qué hay en Oviedo? (L2)

Speaking. In pairs and with books closed, pupils play a memory game. Using the places in town vocabulary from exercise 1, one pupil starts off with, e.g. *Hay un castillo*. The other repeats what they say and adds another place in town: *Hay un castillo y muchas tiendas…* and so on, as the pair create an increasingly long list of places to remember in the correct sequence.

3 ¿Qué hay? ¿Qué no hay? Escucha y apunta los datos en inglés. (1–5) (L3)

Listening. Pupils listen to the five conversations and make notes in English of the facilities that each town has or doesn't have. Make pupils aware that the indefinite article is omitted after *hay* in negative phrases, whereas in English, *No hay museo* would translate 'There isn't **a** museum'.

Audioscript Track 72

1 – ¿Qué hay en tu pueblo o tu ciudad?
– A ver… hay unas plazas, pero no hay piscina.

2 – ¿Qué hay en tu pueblo o tu ciudad?
– Bueno… hay un centro comercial, pero no hay universidad.

3 – ¿Qué hay en tu pueblo o tu ciudad?
– Hay un mercado, pero no hay castillo.

4 – ¿Qué hay en tu pueblo o tu ciudad?
– Hay un estadio muy grande, pero no hay museo.

5 – ¿Qué hay en tu pueblo o tu ciudad?
– Hay muchas tiendas, pero no hay polideportivo.

Answers

1 some squares, no swimming pool
2 shopping centre, no university
3 market, no castle
4 stadium, no museum
5 shops, no sports centre

Starter 2

Aim

To practise transcribing a short dictation.

Dictate the following short sentences to the class and ask pupils to transcribe them. To differentiate, more able pupils can write out the complete sentence, while others write down the place in town.

Hay una piscina.
Hay muchas tiendas.
Hay un estadio.
Hay un centro comercial.
Hay muchos parques.

4 Con tu compañero/a, describe una ciudad. Tu compañero/a dice la letra correcta. (L3)

Speaking. In pairs, pupils take it in turns to describe the facilities in four imaginary towns using the picture prompts supplied. The other person has to guess which town it is. A framework is supplied for support.

5 Lee los textos. Copia y completa la tabla en inglés. (L4)

Reading. Pupils copy the table. They read three people's descriptions of their home towns and fill in the table, noting: where each person lives, what facilities the town has or doesn't have, whether the person likes living there or not and why. Some vocabulary is glossed for support.

Answers			
name	Adrián	Martina	David
town	Santander	Ronda	Almagro
there is…	castle, stadium, parks	monuments, museums	main square
there isn't…		shopping centre, museum	stadium
opinion	likes it	likes it a lot	doesn't like it
reason	on coast, nice city	old, impressive	boring, too small

© Pearson Education Ltd 2013. Copying permitted for purchasing institution only. This material is not copyright free.

Mi ciudad 5.1

Extension

Pupils identify in the exercise 5 texts all instances of connectives, intensifiers, opinions and adjectives, and translate them into English.

6 Escucha la canción y elige la palabra correcta. Luego canta. (L4)

Listening. Pupils listen to the song while following the text. They choose the correct word from two options. *El sitio* is glossed for support. Play the song again to check pupils' answers and encourage them to sing along.

Audioscript Track 73

En el barrio
donde vivo
no hay museo,
no hay castillo.

Es muy bonito
y tranquilo.
Me gusta mucho.
Es mi barrio.

En la gran ciudad
donde vivo,
hay un mercado
y un estadio.

Hay un museo
muy antiguo.
Es mi sitio
favorito.

Answers

1 vivo	2 bonito	3 barrio
4 mercado	5 antiguo	6 favorito

7 Describe tu pueblo o tu ciudad. (L4)

Writing. Pupils write a description of their own home village or town, to include their own opinions and the reasons for them. A writing framework is provided.

Plenary

Split the class into two teams. Have a prepared list of *hay/no hay* + places in town phrases from the unit on the board in Spanish. Teams nominate one person each time to play 'Splat' for them. Ask two pupils to come to the front, you say a phrase in English and the pupils 'splat' the equivalent phrase in Spanish with their hands.

Award two points for the person who splats correctly first. The team with the most points wins.

Workbook 1A, page 47

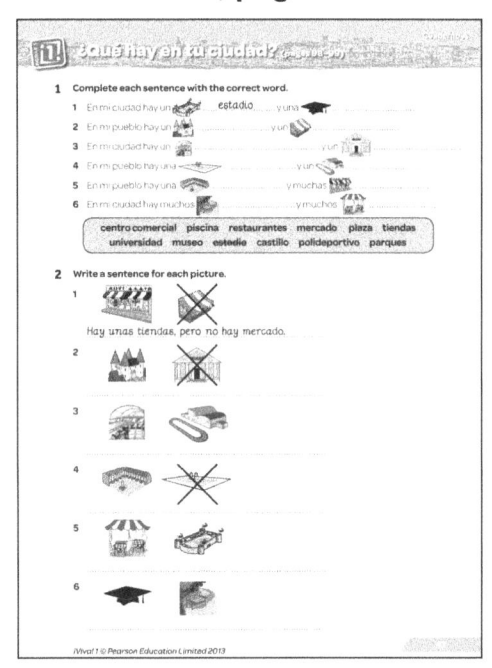

Answers

1
1. estadio, universidad
2. castillo, mercado
3. centro comercial, museo
4. piscina, polideportivo
5. plaza, tiendas
6. parques, restaurantes

2
1. Hay unas tiendas, no hay mercado.
2. Hay un castillo y un museo.
3. Hay un centro comercial y un polideportivo.
4. Hay una plaza, no hay piscina.
5. Hay (muchos) restaurantes y un estadio.
6. Hay una universidad y (muchos) parques.

© Pearson Education Ltd 2013. Copying permitted for purchasing institution only. This material is not copyright free.

Mi ciudad 5.1

Workbook 1B, page 47

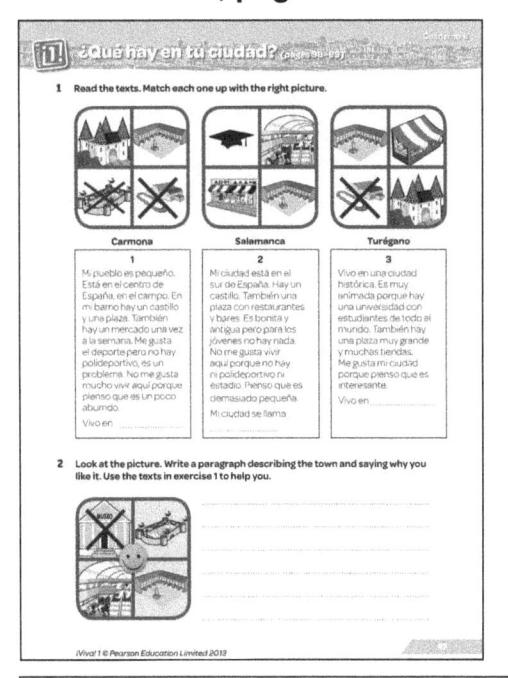

Answers

1 1 Turégano 2 Carmona 3 Salamanca

2 Own answers

¿Qué haces en la ciudad?

Mi ciudad 5.2

Pupil Book pages
Pages 100–101

Learning objectives
- Telling the time
- Using the verb *ir* (to go)

Programme of Study
GV2 Grammatical structures (the verb *ir*, *a + el*)
LC1 Listening and responding
LC5 Speaking coherently and confidently

FCSE links
Unit 2: Education and future plans (Time)
Unit 4: Leisure (Going out)
Unit 7: Local area and environment (Activities)

Grammar
- *ir* – to go (present tense)

Key language
¿Qué hora es?
Es la una.
Son…
las dos
las tres
las cuatro
las cinco
las seis
las siete
las ocho
las nueve
las diez
las once
las doce
y cinco, y diez, y cuarto
y veinte, y veinticinco, y media
menos veinticinco, menos veinte,
menos cuarto, menos diez,
menos cinco
¿Qué haces en la ciudad?
Salgo con mis amigos.
Voy…
al cine
al parque
a la cafetería
a la bolera
a la playa
de paseo con mi familia
de compras
No hago nada.

PLTS
I Independent enquirers

Resources
Audio files:
74_Module5_Unit2_Ex2
75_Module5_Unit2_Ex3
76_Module5_Unit2_Ex5
Workbooks:
Cuaderno 1A & 1B, page 48
ActiveTeach:
p.100 Flashcards
p.101 Video 9
p.101 Video 9 transcript
p.101 Video worksheet 9
p.101 Flashcards
p.101 Grammar presentation
p.101 Grammar worksheet
ActiveLearn:
Listening A, Listening B
Reading A, Reading B
Grammar, Vocabulary

Starter 1

Aim

To review numbers 0–30.

Give pupils two minutes to create three 'Strip' bingo cards, each with six squares in a row, for three games of quick-fire bingo. Instruct pupils to fill in each card in a random order choosing six numbers from 1–15 and 16–30. Starting with the first bingo card, call out numbers, which pupils cross out on their strip. When a pupil has marked off their entire row, he or she calls out *¡Número!*. The pupil then reads those six numbers out loud. He or she can try being the caller for the second bingo card.

1 Empareja las frases con los dibujos. (L2)

Reading. Pupils read the five statements and match them with the pictures, noting the letter of the correct clock. Point out to pupils that *Es la (una)…* is used for any times beginning with one o'clock, while for all other times, *Son las (dos/tres/…*, etc.) is used.

Answers
1 a 2 c 3 e 4 d 5 b

2 Escucha y comprueba tus respuestas. (L2)

Listening. Pupils listen and check their answers to exercise 1.

Audioscript Track 74

1 – *Son las nueve.*
2 – *Son las nueve y cuarto.*
3 – *Son las nueve y media.*
4 – *Son las diez menos cuarto.*
5 – *Son las diez.*

3 Escucha. ¿Qué hora es? Escribe la letra correcta. (1–9) (L2)

Listening. Pupils listen to nine conversations and identify the time given in each, noting the letter of the correct watch.

© Pearson Education Ltd 2013. Copying permitted for purchasing institution only. This material is not copyright free.

Mi ciudad 5.2

Audioscript Track 75

1 – ¿Qué hora es?
 – Son las tres y diez.
2 – ¿Qué hora es?
 – Son las siete y cinco.
3 – ¿Qué hora es?
 – Es la una y veinticinco.
4 – ¿Qué hora es?
 – Son las cuatro y veinte.
5 – ¿Qué hora es?
 – Son las once menos cinco.
6 – ¿Qué hora es?
 – Son las diez menos diez.
7 – ¿Qué hora es?
 – Son las nueve menos veinte.
8 – ¿Qué hora es?
 – Son las seis menos veinticinco.
9 – ¿Qué hora es?
 – Son las tres menos veinte

Answers
1 e 2 a 3 d 4 b 5 h 6 g 7 f 8 c 9 i

Extension
Pupils could write out the times in full sentences for each clock.

4 Con tu compañero/a, juega a las cuatro en raya. (L2)

Speaking. In pairs, pupils play 'Four in a row', using the grid of sixteen digital clock faces. They take it in turns to ask each other what the time is in Spanish, which means that every other question, a pupil gets the opportunity to 'win' a box by correctly stating the time in it. The object of the game is to win four boxes in a row diagonally, horizontally or vertically. The *Pronunciación* box advises pupils to look at p. 8 for a reminder on how to pronounce the letter z.

Starter 2

Aim

To introduce the full paradigm of *ir*.

Present the forms of the verb *ir* on the board in a random order. Allow pupils three minutes to conjugate it, guessing the correct order of all the verb forms based on their knowledge of other verb paradigms.

Pupils then write a couple of sentences in Spanish with two of the verb forms and translate them into English.

Alternative starter 2:

Use ActiveTeach p.100 Flashcards to review and practice telling the time.

5 Escucha y escribe la letra correcta. (1–9) (L2)

Listening. Pupils listen to the nine exchanges and look at the pictures depicting different leisure activities. They note which activity they hear mentioned, matching it to the correct picture (a–i). Point out the Tip box, which explains how when *a* ('to') precedes the definite article *el* ('the'), the two words combine to form a contraction *al* ('to the').

Audioscript Track 76

1 – ¿Qué haces en la ciudad?
 – Voy al cine.
2 – ¿Qué haces en la ciudad?
 – Voy de paseo con mi familia.
3 – ¿Qué haces en la ciudad?
 – Voy a la playa.
4 – ¿Qué haces en la ciudad?
 – Bueno… voy a la cafetería.
5 – ¿Qué haces en la ciudad?
 – Salgo con mis amigos.
6 – ¿Qué haces en la ciudad?
 – Voy de compras. Ji, ji, ji.
7 – ¿Qué haces en la ciudad?
 – Yo voy a la bolera. ¡Me encanta!
8 – ¿Qué haces en la ciudad?
 – A ver… voy al parque.
9 – ¿Y tú?
 – No hago nada.

Answers
1 b 2 g 3 f 4 d 5 a 6 h 7 e 8 c 9 i

Reinforcement
Write up the sentences from exercise 5 (e.g. *salgo con mis amigos*), jumbling the order of the words. With books closed, pupils say the sentences in the correct order.

© Pearson Education Ltd 2013. Copying permitted for purchasing institution only. This material is not copyright free.

Mi ciudad 5.2

Gramática

Use the *Gramática* box to review the full paradigm of *ir*, an extremely useful irregular verb that pupils will need to memorise. There is more information and further practice on p. 112.

6 Lee el texto. Escribe la hora y las letras de los dibujos correctos. (L4)

Reading. Pupils read Luis's account of his perfect Saturday and look at the leisure activity pictures. They identify four key times in Luis's day and note the letters of the activities that he mentions doing at those times. First, read through the Tip box together, which stresses the subtle difference between telling the time (***son** las ocho*) and saying **at** what time something happens (***a** las ocho*). *Hasta* is glossed for support.

Answers

8.00 am, c, b

9.15 am, d, f

1.20 pm, a

5.45 pm, g

8.00 pm, e

7 Prepara una presentación. Describe tu sábado perfecto. Haz tu presentación a tu compañero/a. (L4)

Speaking. Pupils prepare a presentation on their perfect Saturday, to include where they go, what they do, at what time and with whom. They can refer to the text in exercise 6 as a model. Pupils could present their presentation to their partner (who could note down five important details), or to the whole class, as preferred.

Plenary

To review telling the time in Spanish, play 'Time ballet'. Split the class into two teams. Teams nominate one person each time to play for them. The two pupils come to the front, you say a time in Spanish and the pupils 'display' the time using their arms as the hands of the clock. Award two points to the person who shows the correct time first. The team with the most points after a set number of rounds wins.

Workbook 1A, page 48

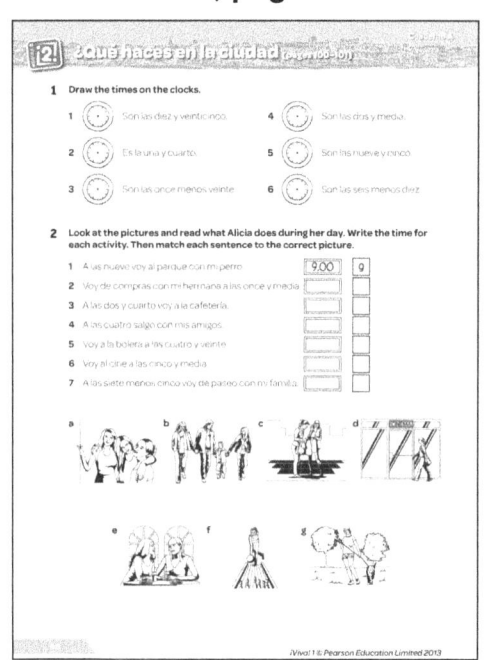

Answers

1 1 10.25	**2** 1.15	**3** 10.40
4 2.30	**5** 9.05	**6** 5.50
2 1 9.00 g	**2** 11.30 c	**3** 2.15 e
4 4.00 a	**5** 4.20 f	**6** 5.30 d
7 6.55 b		

Workbook 1B, page 48

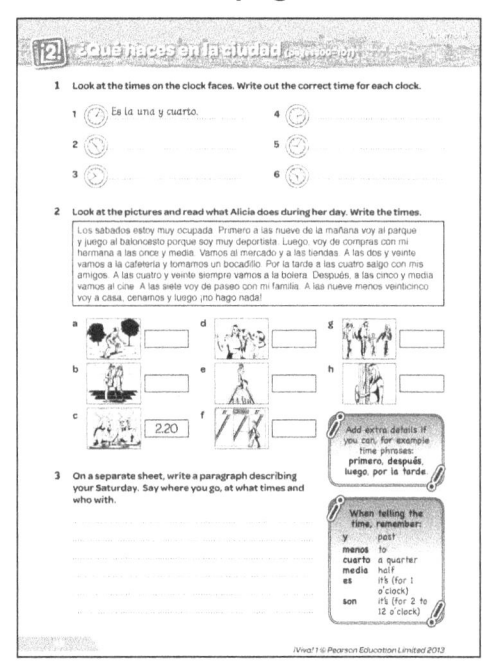

Mi ciudad 5.2

Answers

1 1 *Es la una y cuarto.*
   2 Son las diez y veinticinco.
   3 Son las once menos veinte.
   4 Son las dos y media.
   5 Son las nueve y cinco.
   6 Son las seis menos diez.

2 a 9.00   b 11.30   c *2.20*
   d 4.00   e 4.20   f 5.30
   g 7.00   h 8.35

3 Own answers

Worksheet 5.2 Marta's day in the city

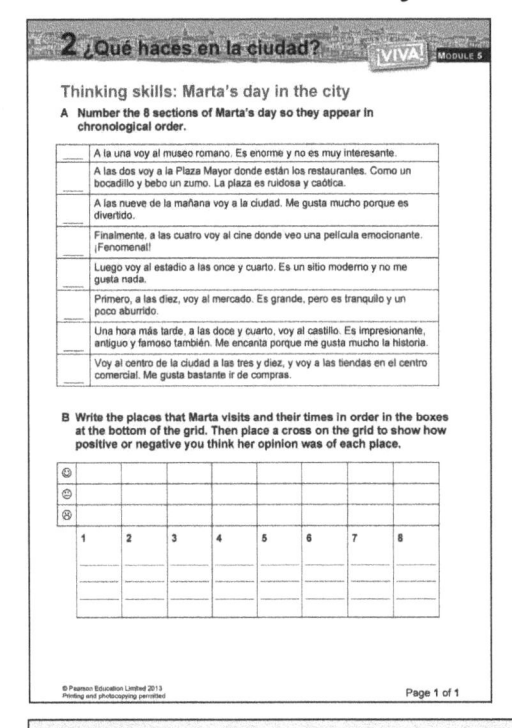

Answers

A

5 A la una voy al museo romano. Es enorme y no es muy interesante.

6 A las dos voy a la Plaza Mayor, donde están los restaurantes. Como un bocadillo y bebo un zumo. La plaza es ruidosa y caótica.

1 A las nueve de la mañana voy a la ciudad. Me gusta mucho porque es divertido.

8 Finalmente, a las cuatro voy al cine, donde veo una película emocionante. ¡Fenomenal!

3 Luego voy al estadio a las once y cuarto. Es un sitio moderno y no me gusta nada.

2 Primero, a las diez, voy al mercado. Es grande, pero es tranquilo y un poco aburrido.

4 Una hora más tarde, a las doce y cuarto, voy al castillo. Es impresionante, antiguo y famoso también. Me encanta porque me gusta mucho la historia.

7 Voy al centro de la ciudad a las tres y diez, y voy a las tiendas del centro comercial. Me gusta bastante ir de compras.

B

	☹	😐	☺
1 ciudad 9:00			x
2 mercado 10:00		x	
3 estadio 11:15	x		
4 castillo 12:15			x
5 museo romano 13:00		x	
6 Plaza Mayor 14:00		x	
7 centro comercial 15:10			x
8 cine 16:00			x

Video

Episode 9: Aquí en Oviedo

Aroa and Marco describe their town and discuss what is there to do for young people in Oviedo. Video worksheet 9 can be used in conjunction with this episode.

Answers to video worksheet (ActiveTeach)

A

1 Answers will vary and may include the twelve places introduced in Unit 1 of the Pupil Book, as well as other places encountered over the course.

2 a) En mi ciudad hay muchas tiendas.
   b) Voy de compras con mis amigos/amigas.
   c) Voy de paseo con mi familia.

B

1 un museo, muchos museos, el museo de arqueología, el museo del queso, una universidad, un centro comercial, las tiendas, la cafetería, muchos cafés, jardines, parques, el parque, el barrio, una catedral, un centro histórico, muchas plazas, los restaurantes, las cafeterías, el cine

2 Aroa says that their city (Oviedo) is <u>fantastic</u> but Marco thinks it's <u>boring</u>.

3 the museum   <u>fascinating</u>
   the university   <u>very old</u>
   (3 adjectives)   <u>very famous</u>
                          <u>very good</u>
   the shopping centre   <u>very big</u>
   Marco's neighbourhood <u>quite modern</u>

Mi ciudad 5.2

C

1. No, he doesn't like museums.
2. a) true
   b) true
   c) false (There are lots of parks and gardens.)
   d) false (Oviedo is a very old city, not a very modern one.)
   e) true
3. to the cinema

D

1. There is nothing for young people.
2. Answers will vary.
3. He says he goes to the cafeteria with his friends. / He goes to restaurants with his family. / He says that the food in Oviedo is very good and very famous. / He asks what there is to eat at the cinema.
4. Answers will vary. Pupils may say 'no' as Marco and Aroa have different opinions about museums / they do different activities after school / she likes shopping whereas he likes playing football, etc. On the other hand, they may say 'yes' as they both like going to cafés and both like going to the park.
5. Answers will vary.

E

Pupils will produce their own report about their town or village.

¡3! En la cafetería

Mi ciudad 5.3

Pupil Book pages
Pages 102–103

Learning objectives
- Ordering in a café
- Using the verb *querer* (to want)

Programme of Study
GV2 Grammatical structures (the verb *querer*)
LC3 Conversation

FCSE links
Unit 5: Healthy lifestyle (Food/drink)
Unit 6: Food and drink (Food/drink vocabulary items, Eating out)

Grammar
- stem-changing verb *querer*

Key language
una bebida
un café
un té
una Fanta limón
un batido de chocolate
un batido de fresa
una Coca-Cola
una granizada de limón
una ración (de)…
gambas
jamón
calamares
croquetas
patatas bravas
tortilla
pan con tomate
¿Qué quieren?
Yo quiero…
¿Algo más?
No, nada más.
¿Y de beber?
¿Cuánto es por favor?
Son… euros…

PLTS
T Team workers

Resources
Audio files:
77_Module5_Unit3_Ex2
78_Module5_Unit3_Ex4
79_Module5_Unit3_Ex5
Workbooks:
Cuaderno 1A & 1B, page 49
ActiveTeach:
p.102 Flashcards
p.103 Grammar presentation
p.103 Grammar worksheet
ActiveLearn:
Listening A, Listening B
Reading A, Reading B
Grammar, Vocabulary

Starter 1

Aim

To review numbers 1–100.

Practise a few drills with the class to review numbers up to 100 in Spanish. In pairs, pupils count through the five, ten (and any other multiple you wish) times tables forwards and backwards; you say a sequence of numbers and stop (or insert a 'beep') for pupils to complete it; you make a deliberate mistake in a sequence of numbers, and pupils put up their hands as soon as they spot it.

1 Empareja las imágenes con el menú y escribe los precios correctos. (L2)

Reading. Read through the *Zona Cultura* box before starting this exercise. Pupils read the menu and write down the correct prices for the drinks and tapas listed.

Answers

Bebidas	Raciones
a un café (1,50 €)	g gambas (9,50 €)
b un té (1,50 €)	h jamón (10,50 €)
c una Fanta limón (1,75 €)	i calamares (5,50 €)
d un batido de chocolate/fresa (3,00 €)	j croquetas (3,50 €)
e una Coca-Cola (1,75 €)	k patatas bravas (3,50 €)
f Especial del día: granizada de limón (2,75 €)	l tortilla (4,00 €)
	m pan con tomate (4,50 €)

Reinforcement

Working in pairs, pupils take turns to prompt with one of the items of food/drink pictured on p. 102 and to give the price in Spanish.

2 Escucha y comprueba tus respuestas. (L3)

Listening. Pupils listen and check their answers to exercise 1.

© Pearson Education Ltd 2013. Copying permitted for purchasing institution only. This material is not copyright free.

Mi ciudad 5.3

Audioscript Track 77

– Las bebidas...
– Un café, ¿cuánto es, por favor?
– 1,50 €.

– Y ¿un té?
– Un té, 1,50 € también.

– Una Fanta limón, ¿cuánto es?
– Son 1,75 €.

– ¿Y un batido de chocolate?
– Son 3,00 €.

– Una Coca-Cola, ¿cuánto es?
– 1,75 €

– ¿Y una granizada de limón?
– Una granizada de limón son 2,75 €.

– Y las raciones...

– Una ración de gambas, ¿cuánto es, por favor?
– Son 9,50 €.

– ¿Y una ración de jamón?
– ¿Una ración de jamón? Son 10,50 €.

– Una ración de calamares ¿cuánto es, por favor?
– Son 5,50 €.

– ¿Y Una ración de patatas bravas?
– Son 3,50 €.

– Una ración de croquetas, ¿cuánto es?
– Son 3,50 €.

– ¿Y una ración de tortilla?
– Son 4,00 €.

– Pan con tomate ¿cuánto es?
– Son 4,50 €.

3 Con tu compañero/a, pregunta y contesta. (L3)

Speaking. In pairs, pupils practise short café dialogues. They take it in turns to play the customer, asking the price of food and drinks, and the waiter/waitress, taking orders and stating the prices. A framework is supplied. Point out the Tip box at the top of the page, which explains how to pronounce *euros* correctly.

4 Escucha. ¿Qué quieren? Hay un error en las notas del camarero cada vez. (1–5) (L3)

Listening. Pupils listen to the five conversations and read the waiter's order pad notes. They note in Spanish what is actually ordered, identifying one error in the waiter's notes each time.

Audioscript Track 78

1 – Buenos días, ¿qué quieres?
– Quiero una ración de patatas bravas y una Coca-Cola.

2 – Buenos días, ¿qué quieres?
– A ver... una ración de gambas por favor y un té.

3 – ¡Hola! ¡Hola! ¿Qué quieres?
– Bueno... una ración de croquetas y una Fanta limón.

4 – Buenas tardes, ¿qué quieres?
– Queremos una ración de tortilla y dos batidos de chocolate.

5 – Buenos días, ¿qué quieres?
– Quiero una ración de jamón y un café.

Answers

1 ~~1 x limonada~~ ⇒ 1 x Coca-Cola
2 ~~1 x tortilla~~ ⇒ 1 x gambas
3 ~~1 x Coca-Cola~~ ⇒ 1 x Fanta limón
4 ~~1 x calamares~~ ⇒ 1 x tortilla
5 ~~1 x Fanta limón~~ ⇒ 1 x café

Extension

Write up the following prices on the board, with the first one given as a model. Pupils write out each price in words.

1 8,90 € *ocho euros noventa*
2 30,45 €   3 14,75 €   4 11,60 €
5 20,30 €   6 3,40 €   7 1,55 €

Mi ciudad 5.3

Starter 2

Aim

To revise pronunciation of the letter *c*.

Working in pairs, ask pupils to come up with three or four tips for pronouncing the letter *c* in Spanish to share with the class.

Alternative starter 2:

Use ActiveTeach p.103 Grammar presentation to introduce the stem-changing verb *querer*.

Gramática

Use the *Gramática* box to teach the full paradigm of the irregular stem-changing verb *querer*, meaning 'to want' or 'to love' – an important verb to memorise as it is so common.

5 Escucha y lee el diálogo. Escribe las letras correctas del ejercicio 1 en los espacios en blanco. (L4)

Listening. Pupils listen and read the café dialogue at the same time. They fill in the gaps in the dialogue, using the correct letters for items of food and drink from exercise 1.

Audioscript Track 79

– Buenos días, ¿qué queréis?
– A ver… ¿Qué quieres, Raúl?
– Quiero una ración de calamares y una ración de croquetas, por favor.
– Muy bien…
– Yo quiero una ración de tortilla.
– ¿Algo más?
– Eh… Sí, una ración de jamón, por favor. Raúl, ¿algo más?
– No, nada más.
– ¿Y de beber?
– Quiero una Coca-Cola.
– Yo quiero una granizada de limón

Un poco más tarde…
– ¿Cuánto es, por favor?
– Bueno… Son 28 euros.
– Gracias. ¡Me encanta ir de tapas!

Answers

1 i 2 j 3 l 4 h 5 e 6 f

6 Escribe un diálogo utilizando el ejercicio 5 como modelo. (L4)

Writing. Pupils write their own café dialogue, using the one in exercise 5 as a model. Once complete, pupils can practise their dialogues with their partners, in preparation for the plenary.

7 ¡Juega! Trabaja en un grupo de cuatro personas. (L4)

Speaking. In groups of four, pupils play a board game to practise the café language they have learned. The rules of the game are provided and some vocabulary is glossed for support. The first pupil to reach the final square wins.

Plenary

Ask pupils to write three multiple-choice questions focusing on food and drink items for their partner, giving four options to choose from. For example:

How do you say 'strawberry milkshake' in Spanish?
(a) *Una Coca-Cola*
(b) *Un batido de chocolate*
(c) *Un batido de fresa*
(d) *Una granizada de limón*

Workbook 1A, page 49

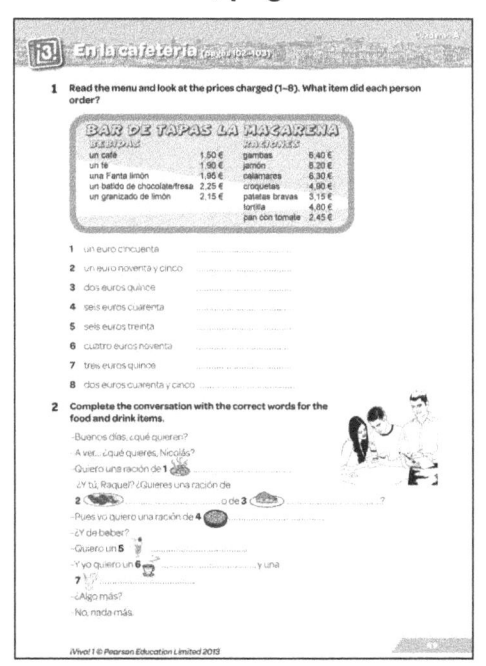

Answers

1 1 un café   2 una Fanta limón
   3 un granizado   4 gambas
     de limón
   5 calamares   6 croquetas
   7 patatas bravas 8 pan con tomate

Mi ciudad 5.3

2
1 croquetas 2 jamón
3 tortilla 4 gambas
5 batido de fresa 6 café
7 Fanta limón

Workbook 1B, page 49

Answers

1 1 un té 2 un *euro* noventa y cinco
3 un granizado de limón 4 gambas
5 seis *euros* treinta 6 croquetas
7 tres *euros* quince
8 dos *euros* cuarenta y cinco

2 2, 11, 8, *1*, 10, 6, 3, 5, 7, 9, 4

3 Own answers

Worksheet 5.3 Stem-changing verbs

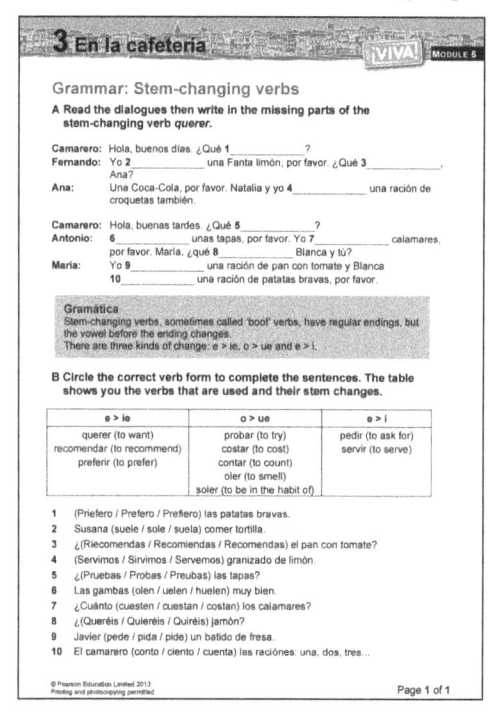

Answers

A

1 queréis/quieren 2 quiero
3 quieres 4 queremos
5 queréis/quieren 6 Queremos
7 quiero 8 queréis
9 quiero 10 quiere

B

1 Prefiero 2 suele 3 Recomiendas
4 Servimos 5 Pruebas 6 huelen
7 cuestan 8 Queréis 9 pide
10 cuenta

4 ¿Qué vas a hacer?

Mi ciudad 5.4

Pupil Book pages
Pages 104–105

Learning objectives
- Saying what you are going to do at the weekend
- Using the near future tense

Programme of Study
GV1 Tenses (the near future tense)
LC3 Conversation
LC6 Translation into English

FCSE links
Unit 4: Leisure (Going out)

Grammar
- the near future tense (*voy, vas, va*, etc. + infinitive)

Key language
¿Qué vas a hacer este fin de semana?
el sábado por la mañana
el viernes por la tarde
(No) Voy a…
jugar a los videojuegos
ir de compras
ir de paseo
ir al parque
bailar
salir con mis amigos
navegar por Internet
ver la televisión
hacer los deberes
montar en bici
jugar al fútbol
chatear

PLTS
T Team workers

Cross-curricular
English: verb tenses

Resources
Audio files:
80_Module5_Unit4_Ex1
81_Module5_Unit4_Ex5
Workbooks:
Cuaderno 1A & 1B, page 50
ActiveTeach:
p.104 Grammar presentation
p.104 Extension reading
p.105 Grammar worksheet
p.105 Video 10
p.105 Video 10 transcript
p.105 Video worksheet 10
ActiveLearn:
Listening A, Listening B
Reading A, Reading B
Grammar, Vocabulary

Starter 1

Aim

To revise the temporal phrases (weekend days + *por la mañana/por la tarde*).

The teacher mimes all of the weekend activities for pupils, who have to guess when they think he or she does them, for example: ¿*el viernes por la tarde?*, ¿*el sábado por la mañana?*, ¿*el domingo por la tarde?* This could be a class team activity where you award points for a correct answer and deduct them for a wrong answer. The team with the most points wins.

1 Escucha y lee. (L5)

Listening. Pupils listen and follow the text at the same time. *Muchas cosas interesantes* is glossed for support.

Audioscript Track 80

Me llamo Manuel. ¡Hola! ¿Qué tal?

Este fin de semana voy a hacer muchas cosas interesantes.

Por ejemplo, el sábado por la mañana, voy a jugar a los videojuegos.

Luego, a las once voy a ir de compras con mi hermano.

A las siete voy a salir con mis amigos. Vamos a bailar. ¡Me encanta bailar! Es estupendo. ¡Ja, ja, ja!

El domingo por la mañana, primero voy a navegar por Internet y luego, voy a ver la televisión.

No voy a hacer los deberes. ¡Ji, ji, ji, ji! ¡Qué aburrido!

A las tres de la tarde voy a montar en bici. Voy a ir al parque, donde voy a jugar al fútbol.

¡Va a ser guay!

¿Y tú? ¿Qué vas a hacer este fin de semana?

Gramática

Use the *Gramática* box to introduce the concept of the near future tense to pupils – a tense that describes something that is about to occur and one that is relatively simple to learn.

Voy a *comer ahora* – **I'm going** to eat now.

Vamos a *bailar este tarde.* – **We're going** to dance this evening.

Pupils will be more familiar with the tense once they have completed exercise 2, but there is also more information and further practice on Pupil Book p. 113.

© Pearson Education Ltd 2013. Copying permitted for purchasing institution only. This material is not copyright free.

Mi ciudad 5.4

2 Busca trece ejemplos del futuro inmediato en el ejercicio 1. Tradúcelos al inglés. (L5)

Reading. Pupils look for thirteen examples of the near future tense in the exercise 1 text, then translate them into English.

Answers

voy a hacer	I am going to do
voy a jugar	I am going to play
voy a ir (de compras)	I am going to go (shopping)
voy a salir	I am going to go out
Vamos a bailar	We are going to dance
voy a navegar por Internet	I am going to surf the net
voy a ver la televisión	I am going to watch TV
No voy a hacer (los deberes)	I am not going to do (my homework)
voy a montar en bici	I am going to ride my bike
voy a ir (al parque)	I am going to go (to the park)
voy a jugar	I am going to play
va a ser	It is going to be
¿Qué vas a hacer?	What are you going to do?

Reinforcement

Working in pairs with their books closed, pupils try to remember the thirteen activities that Manuel is going to do at the weekend (using *este fin de semana* + the near future tense).

3 Busca las palabras en español en el ejercicio 1. (L2)

Reading. Pupils find in the exercise 1 text the Spanish translations of the time expressions listed.

Answers

1 Este fin de semana	2 Por ejemplo
3 Luego	4 A las siete
5 El domingo por la mañana	6 primero

Starter 2

Aim

To review infinitive forms.

Provide the following list of verb forms on the board (omitting the answers). Give pupils a few minutes to write the infinitive form of each verb.

1 van (ir)   2 tiene (tener)
3 hago (hacer)   4 jugamos (jugar)
5 beben (beber) 6 escuchas (escuchar)
7 soy (ser)   8 vivís (vivir)

Next, prompt pupils to offer examples of sentences that contain an infinitive. They might need to be reminded of the structures *me gusta/ me encanta*. Remind them also that the infinitive is the verb form found in a dictionary.

4 Con tu compañero/a, haz un diálogo. Eres Manuel y tu compañero/a es un amigo/una amiga. (L5)

Speaking. Pupils alternate playing the role of Manuel from exercise 1, and take turns to be asked what they (or Manuel) are going to do at the weekend, and specifically on Saturday and Sunday morning and afternoon. A framework is supplied.

Pronunciación

Draw pupils' attention to the *Pronunciación* box, to remind them that, in Spanish, *b* and *v* are essentially pronounced the same and sound like a *b* in English.

5 ¿Qué van a hacer este fin de semana? Copia y completa la tabla. (1–4) (L4)

Listening. Pupils copy out the table. They listen to four people talking about the weekend, then fill in the table, noting what their planned activities are and when they will happen.

Audioscript Track 81

1 – ¿Qué vas a hacer este fin de semana, Laura?
  – El sábado por la mañana voy a salir con mis amigas y vamos a ir al cine.

2 – ¿Qué vas a hacer este fin de semana, Samuel?
  – El domingo por la tarde voy a navegar por Internet y luego, voy a ver la televisión.

3 – ¿Qué vas a hacer este fin de semana, Carla?

Mi ciudad 5.4

- *A ver… el sábado por la tarde, voy a ir al parque, donde voy a jugar al fútbol.*
- **4** – *¿Qué vas a hacer este fin de semana, Álvaro?*
- *El domingo por la mañana, voy a escuchar música y luego, voy a cantar karaoke.*

Answers		
	¿Cuándo?	¿Qué?
Laura	sábado por la mañana	salir con amigas, ir al cine
Samuel	domingo por la tarde	navegar por Internet, ver la televisión
Carla	sábado por la tarde	ir al parque, jugar al fútbol
Álvaro	domingo por la mañana	escuchar música, cantar karaoke

6 Con tu compañero/a, juega a los barcos. (L3)

Speaking. Pupils follow the instructions provided in English with the aim of playing a game of battleships with their partner. Instructions on how to make a battleships grid are given and a framework for the dialogue is provided.

7 Eres una persona famosa. ¿Qué vas a hacer el sábado por la mañana/por la tarde? Escribe un párrafo. (L5)

Writing. Pupils imagine they are a celebrity and write a description of their weekend plans. A list of what to feature and a writing framework are provided. Encourage pupils to use connectives and intensifiers in their writing, as well as sequencers to make their sentences more interesting and chronological.

Extension

Pupils can also write a short paragraph about a friend or a family member, describing what he or she is going to do on Saturday with verbs in the third person singular form.

Plenary

Ask pupils to create five sentences for their partner to decipher using single letter prompts for phrases from the unit, for example:

Vaialp = **Voy a ir a la piscina**

Workbook 1A, page 50

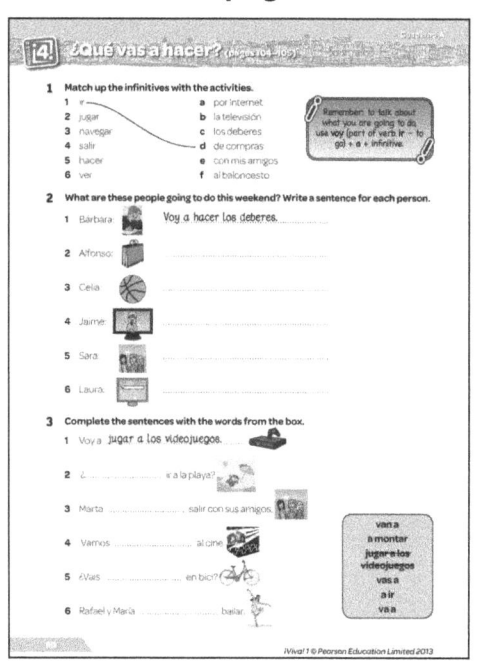

Answers
1 1 d 2 f 3 a 4 e 5 c 6 b
2 1 *Voy a hacer los deberes.*
   2 Voy a ir de compras.
   3 Voy a jugar al baloncesto.
   4 Voy a ver la televisión.
   5 Voy a salir con mis amigos.
   6 Voy a navegar por Internet.
3 1 *jugar a los videojuegos*   2 vas a
   3 va a   4 a ir   5 a montar   6 van a

Workbook 1B, page 50

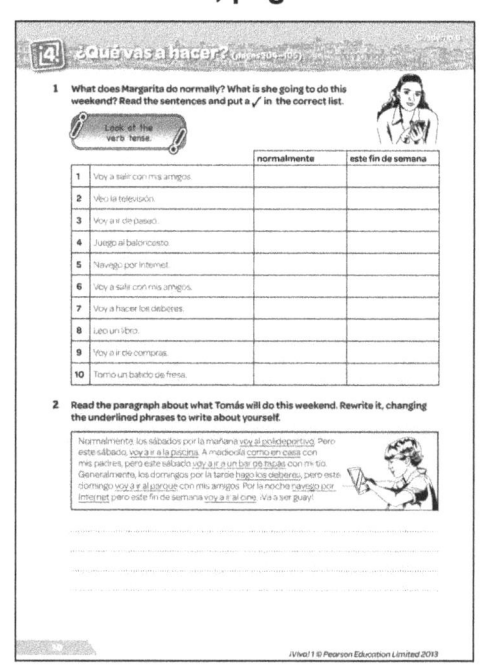

© Pearson Education Ltd 2013. Copying permitted for purchasing institution only. This material is not copyright free.

Mi ciudad 5.4

Answers

1
1. este fin de semana 2. normalmente
3. este fin de semana 4. normalmente
5. normalmente 6. este fin de semana
7. este fin de semana 8. normalmente
9. este fin de semana 10. normalmente

2 Own answers

Worksheet 5.4 Holiday in Chile

Answers

A

1 voy a viajar	2 vamos a ir
3 vamos a ver	4 van a ir
5 vamos a jugar	6 voy a ir
7 vamos a viajar	8 va a hacer
9 van a bailar	10 van a beber
11 Voy a escribir	12 van a encantar

B
1. excited
2. the neighbourhood
3. the ski resorts
4. the name of the (Chilean) national dance/ the national dance
5. postcards

ActiveTeach, Extension Reading

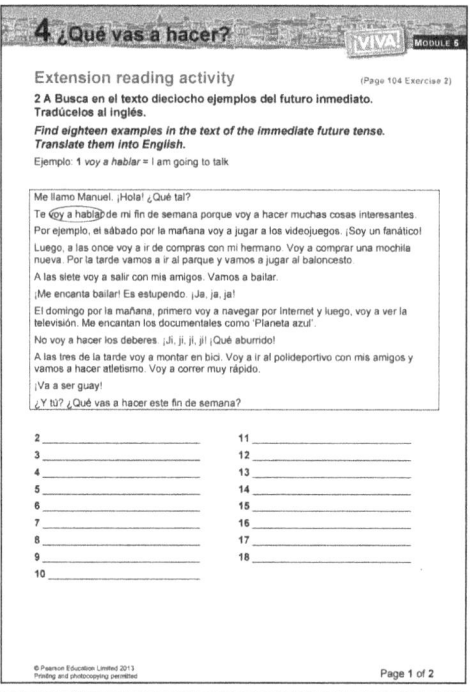

Answers

A

1. voy a hablar = I am going to talk
2. voy a hacer = I am going to do
3. voy a jugar = I am going to play
4. voy a ir = I am going to go
5. voy a comprar = I am going to buy
6. vamos a ir = we are going to go
7. vamos a jugar = we are going to play
8. voy a salir = I am going to go out

Mi ciudad 5.4

9 vamos a bailar = we are going to dance
10 voy a navegar por Internet = I am going to surf the net
11 voy a ver = I am going to watch
12 voy a hacer = I am going to do
13 voy a montar en bici = I am going to ride my bike
14 voy a ir = I am going to go
15 vamos a hacer = we are going to do
16 voy a correr = I am going to run
17 va a ser = it is going to be
18 ¿Qué vas a hacer? = What are you going to do?

B

1 por ejemplo
2 el sábado por la mañana
3 ¡Soy un fanático!
4 una mochila nueva
5 me encanta bailar
6 El domingo por la mañana
7 Me encantan los documentales como 'Planeta azul'.
8 correr muy rápido

Video

Episode 10: ¡Al futuro!

The ¡TeleViva! team celebrate their last report from a café, and talk about their plans for what to do next. Video worksheet 10 can be used in conjunction with this episode.

Answers to video worksheet (ActiveTeach)

A

1 Answers will vary and may include the six drinks introduced in Unit 3 of the Pupil Book, as well as drinks that they have seen previously in the context of school (page 60 of the Pupil Book).

2 'Tapas' are snacks. See page 102 of the Pupil Book for a fuller explanation.
   a) jamón
   b) pan con tomate
   c) patatas bravas
   d) tortilla
   e) calamares

3 a) Voy a ver la televisión.
   b) Voy a ir al cine.
   c) Voy a jugar al fútbol.

B

1 un batido de chocolate, un batido de fresa, un té, un granizado de limón, un agua, una Coca-Cola

2 gambas (prawns), croquetas (croquettes)

3
1 chocolate milkshake
~~2 strawberry milkshakes~~
1 strawberry milkshake
~~1 coffee~~
1 tea
~~1 iced lemon drink~~
2 iced lemon drinks
1 mineral water
1 Coca-Cola

5. Listening Skills: ¿Te gusta tu ciudad? Mi ciudad 5.5

Pupil Book pages
Pages 106–107

Learning objectives
- Understanding people describing their town
- Listening for detail

Programme of Study
GV3 Opinions and discussions
LC1 Listening and responding

Key language
Review of language from Units 1–4

PLTS
R Reflective learners

Resources
Audio files:
82_Module5_Unit5_Ex1
83_Module5_Unit5_Ex3
84_Module5_Unit5_Ex4
85_Module5_Unit5_Ex6
86_Module5_Unit5_Ex8
87_Module5_Unit5_Ex9
ActiveTeach:
Starter 2 resource

Starter 1

Aim

To review negative phrases.

Provide the following negative sentence starters on the board and give pupils three minutes, working in pairs, to write suitable endings for them. Check pupils' answers and discuss the grammatical differences between each one (suggestions in brackets). Ask pupils to translate the sentences into English.

(**followed by**)

No quiero… (+ infinitive)
No hay… (+ noun, with no indefinite article)
No tiene… (+ noun, with no indefinite article)
No me gusta…(+ infinitive)
No soy… (+ adjective)
No es… (+ adjective)

1 Escucha. ¿Entiendes 'no' en estas frases? (1–6) (L2)

Listening. Read through the Skills box together on how small words can easily alter the whole meaning of what someone is saying. Pupils listen to the six statements and identify whether they hear the word 'no' in them. *Mucho que hacer* is glossed for support.

Audioscript Track 82

1 – *Hay muchos museos.*
2 – *Hay un mercado.*
3 – *No voy a la bolera.*
4 – *Quiero una Coca-Cola.*
5 – *No es tranquilo.*
6 – *No hay mucho que hacer.*

Answers
'No' is used in sentences 3, 5 and 6.

2 Escribe las frases del ejercicio 1 en inglés. (L3)

Writing. Pupils translate the sentences from exercise 1 into English. Point out how easy it is to write the opposite of each of the sentences by either adding or removing *no*.

Answers
1 There are many museums.
2 There is a market.
3 I am not going to the bowling alley.
4 I want a Coke.
5 It is not quiet.
6 There is not a lot to do.

3 ¿A dónde no va Daniel? Escribe las dos letras correctas. (L3)

Listening. Pupils listen to Daniel and identify which two activities he does not do on a Saturday, noting the correct letters of the activities.

Audioscript Track 83

Todos los sábados, voy a la bolera por la mañana y voy al centro comercial por la tarde. Luego voy al cine con mis amigos. No voy al estadio porque no me gusta. Los domingos voy a la cafetería, pero no voy al parque, prefiero ver la televisión.

Answers
a, e

© Pearson Education Ltd 2013. Copying permitted for purchasing institution only. This material is not copyright free.

Mi ciudad 5.5

4 Escucha y lee. ¿Qué piensan de la ciudad? Escribe P (positivo), N (negativo) o P/N (positivo y negativo). (L4)

Listening. Pupils listen and follow the text. They decide whether the young people have a positive opinion of their town (P), a negative one (N) or both (P/N). Read through the Skills box first, which highlights that they might not hear *me gusta* or *no me gusta* as they might expect. There may be other clues to draw from, such as adjectives or intonation.

Audioscript Track 84

1 – No me gusta porque no hay estadio. En mi opinión no es interesante.

2 – En mi ciudad hay muchas cosas que hacer. Los fines de semana voy a la bolera con mis amigas o vamos al cine. Es fenomenal.

3 – Me encantan los museos y los monumentos, pero no hay piscina y el centro comercial es un poco feo.

Answers
1 N 2 P 3 P/N

Extension
Pupils rework the first two texts in exercise 4 converting the first into a positive text and the second into a negative one. This can be done orally or in writing.

5 Escribe las expresiones que indican la opinión (P, N, P/N) de las personas del ejercicio 4. (L4)

Writing. Pupils write out the phrases that show the opinions of the people in exercise 4.

Answers
1 *No me gusta*, En mi opinión, no es interesante.

2 Es fenomenal.

3 Me encantan, es un poco feo.

Starter 2

Aim

To revise time markers and expressions of frequency.

Provide the following on the board and give pupils three minutes to come up with sentences for six of them, either orally or written (Starter 2 resource).

A las ocho de la mañana,	En diez minutos,
A las cinco de la tarde,	Ahora,
Este fin de semana,	En verano
Los sábados,	Todos los días
El viernes por la tarde,	A veces
Primero... luego...	Nunca

6 Escucha y elige la respuesta correcta. (L4)

Listening. Pupils listen and choose the correct answer from the multiple-choice options. Make pupils aware of the Skills box and the need to not only listen carefully to avoid 'red herrings', but also to read the question carefully.

Audioscript Track 85

1 – Voy a ir a la piscina con mi padre a las seis y media de la tarde.

2 – Voy a ir de compras con mi madre el sábado por la mañana, a las once menos cuarto.

Answers
1 c 2 a

Reinforcement
Ask pupils to translate the following into Spanish:

1 at 8.30 am on Monday morning

2 at 4.45 pm on Friday afternoon

3 on Wednesdays at 3.00 pm

4 on Sundays at 11.15 am

5 at 2.10 pm on Thursday afternoon

7 Escribe una pregunta de respuesta múltiple para tu compañero/a. (L4)

Writing. Pupils write their own sentence in Spanish, with three multiple-choice answer options in English. They then read the sentence aloud to their partner, who chooses the correct answer.

Mi ciudad 5.5

8 Escucha. ¿Qué quieren Emilio y Paulina? Escribe las dos letras correctas para cada persona. (L3)

Listening. Pupils listen to the café conversation between Emilio and Paulina and look at the pictures. They note the letters of the food and drink items that they order.

Audioscript Track 86

- Buenos días, ¿qué queréis?
- A ver… ¿qué quieres, Paulina?
- Quiero una ración de croquetas, por favor. Y tú, ¿qué quieres, Emilio?
- Quiero una ración de jamón, por favor.
- Muy bien…
- ¿Y de beber?
- Quiero una Coca-Cola.
- Yo quiero un té.
- ¿Cuánto es, por favor?
- Bueno…son diez… catorce… 26 euros cincuenta.

Answers
Emilio: d, e **Paulina:** a, f

9 Escucha y elige la respuesta correcta. (L4)

Listening. Pupils listen to Martina talk about her home town of Nerja, then answer the multiple-choice questions.

Audioscript Track 87

Me llamo Martina y vivo en Nerja. Es un pueblo que está en el sur de España. En Nerja hay muchos monumentos y muchos museos, pero no hay centro comercial.

Me gusta mucho vivir aquí porque es muy antiguo y muy impresionante. Es un pueblo precioso. Es mi pueblo favorito.

Answers
1 c 2 b 3 c

Plenary

In pairs, pupils discuss what they have learned about listening strategies from the unit. Ask them to create a wall poster to share three of their key ideas.

6 Writing Skills: Mi vida en La Habana — Mi ciudad 5.6

Pupil Book pages
Pages 108–109

Learning objectives
- Writing a blog about your town and activities
- Using two tenses together

Programme of Study
GV4 Accuracy (spelling, grammar)
LC4 Expressing ideas (writing)
LC8 Writing creatively

Key language
Review of language from Units 1–4

PLTS
S Self-managers

Cross-curricular
English: verb tenses; writing fluently

Resources
Audio files:
88_Module5_Unit6_Ex1
89_Module5_Unit6_Ex5
Workbooks:
Cuaderno 1A & 1B, page 51
ActiveTeach:
p.109 Grammar presentation

Starter 1

Aim

To review temporal phrases with the near future and present tenses.

Present the following time expressions on the board. Allow pupils three minutes to match them to verbs in the appropriate (present or near future) tense.

Normalmente	salgo/voy a salir
el domingo por la tarde…	hago/voy a hacer
…y luego	veo/voy a ver
este fin de semana	juego/voy a jugar
todos los días	escucho/voy a escuchar
los lunes	voy/voy a ir

1 Escucha y lee. (L5)

Listening. Pupils listen and follow the text on p. 108 of the Pupil Book at the same time. *Nadar* is glossed for support.

Audioscript Track 88

¿Qué tal?

Me llamo Lucía y tengo trece años. Soy bastante simpática y muy divertida. No soy tímida. ¿Y tú? ¿Cómo eres?

Vivo en Cuba, en la capital, La Habana. Está en el oeste de Cuba, en la costa. Me gusta vivir en La Habana porque todos los días hace sol. Hay un castillo y unos museos interesantes. También hay una universidad y muchas plazas.

Vivo en un piso moderno con mi familia. No me gusta nada porque es muy pequeño

En mi tiempo libre salgo con mis amigas. Montamos en bici o vamos a la playa, donde jugamos al voleibol. Me gusta mucho escuchar música y mi pasión es la salsa. Toco el piano y también canto en un coro. ¿Y tú? ¿Qué haces en tu tiempo libre?

Normalmente los sábados, canto en el coro y luego voy de paseo con mi madre, pero este fin de semana voy a ir a la playa con mis amigas, porque es mi cumpleaños. Vamos a nadar. ¡Va a ser estupendo! ¿Y tú? ¿Qué vas a hacer este fin de semana?

Extension

Pupils read aloud the Spanish text in exercise 1 round the class, a sentence at a time, translating it into English.

2 Completa las frases en inglés. (L5)

Reading. Pupils read the text in exercise 1 again, then complete the gap-fill sentences in English.

Answers
1. Lucía is quite nice and **very funny**.
2. Havana is the capital of Cuba. It is in the **west on the coast.**
3. She likes Havana because **it's sunny** every day.
4. She doesn't like her flat because **it's very small.**
5. Lucía likes to listen to music and her passion is **salsa**.
6. Lucía plays piano and on Saturdays she **sings in a choir**.
7. Normally after choir Lucía goes for **a walk** with **her mother**.
8. But this weekend she is going to go **to the beach (with her friends)** because **it's her birthday**.

Mi ciudad 5.6

3 Busca en el texto: (L5)

Reading. Pupils find in the exercise 1 text examples of Spanish verbs in the present and near future tenses, in both the 'I' and 'we' forms.

Answers

Present tense 'I' form: *me llamo, tengo, soy, vivo, salgo, toco, canto*

Present tense 'we' form: *montamos, vamos, jugamos*

Near future tense 'I' form: *voy a ir*

Near future tense 'we' form: *vamos a nadar*

4 Eres Lucía. Con tu compañero/a, pregunta y contesta. (L5)

Speaking. Pupils alternate playing the role of Lucía from exercise 1, and take it in turns to be asked a series of questions about her, including details about her town, free time and weekend plans.

Starter 2

Aim

To practise improving sentences with extra detail.

Provide the following list of sentences on the board. Ask pupils to improve them by adding connectives, intensifiers, time expressions and/or two different tenses where appropriate.

1 *Vivo en una casa.*
2 *Soy simpático.*
3 *Juego al fútbol.*
4 *Voy a la bolera.*
5 *Voy de paseo.*
6 *Hay un castillo.*

5 Escucha y escribe las letras correctas. (1–5) (L5)

Listening. Pupils listen to five statements with a mixture of present and near future tenses, and identify the pictures of the activities that each person mentions, writing the appropriate letters. Draw pupils' attention to the Skills box and explain that being able to use two tenses together will help them to attain a higher level.

Audioscript Track 89

1 – *Normalmente, los fines de semana hago los deberes, pero este fin de semana voy a nadar.*

2 – *Normalmente, los sábados monto en bici, pero este fin de semana voy a jugar al tenis.*

3 – *Normalmente, los fines de semana voy al parque, pero este fin de semana voy a ir al cine.*

4 – *Normalmente, los domingos veo la televisión, pero este fin de semana voy a cantar karaoke.*

5 – *Normalmente, los fines de semana salgo con mis amigos, pero este fin de semana voy a salir con mi familia.*

Answers
1 d, f   2 b, i   3 a, j   4 c, g   5 e, h

Reinforcement

Pupils rework sentences a–j in exercise 5 using the third person singular orally or in writing.

6 Lee el texto del ejercicio 1 otra vez. Copia y completa la tabla. (L3)

Reading. Pupils reread the text in exercise 1 and complete the table, listing all the connectives, intensifiers and time expressions they can find.

Answers

connectives	intensifiers	time expressions
y	bastante	todos los días
también	muy	normalmente
porque		los sábados
donde		luego
pero		este fin de semana

7 Escribe una entrada de blog sobre ti. ¡Cuidado con la ortografía y la gramática! (L5)

Writing. Pupils write a blog entry about themselves, to include details of their house, home town, leisure interests and plans for the weekend, using the text in exercise 1 as a model. A list of topics to include is provided.

Mi ciudad 5.6

8 Lee la entrada de blog de tu compañero/a. Comprueba y comenta su trabajo. (L5)

Reading. Pupils swap their texts from exercise 7 with a partner and check and correct each other's work, specifically looking at spelling, accents, endings on articles and adjectives, verb endings and tenses. Pupils comment on their partner's work, awarding marks out of 3.

Plenary

Put one pupil in the 'hot seat' as an expert – the other pupils ask him or her questions on anything that has been taught in the book. If the pupil answers them correctly, he or she gets to nominate another pupil to take the hot seat.

Workbook 1A, page 51

Answers

1 1 b 2 a 3 d 4 c 5 e 6 h 7 f 8 g
   9 i 10 j

2 1 Barcelona   2 it's a very interesting city
   3 his flat is quite small
   4 the swimming pool or the beach
   5 his homework
   6 go to the cinema with his family and then they're going to eat in a restaurant

3 Own answers.

Workbook 1B, page 51

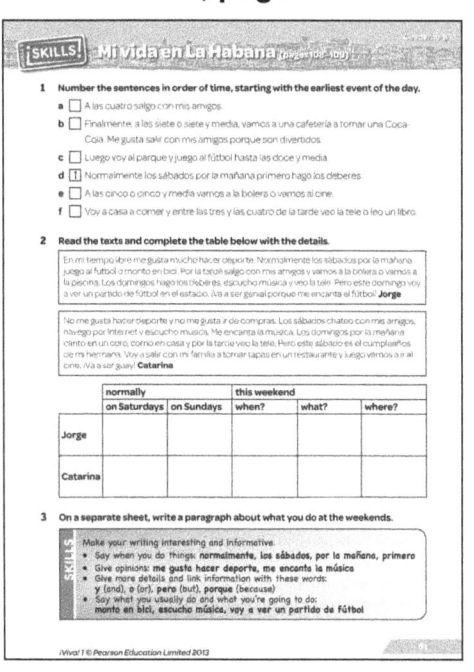

Answers

1 a 4 b 6 c 2 d 1 e 5 f 3

2

	Jorge	Catarina
on Saturdays	plays football, rides his bike, goes out with friends, they go bowling or swimming	chats with her friends, surfs the Internet, listens to music
on Sundays	plays football, rides his bike, goes out with friends, they go bowling or swimming	sings in a choir, has lunch at home, watches TV
when?	on Sunday	on Saturday
what?	going to a football match	her sister's birthday, going out for tapas with her family
where?	at the stadium	at a restaurant

3 Own answers.

Mi ciudad 5

Pupil Book pages
Pages 110–111

Resumen
Pupils use the checklist to review language covered in the module, working on it in pairs in class or on their own at home. Encourage them to follow up any areas of weakness they identify. There are Target Setting Sheets included in the Assessment Pack and an opportunity for pupils to record their own levels and targets on the Self-assessment pages in the Workbooks, p. 55. You can also use the *Resumen* checklist (available in the ActiveTeach) as an end-of-module plenary option.

Prepárate
These revision exercises can be used for assessment purposes or for pupils to practise before tackling the assessment tasks in the Assessment Pack.

Resources
Audio file:
90_Module5_Prep_Ex1
Workbooks:
Cuaderno 1A & 1B, pages 52 & 53
ActiveTeach:
p.110 *Resumen* checklist

1 Escucha y completa la tabla en inglés. (1–4) (L4)

Listening. Pupils copy out the table. They listen to four people talking about where they live – for each person they note what attractions there are in their town and whether they like living there and why.

Audioscript Track 90

1 – ¡Hola! Soy Alejandro. Vivo en Barcelona, en el este de España. En mi ciudad hay un castillo, un estadio y muchas tiendas. Me gusta vivir en Barcelona porque está en la costa y es una ciudad muy interesante.

2 – Me llamo Lola y vivo en Cútar. Es un pueblo que está en el sur de España. En Cútar no hay nada. No hay tiendas, no hay museos, no hay castillo. No me gusta nada porque es muy aburrido.

3 – Soy Miguel. Vivo en Sevilla, en el sur de España. Hay un mercado y una universidad. Hay muchas plazas y parques. Me gusta mucho vivir en Sevilla porque es muy antiguo y muy impresionante.

4 – Me llamo Daniela. Vivo en Valladolid. Está en el centro de España. Hay muchos parques y restaurantes. Hay un polideportivo pero no hay bolera. Me gusta vivir en Valladolid porque tengo muchas amigas aquí.

Answers

	things in town	opinion	reason
Alej.	castle, stadium, shops	likes it	it's interesting
Lola	nothing, no shops, no museums, no castle	doesn't like it at all	it's boring
Miguel	market, uni, squares, parks	likes it a lot	it's old, impressive
Daniel	parks, restaurants, sports centre but no bowling alley	likes it	has lots of friends there

2 Con tu compañero/a, haz tres diálogos utilizando las imágenes. (L3)

Speaking. In pairs, using the pictures supplied, pupils make up three dialogues. A sample exchange is given.

3 Lee el texto. ¿Verdadero o falso? Escribe V o F. (L5)

Reading. Pupils read the text, then decide whether the English statements that follow are true (V) or false (F).

Answers
1 F 2 V 3 V 4 F 5 F 6 V

© Pearson Education Ltd 2013. Copying permitted for purchasing institution only. This material is not copyright free.

Mi ciudad 5

4 Escribe un párrafo sobre tus actividades. (L5)

Writing. Pupils write a paragraph about their own weekend plans, using the present tense to describe what they normally do, and the near future tense to describe what they are going to do. Sentence starters are supplied.

Workbook 1A, page 52

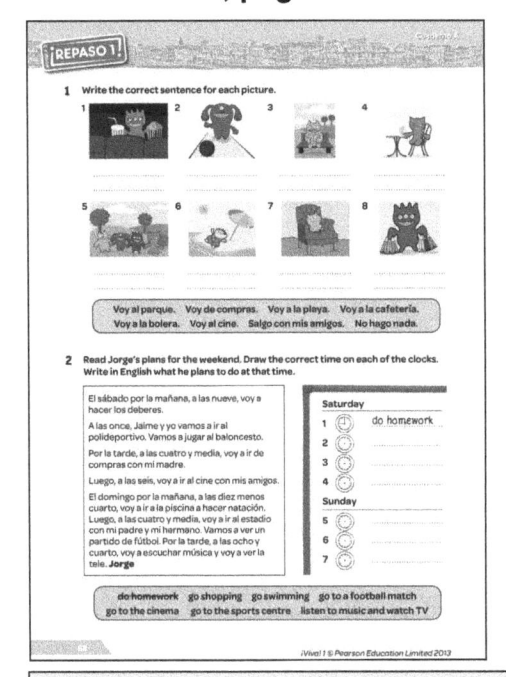

Answers

1. 1 Voy al cine.
   2 Voy a la bolera.
   3 Voy al parque.
   4 Voy a la cafetería.
   5 Salgo con mis amigos.
   6 Voy a la playa.
   7 No hago nada.
   8 Voy de compras.

2. **Saturday**
   1 9.00, do homework
   2 11.00, go to the sports centre
   3 4.30, go shopping
   4 6.00, go to the cinema
   Sunday
   5 9.45, go swimming
   6 4.30, go to a football match
   7 8.15, listen to music and watch TV

Workbook 1A, page 53

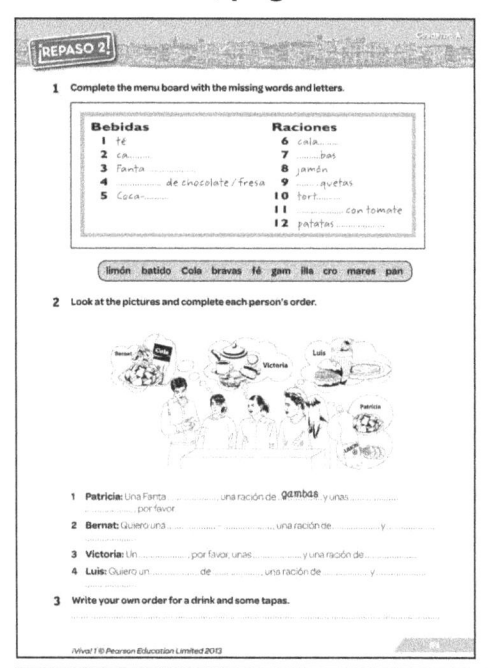

Answers

1. **Bebidas**
   1 té 2 café 3 Fanta **limón**
   4 batido de chocolate/fresa 5 Coca-**Cola**
   Raciones
   6 cala**mares** 7 **gam**bas
   8 jamón 9 cro**quetas**
   10 tortilla 11 **pan** con tomate
   12 patatas **bravas**

2. 1 **Patricia:** limón, *gambas*, patatas bravas
   2 **Bernat:** Coca-Cola, calamares, patatas bravas
   3 **Victoria:** té, croquetas, tortilla
   4 **Luis:** batido de fresa, jamón, pan con tomate

3. Own answers.

Mi ciudad 5

Workbook 1B, page 52

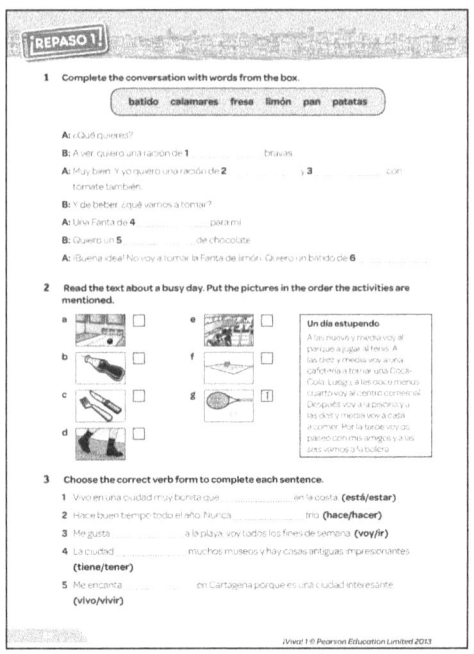

Workbook 1B, page 53

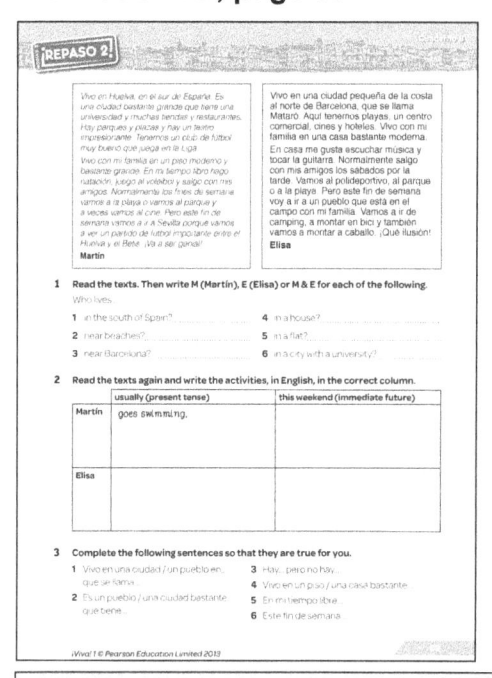

Answers

1 1 patatas   2 calamares   3 pan   4 limón
   5 batido   6 fresa

2 g 1   b 2   e 3   f 4   c 5   d 6   a 7

3 1 está   2 hace   3 ir
   4 tiene   5 vivir

Answers

1 1 M   2 M & E   3 E   4 E
   5 M   6 M

2

	usually (present tense)	this weekend (immediate future)
Martín	goes swimming, plays volleyball, goes out with friends, goes to the beach, park, or cinema	he's going to Sevilla to see a football match between Huelva and Betis
Elisa	listens to music, plays the guitar, goes out with friends, they go to the sports centre, park or beach	she's going to a village in the country with her family, they're going to camp, go cycling and horse riding

3 Own answers.

¡GRAMÁTICA!

Mi ciudad 5

Pupil Book pages	Grammar topics	Resources
Pages 112–113 The *Gramática* section provides a more detailed summary of the key grammar covered in the module, along with further exercises to practise these points.	• 'a' (*un/una*), 'some' (*unos/unas*) and 'many' (*muchos/muchas*) • the verb *ir* (to go) • the near future tense • using two tenses together	Workbooks: Cuaderno 1A & 1B, page 54 ActiveTeach: p.112 Grammar presentation p.112 Grammar presentation p.113 Grammar presentation p.113 Grammar presentation

'a', 'some', 'many'

1 Choose the correct version of each word and complete the sentences.

Pupils complete the gap-fill sentences by supplying the correct form of the indefinite articles (*un/una/unos/unas*) or adjectives of quantity (*muchos/muchas*) given each time.

Answers
1 un estadio
2 una piscina
3 un polideportivo
4 unos museos
5 muchas tiendas
6 muchas plazas
7 unos parques
8 muchos restaurantes

The verb *ir* (to go)

2 Write six sentences each containing one element from each box. Translate your sentences into English.

Pupils write six sentences containing one element from the three boxes (a time phrase, a form of *ir* and a place). Pupils then translate the sentences into English. Point out the Tip box, which explains how when *a* ('to') precedes the definite article *el* ('the'), the two words combine to form a contraction *al* ('to the').

3 Translate these sentences into Spanish.

This exercise provides further practice of the verb *ir*. Pupils translate the sentences into Spanish, referring to the model paradigm as necessary.

Answers
1 Vamos a la playa.
2 (Ella) va de compras.
3 Voy al cine.
4 Los sábados van al parque.
5 A veces vas a la piscina.
6 Los fines de semana vais a la bolera.

The near future tense

4 Write out these sentences in the near future tense.

Pupils look at the summary of the near future tense on this page. They then write out the sentences using the pictures and the single letter prompts for each word in the sentence.

Answers
1 Vamos a jugar al voleibol.
2 Ella va a hacer los deberes.
3 Voy a salir con mis amigos.
4 Vas a ir de paseo.
5 Van a ir a la bolera.
6 Vais a navegar por Internet.

Using two tenses together

5 Copy the table and fill in the gaps.

Pupils copy and complete the table with the correct verb forms in the present and near future tenses.

Answers

infinitive	present tense	near future tense
escuchar (to listen)	escucho (I listen)	**1 voy a escuchar** (I am going to listen)
bailar (to dance)	bailo (I dance)	**2 voy a bailar** (I am going to dance)
comer (to eat)	**3 como** (I eat)	voy a comer (I am going to eat)
jugar (to play)	juego (I play)	**4 voy a jugar** (I am going to play)
hacer (to do)	**5 hago** (I do)	**6 voy a hacer** (I am going to do)
ir (to go)	**7 voy** (I go)	**8 voy a ir** (I am going to go)

© Pearson Education Ltd 2013. Copying permitted for purchasing institution only. This material is not copyright free.

Mi ciudad 5

6 Copy and complete the text using the correct verb forms.

Pupils copy and complete the gap-fill text using the picture prompts and the present or near future tense each time.

Answers

1 salgo con mis amigos	2 juego al fútbol
3 hago artes marciales	4 voy a ir al cine
5 voy a montar en bici	6 Voy a ir a la playa
7 voy a nadar	8 voy a comer algo
9 leo	10 voy a leer

Workbook 1A, page 54

Answers

1 1 al   2 a la   3 al   4 a la   5 al   6 a la

2 ir (to go)

voy	I go
vas	you go
va	**he/she goes**
vamos	**we go**
vais	you go
van	they go

3 1 muchos   2 una   3 un   4 muchas
   5 unas   6 unos   7 una   8 muchos
   9 un   10 unas

Workbook 1B, page 54

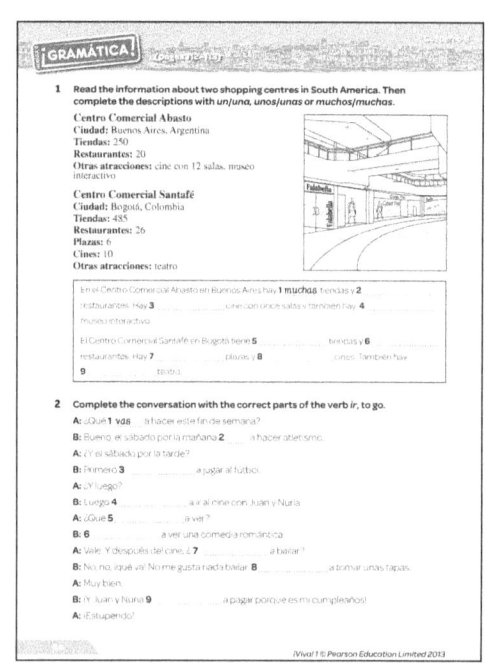

Answers

1 1 *muchas*   2 muchos   3 un
   4 un   5 muchas   6 muchos
   7 unas   8 unos   9 un

2 1 *vas*   2 voy   3 voy
   4 voy   5 vais   6 Vamos
   7 Vais   8 Vamos   9 van

¡Pasaporte fiesta!

Mi ciudad 5

Pupil Book pages	Programme of Study	Cross-curricular
Pages 116–117	LC6 Reading comprehension	**English:** poetry
Learning objectives	LC7 Literary texts	**Computing:** internet research
• Learning about Spanish festivals	**FCSE links**	**Resources**
• Creating a brochure about a fiesta	Unit 8: Celebrations (Various festivals, Special celebrations)	Audio files:
	PLTS	91_Module5_ZP1_Ex2
	I Independent enquirers	92_Module5_ZP1_Ex4

Starter 1

Aim

To review question words.

Allow pupils four minutes to brainstorm as many question words as they can remember and decide what information they need to know about Spanish fiestas. Pupils feed back their thoughts and discuss the findings as a class.

1 Lee el pasaporte fiesta y completa las frases en inglés. (L4)

Reading. First read together through the *Zona Cultura* box on Spanish fiestas. Pupils then read the text in exercise 1 and complete the gap-fill sentences that follow in English. Some vocabulary is glossed for support.

Answers

1 This fiesta is called **la Tomatina**.
2 It takes place in Buñol, which is in **the west of Spain**.
3 It takes place on the last **Wednesday** of **August** at **11am**.
4 It lasts **one hour**.
5 For one hour, we **throw tomatoes**.
6 It is **very funny/lots of fun!**

2 Escucha. Elige la respuesta correcta. (L4)

Listening. Pupils listen to a radio jingle advertising the Cadiz festival, then complete the gap-fill sentences that follow in Spanish. *Salimos* is glossed for support.

Audioscript Track 91

– *Ahora: pasaporte fiesta…*
– *¿Cómo se llama la fiesta?*
– *Se llama el carnaval de Cádiz.*
– *¿Dónde tiene lugar?*
– *Tiene lugar en Cádiz, en el sureste de España.*
– *¿Cuándo es?*
– *En febrero o marzo.*
– *¿Cuánto tiempo dura?*
– *Dura diez días.*
– *¿Qué pasa?*
– *Salimos disfrazados, bailamos, cantamos y comemos cosas muy buenas.*
– *¿Cómo es?*
– *Es estupendo.*

Answers

1 a el carnaval de Cádiz	2 a Cádiz
3 a sureste de España	4 b febrero o marzo
5 a diez días	6 a bailamos
7 b comemos	8 b estupendo

3 Con tu compañero/a, describe la Feria de Málaga. Utiliza las preguntas del ejercicio 2. (L4)

Speaking. In pairs, pupils take it in turns to ask and answer each other questions about the Málaga fiesta, using the questions from exercise 2 as a model. Pupils choose the answers from the box provided, but point out that they will need to conjugate the verbs *bailar* and *escuchar* into the first person plural forms.

Starter 2

Aim

To review verbs from the unit.

Allow pupils four minutes to write down the infinitive and first person singular forms of these verbs:

| salimos | bailamos | paseamos |
| cantamos | lanzamos | comemos |

Mi ciudad 5

4 Escucha y lee el texto, y mira la foto. Busca las frases en español. (L4)

Listening. Pupils look at the photo on p. 117 of the Pupil Book and listen, following the text at the same time. They then look for the Spanish phrases in the text. Some vocabulary is glossed for support.

Audioscript Track 92

En esta foto ves mi mejor amiga, Alicia, durante la Feria de Abril, en Sevilla.

Tiene el pelo castaño y liso. Es una chica muy guapa, ¿verdad?

Durante la Feria llevamos ropa tradicional y bailamos sevillanas. También tocamos instrumentos y cantamos. Comemos cosas muy buenas y hay un espectáculo de fuegos artificiales. ¡Es fenomenal! Me encanta la Feria.

Answers
1 llevamos ropa tradicional
2 bailamos
3 tocamos instrumentos
4 cantamos
5 comemos cosas muy buenas
6 hay un espectáculo de fuegos artificiales.

5 Lee el texto otra vez. Corrige los errores en estas frases. (L4)

Reading. Pupils rewrite the Spanish sentences that summarise the text in exercise 4, correcting the errors in each of them.

Answers
1 La chica de la foto se llama **Alicia**.
2 La Feria de Abril tiene lugar en **Sevilla**.
3 Alicia tiene el pelo **liso**.
4 En la foto Alicia lleva ropa **tradicional**.
5 Durante la Feria bailamos **sevillanas**.
6 En la opinión de Silvia, el espectáculo de fuegos artificiales es **fenomenal.**

6 Haz un folleto sobre una fiesta. (L4)

Writing. Before starting this exercise, read together through the extract of García Lorca's poem about Seville in the *Zona Cultura* box. Pupils research a famous Spanish fiesta from a choice of four alternatives. They then create and decorate a *Pasaporte Fiesta* booklet, covering detailed answers to the list of questions that are provided. Draw pupils' attention to the text in exercise 1, which can be used as a model.

Plenary

Allow pupils four minutes to test each other on what they have learned about Spanish fiestas.

© Pearson Education Ltd 2013. Copying permitted for purchasing institution only. This material is not copyright free.

¡PROYECTO! El Día de los Muertos — Mi ciudad 5

Pupil Book pages
Pages 118–119

Learning objectives
- Learning about *el Día de los Muertos*
- Making a skull mask or paper flowers

Programme of Study
LC1 Listening and responding
LC6 Reading comprehension

FCSE links
Unit 8: Celebrations (Various festivals, Special celebrations)

PLTS
E Effective participators

Cross-curricular
Religious Studies: festivals
Art and design: crafts

Resources
Audio files:
93_Module5_ZP2_Ex1
94_Module5_ZP2_Ex3
95_Module5_ZP2_Ex4
ActiveTeach:
Starter 2 resource

Starter 1

Aim
To learn about Mexico.

With books closed, pupils work in pairs to brainstorm all that they know about Mexico – where it is, what it's like, the food, traditions, climate, etc. Ask pupils to feed back their knowledge and discuss the findings as a class.

1 ¿Qué pasa el Día de los Muertos? Escucha y pon las fotos en el orden correcto. (1–6) (L3)

Listening. First, read together through the *Zona Cultura* box on the Day of the Dead. Pupils listen and follow the text at the same time. They then put the photos in the order that they are mentioned. *Ponemos* is glossed for support.

Audioscript Track 93

¿Qué pasa el Día de los muertos?
1 – Decoramos las tumbas con flores…
2 – …y ponemos velas.
3 – Hacemos el pan de muerto.
4 – Decoramos calaveras de azúcar.
5 – A veces hacemos flores de papel.
6 – Hacemos máscaras de calaveras que decoramos.

Answers
1 b 2 d 3 c 4 a 5 f 6 e

2 Busca las frases en español en ejercicio 1. (L3)

Reading. Pupils find in the exercise 1 text the Spanish for the English words or phrases given.

Answers
1 calaveras de azúcar   2 tumbas
3 pan de muerto   4 velas
5 máscaras de calaveras 6 flores de papel

3 Escucha y lee el texto. Contesta a las preguntas en inglés. (L4)

Reading. Pupils listen to Santi talk about the Day of the Dead festival, following the text at the same time. They then answer the questions that follow in English. *Lo pasamos bien* is glossed for support.

Audioscript Track 94

Me llamo Santi y vivo en México. El Día de los Muertos es una celebración muy importante en México. También es importante en Guatemala y en los Estados Unidos.

Dura dos días, el uno y el dos de noviembre. Hay muchos preparativos: decoramos las tumbas con flores, velas y calaveras de azúcar.

El Día de los Muertos voy al cementerio con mi familia, donde comemos y bebemos. Además, tocamos música y bailamos. Lo pasamos bien.

Me encanta el Día de los Muertos. En mi opinión, es una celebración fenomenal.

Answers
1 Mexico
2 Guatemala, USA
3 1st and 2nd November, 2 days
4 (any two of) candles, flowers, sugar skulls
5 (any two of) go to the cemetery, eat, drink, play music, dance
6 He loves it. It's great.

Mi ciudad 5

Starter 2

Aim

To review the Day of the Dead festival.

Put the following wordsnake up on the board (Starter 2 resource).

calaverasdeazúcarfloresdepapelpandemuertovelasmáscarasdecalaveras

Allow pupils four minutes to unravel it to identify five things associated with the festival. Ask pupils to translate the words in English.

4 Escucha a Elena y Juan. ¿Qué van a hacer el Día de los Muertos? Apunta los detalles en inglés. (L5)

Listening. Pupils listen to Elena and Juan talk about their plans for the Day of the Dead festival. They note the details for each person in English.

Audioscript Track 95

1 – Elena, ¿qué vas a hacer por el Día de los Muertos?

– Primero voy a hacer el pan de muerto con mi madre. Luego, con mi padre, voy a decorar la tumba de mi abuela. Vamos a poner flores y velas. También mi hermana y yo vamos a decorar una calavera de azúcar. Me encanta esta tradición. Es muy interesante.

2 – ¿Y tú, Juan?

– Voy a hacer una máscara. Voy a decorar la máscara con colores muy fuertes: rojo, naranja, amarillo... y también voy a hacer unas flores de papel. El Día de los Muertos voy a ir con mi familia al cementerio y vamos a cantar y bailar. Me gusta mucho el Día de los Muertos.

Answers

Elena – make bread, decorate (grandmother's) grave, put flowers and candles (on grave), decorate a sugar skull

Juan – make a mask, decorate it (with strong colours), make paper flowers, go to the cemetery with family, sing and dance

5 Empareja las palabras en español con las palabras en inglés. Utiliza el minidiccionario si es necesario. (L2)

Reading. Pupils match up the Spanish words with their English equivalents, using the mini-dictionary provided, if necessary. *Vas a necesitar* is glossed for support.

Answers

1 c 2 g 3 a 4 d 5 f 6 e 7 b

6 Haz una máscara o unas flores de papel para el Día de los Muertos. (L3)

Reading. Pupils follow the instructions and photos given and make their own masks and paper flowers for the Day of the Dead. Some vocabulary is glossed for support.

7 Haz un folleto de 'Pasaporte fiesta' sobre el Día de los Muertos. Mira el ejercicio 6 de la página 117. (L5)

Writing. Pupils create and decorate a *Pasaporte Fiesta* booklet for the Day of the Dead festival, covering detailed answers to the list of questions that are provided in exercise 6 on page 117.

Plenary

Pupils write two sentences about the Day of the Dead for their partners, each containing two errors. They swap their work and attempt to make the necessary corrections.

¡TE TOCA A TI!

Mi ciudad 5

Pupil Book pages
Pages 128–129

Self-access reading and writing

A Reinforcement

1 Copia y completa la tabla. (L2)

Reading. Pupils read the sentences and fill in the table, choosing letters that denote the time and activity mentioned in each sentence.

Answers		
	time	place
1	c	h
2	e	i
3	b	g
4	a	f
5	d	j

2 Copia y completa el diálogo con palabras del cuadro. (L3)

Reading. Pupils write out the dialogue, supplying the Spanish for the picture prompts and using the words provided in the box.

Answers
1 *una ración de patatas bravas*
2 una ración de gambas
3 una ración de calamares
4 una ración de jamón
5 una Coca-Cola
6 un té

3 Escribe otro diálogo utilizando los dibujos. (L3)

Writing. Pupils write their own café dialogue using the pictures given as prompts and adapting the dialogue in exercise 2.

B Extension

1 Escribe las frases en el orden correcto. Luego tradúcelas al inglés. (L3)

Reading. Pupils write out the jumbled sentences in the correct order, then translate them into English.

Answers
1 Me gusta mucho vivir en Madrid porque hay muchos monumentos.
   I really like living in Madrid because there are many/a lot of monuments.
2 No me gusta nada vivir en Tarragona porque es muy aburrido.
   I don't like living in Tarragona at all because it is very boring.
3 Me encanta vivir en Barcelona porque hay muchos restaurantes.
   I love living in Barcelona because there are a lot of/many restaurants.
4 Me gusta vivir en Ibiza porque es muy interesante.
   I like living in Ibiza because it is very interesting.
5 Me gusta mucho vivir en Málaga porque hay muchas tiendas.
   I really like living in Malaga because there are many/a lot of shops.
6 No me gusta vivir en Órgiva porque no hay centro comercial.
   I don't like living in Órgiva because there is no/there isn't a shopping centre.

© Pearson Education Ltd 2013. Copying permitted for purchasing institution only. This material is not copyright free.

Mi ciudad 5

2 Escribe estas frases. (L3)

Writing. Pupils write out the sentences, supplying the Spanish for the picture prompts.

> **Answers**
>
> 1 Me gusta vivir en Ampurias porque hay un castillo y también hay unos museos.
> 2 Me encanta/Me gusta mucho vivir en Madrid porque hay muchos restaurantes y muchas tiendas.
> 3 Me encanta/Me gusta mucho vivir en Valencia porque hay una piscina y también hay un estadio.
> 4 Me gusta vivir en Málaga porque hay un centro comercial y también hay un polideportivo.
> 5 No me gusta nada vivir en Capileira porque no hay piscina. No hay nada.

3 Lee el texto y contesta a las preguntas. (L5)

Reading. Pupils read Blanca's description of her town and leisure activities and answer the questions that follow in English. *Recaudar dinero* is glossed for support.

> **Answers**
>
> 1 In the northeast of Spain, on the coast.
> 2 She goes to the sports centre and plays basketball with her friends.
> 3 A museum, squares and a cathedral.
> 4 She goes to the shopping centre, talks, listens to music.
> 5 She goes to the beach.
> 6 She is going to go cycling, to raise money for Oxfam.

4 Escribe un correo utilizando el texto electrónico de Blanca como modelo. (L5)

Writing. Pupils write an email describing their town and leisure activities, using Blanca's text from exercise 3 as a model. A list of topics to include is provided.